The Art of English

A Certificate Course for Secondary Schools
BOOK 2 Revised edition

KEITH NEWSON M.A. Dip.Ed.

There is an art of reading
as well as an art of thinking
and an art of writing
ISAAC D'ISRAELI

Illustrated by Derek Collard

Schofield & Sims Ltd Huddersfield

Printed in Great Britain at the Alden Press, Oxford

Contents

Each chapter contains an extract for reading and the following sections:
For discussion
For written answers
For learning about language
For your own writing
For talk and action
For further reading.
Most chapters include a poem and a section **Discussing the poem**.

The following Contents List includes the new work and most of the revision to be found in the **Learning about language** section in each chapter.

4

Acknowledgements

The author and publishers wish to thank the following for permission to include the copyright material listed below:

The Bodley Head for an extract from **The Otterbury Incident** by C. DAY LEWIS.

Faber & Faber Ltd. for the poem CHILD ON TOP OF A GREENHOUSE from **Collected Poems** by THEODORE ROETHKE.

Leslie Norris and Chatto & Windus Ltd. for the poem THE BALLAD OF BILLY ROSE from **Finding Gold** by LESLIE NORRIS.

Oxford University Press for an extract from **Tom's Midnight Garden** by A. PHILIPPA PEARCE.

The Literary Trustees of Walter de la Mare and The Society of Authors as their representative for the poems THE LISTENERS and SNOW by WALTER DE LA MARE.

Victor Gollancz Ltd. for two extracts from **Annerton Pit** by PETER DICKINSON, for an extract from **Z for Zachariah** by ROBERT O'BRIEN and for an extract from **The Tombs of Atuan** by URSULA LE GUIN.

ACKNOWLEDGEMENTS

Harcourt Brace Jovanovich, Inc. for the poem CALIBAN IN THE COAL MINES by LOUIS UNTERMEYER, reprinted from his volume **Long Feud** by permission of the publishers. (© 1914 by Harcourt Brace Jovanovich, Inc.; renewed 1942 by Louis Untermeyer.)

Mrs Sonia Brownell Orwell and Martin Secker & Warburg for an extract from **The Road to Wigan Pier** by GEORGE ORWELL.

Harmony Music Ltd. for an extract from the ballad SPRING HILL DISASTER by EWAN MACCOLL and PEGGY SEEGER.

Granada Publishing Ltd. for an extract from **Greeks and Trojans** by REX WARNER.

William H. Wise & Co. Inc. for the poem THE DAVID JAZZ by EDWIN MEADE ROBINSON from **A Book of American Poetry.**

Edinburgh University Press for the poem THE COMPUTER'S FIRST CHRISTMAS CARD from **The Second Life** by EDWIN MORGAN.

The Hogarth Press Ltd. for an extract from **Cider with Rosie** by LAURIE LEE.

Harrap Ltd. for an extract from **The Haircut** in **The Goalkeeper's Revenge** by BILL NAUGHTON.

Alan Brownjohn for the poem TO SEE THE RABBIT from **The Railings** by ALAN BROWNJOHN.

Penguin Books Ltd. for an extract from **Lorna Doone** by R. D. BLACKMORE abridged by Stephanie Nettell, and for an extract from **Devil-in-the-Fog** by LEON GARFIELD.

Robert Finch, Author, and Sybil Hutchinson, Literary Agent, for the poem **PROTOCOL** from **Silverthorn Bush** (Macmillan, Canada) by ROBERT FINCH.

Lady|Gwendoline Herbert and A. P. Watt Ltd. Literary Agents for the poem AT THE THEATRE by A. P. HERBERT.

A. Deutsch Ltd. for an extract from **Facts about a Theatre Company** by PETER LEWIS.

William Heinemann Ltd. for an extract from **The Saturdays** by ELIZABETH ENRIGHT, for an extract from **The Maythorn Story** by GEOFFREY TREASE and for the poem BREATHLESS from **South Col** by WILFRID NOYCE.

The Estate of the late Richard Church and William Heinemann Ltd. for an extract from **Over the Bridge** by RICHARD CHURCH.

Mrs E. F. Starkey for the poem NELSON STREET by SEUMAS O'SULLIVAN.

The Estate of the late Mary O'Hara and Eyre Methuen Ltd. for an extract from **My Friend Flicka** by MARY O'HARA.

The Estate of Robert Frost, the editor, Jonathan Cape Ltd., Publishers, and Holt, Rinehart & Winston Inc., Proprietors, for the poem THE RUNAWAY from **The Poetry of Robert Frost.**

Ian Serraillier and Jonathan Cape Ltd. for an extract from **The Silver Sword** by IAN SERRAILLIER.

Miss J. Freeman for the poem MUSIC COMES by JOHN FREEMAN from **Fresh Fields.**

Hodder & Stoughton Ltd. for an extract from **Everest the Hard Way** edited by CHRIS BONINGTON.

Wayland Publishers Ltd. for an extract from **Running Out of Fuel – Solving the Energy Puzzle** by RAY DAFTER.

National Geographic Magazine for an extract from the article **Hurricane** by BEN FUNK.

Mollie Hunter and Hamish Hamilton Ltd. for an extract from **The Third Eye** by MOLLIE HUNTER.

Methuen Children's Books for the poem SMELLS from **Chimney Smoke** by CHRISTOPHER MORLEY.

Ministry of Transport signs, p. 20, by permission.

The revised Art of English and GCSE

The **Art of English** is a well-established five-year English series for Secondary schools now radically revised and updated to meet the aims and objectives of the General Certificate of Secondary Education in English and English Literature. It comprises two complete and self-contained sequences of five books, the *Certificate Course* and the *General Course,* which between them will stretch pupils across the whole range of GCSE grades. There is much common ground, but the *Certificate Course* is intended particularly for those pupils who should aim at grade C or above in written language and Literature (and grades 2 or 1 in oral communication), and are capable of the former GCE O Level standard in English. The course is aimed at the objectives set out in the National Criteria in 1985.

The **Art of English** has always reflected the authors' conviction that good written and spoken communication in English is rooted in wide reading, critical listening and clear understanding. Imaginative and factual writing using language in a variety of modes and contexts stimulates discussion and other group and individual activities. These lead students to a greater awareness of themselves and sensitivity to the views and feelings of others. Critical appreciation of books, poems, plays and other media develops ideas, understanding, opinions and values, and helps students to find a personal place in a now shrinking, multi-cultural world.

In *both courses,* each chapter is based on an extract from a suitable, usually modern, book of acknowledged merit; this is supported by one or more poems on a similar theme. Extracts and poems are then used to develop understanding of information, emotions, ideas and/or opinions. The language is studied and evaluated in context, and the appropriate conventions of written and spoken English are reinforced. Students are invited to respond and articulate their own ideas, communicating in writing and orally, and through drama and other group activities. The main extracts should prove exciting and thought-provoking enough to make students want to read the books for themselves, and each chapter ends with suitable and varied further reading suggestions.

In the *Certificate Course*, the language work and the communication activities promote awareness of style and usage for different purposes, and help students to evaluate and discriminate, sharpening their own skills in controlling style and structure. The requirements of further training and higher education are fully met, but material is kept directly relevant to the immediate needs and interests of most young people.

Together, the two Courses of the **Art of English** form a unique series, covering the common ground of English teaching that is now the basis of assessments in GCSE. They offer ample material for course-work and final examinations, including objective techniques of testing.

1   Caught in the Act

Ted and Toppy are on the trail of a vicious criminal called Johnny Sharp and his accomplice, the Wart. The boys have ventured into the cellar of Skinner's warehouse where they discover cases of stolen cigarettes and a coiner's den. Suddenly they hear the criminals returning . . .

"The trapdoor. Quick!" said Toppy.

They tore up the chute. But, as they reached the top, they saw the big warehouse door beginning to open. Toppy, who was ahead, managed to scramble through the trap; he flitted like a bat towards the staircase that led up to the workshop. In the mad *sauve-qui-peut*, his foot had accidentally thrust against Ted, who slid a little way down the chute. By the time he had scrambled up to the trapdoor again, the Wart and Johnny Sharp, their backs turned to him, were in the warehouse, only six yards away. Frantically, Ted tugged at the trapdoor. It would be fatal if the men found it open. It slid back silently over his head. This was a respite at any rate. He careered down the chute, through the vault, into the passage beyond, bumping and bruising himself against the edge of a packing-case, for the sliding-to of the trap had automatically switched off the electric lights in the vault. He paused a moment by the door of the coiner's den. There seemed to be no sounds of pursuit. Perhaps the roar of the lorry's engine had covered up the noise he made on the chute. He remembered he'd brought a pocket-torch. Switching it on, he turned off the light in the den, closed the splintered door, and crept off along the passage away from the vaults.

The passage took him about twenty paces. Then there was a flight of stone steps. Climbing up these, he found a blank wall, a grating set high up in it, and a small door. Desperately he tugged at its handle. The door was locked.

Ted knew it was only a matter of minutes before the gang realised something was wrong. The dressing-table moved out of position in the warehouse; the packing-case Toppy had opened; the splintered door of the coiner's den – there were too many signs betraying him. He sat down on the stone steps, his head in his hands, trying to steady his nerve. There was only one hope – that the gang would go upstairs first, find the scout-rope dangling from the workshop sky-light, and assume that their birds had flown. But would Toppy have the sense to leave the rope there? Wouldn't his instinct be to remove this indication of their presence?

Then Ted caught at another straw of hope. Up above, in a cubby-hole off the workshop, there was a telephone. Perhaps Toppy had had time and sense enough to ring up the police before making his escape. If the gang found him, Ted determined that he would play this card, even though it might only be a bluff.

Even as he made this decision, he heard footsteps approaching along the passage, and a voice – the soft, cold voice of Johnny Sharp – saying, "Come out! Come on out! And no tricks."

(from The Otterbury Incident by C. DAY LEWIS)

For discussion

1 As far as you can tell from the extract, how had the boys reached the coiner's den (from their first entry into the warehouse)?

2 What do you think had been the dressing-table's position, before they moved it?

3 What was above the warehouse?

4 Where were the gang about to find Ted?

5 What kind of person do you imagine (a) Ted, (b) Johnny Sharp to be?

6 What do these expressions mean?

"their birds had flown"   "play this card"

"straw of hope"   "a bluff"

7 *Sauve-qui-peut* means "flight in which every man cares only about his own safety". Why is it printed in italics? Why did the author use this French phrase instead of an English word or phrase?

8 Explain: "Wouldn't his instinct be to remove this indication of their presence?" What does "instinct" mean here?

9 What damage had the boys done?

10 How do you react when you see a notice that says "Private Property"? What does the expression "An Englishman's home is his castle" mean? How do you think Ted and Toppy's entry into Skinner's warehouse could be justified? How much privacy do you think people are entitled to?

For written answers

1 Write out the three or four words that tell us how Toppy ran from the trapdoor to the staircase.

2 Write down (a) the adverb that tells us that Toppy did not mean to push Ted back down the chute, and (b) the adverb that shows us that the electric lights were beyond Ted's control.

3 Write down the other word used in the extract instead of "cellar". (Answer questions 4 and 5 fully, in complete statement sentences.)

4 Why was Ted in the dark?

5 What do you think Ted and Toppy heard to warn them of the criminals' return?

CHILD ON TOP OF A GREENHOUSE

The wind billowing out the seat of my britches,
My feet crackling splinters of glass and dried putty,
The half-grown chrysanthemums staring up like accusers,
Up through the streaked glass, flashing with sunlight,
A few white clouds all rushing eastward,
A line of elms plunging and tossing like horses,
And everyone, everyone pointing up and shouting!

THEODORE ROETHKE

Discussing the poem

1 Who is supposed to be speaking here? What has happened to him and how does the poem emphasise his feelings?
2 What kind of day is it? How does the poem emphasise this?
3 Can you describe a similar experience?

For learning about language

By discussion, see if you can sort out the following lines from the extract into statements, questions, incomplete statements; commands, incomplete commands; and exclamations.

"The trapdoor. Quick!"
They tore up the chute.
Frantically, Ted tugged at the trapdoor.
It slid back silently over his head.
But would Toppy have the sense to leave the rope there?
Wouldn't his instinct be to remove this indication of their presence?
Perhaps Toppy had had time and sense enough to ring up the police before making his escape.
"Come on out! And no tricks."

What is missing (or understood) where the statement or command is incomplete?

Exercise 1(a) The following are incomplete or condensed sentences that might appear as newspaper or advertisement headlines. Rewrite them as full sentences, to give the full meanings.

For example: ELECTION SOON
means: There will soon be an election.
(or: An election will soon take place.)
Those marked with an asterisk* could have two different meanings.

(1) NO HOPE FOR MINE VICTIMS

(2)* BEST CAR BARGAINS HERE

(3) COUPLE MARRIED TWICE

(4) ARSENAL WON, CHELSEA TOO

(5) ARSENAL ONE, CHELSEA TWO

(6)* MEAT TALKS IN WHITEHALL

(7)* BEST BUYS AT BOTTOMLEY'S

(8) COUNCIL RUNNING LOTTERY

(9) PRICE'S PRICES DOWN

(10)* STUDENT RIOTS IN OXFORD

(b) Nouns are names of persons, places, things or ideas. Those that name particular persons, places or things are called **proper nouns**. How can we recognise the proper nouns in the following sentence?

> Mr Smith went to the smith who worked in the forge in Forge Lane.

Can you find twenty-one instances of a capital letter used for a proper noun in the introductory note and the extract from **The Otterbury Incident**?

Exercise 2 Rewrite the following, putting in all the capital letters, full stops, question marks and exclamation marks that are necessary (50 changes or additions in all).

"did you have a good holiday, ray" asked his friend, mark, when they met for the first time that term

"you bet" ray replied his eyes lit up with enthusiasm "terry and i went to france, to paris, with the school party we climbed the eiffel tower, saw the mona lisa, were nearly run over at the arc de triomphe, went round notre dame, were photographed in montmartre, took a coach out to versailles for the day and went on a cruise up the river seine i reckon we saw just about everything"

"you didn't go to the folies bergeres" mark said, doubtfully

"no, but mr pearce and mr jenkins took some of the sixth formers out late on friday, and roberts says he saw one of them with a programme from there on saturday morning"

"huh that proves nothing," commented mark

Exercise 3(a) English is a very flexible language. Many words can be either nouns (names of persons or places or things) or adjectives (describing words) according to the way they are used.

For example:

His father had bought a new *car*.

The *car* roof leaked.

In the first sentence "car" is a noun; in the second "car" is an adjective going with "roof" (it tells you what kind of roof). Say whether each of the words in italics in the following sentences is a noun or an adjective. If they are adjectives, say what they describe.

(1) They pulled down the *blind*.

(2) A *blind* man came to tune the piano.

(3) You will need a *metal* rod.

(4) Some *metals* are very expensive.

(5) They imposed a *pound fine* for each offence.

(6) She had a *fine* new hat that cost a lot more than a *pound*.

(7) The children in the *wood* put on *paper* masks.

(8) *Paper* is made from *wood* pulp.

(9) To make this *pudding*, take *sugar*, fat, flour and *eggs*.

(10) You will also require a *pudding* basin, an *egg* beater and a *sugar* thermometer.

(b) State whether the words in italics in the following sentences are nouns or adjectives. If the word is a noun, compose a sentence using it as an adjective; if it is an adjective, compose a sentence using it as a noun.

For example:

He was a well-known *television* personality.
Here "television" is an adjective. Using it as a noun you might put:

Television has brought great changes in our way of life.

(1) We travelled on a *London* bus.

(2) The *rich* can look after themselves.

(3) Let the cobbler stick to his *last*.

(4) The *student* teachers were all present.

(5) The *roof* beams were rotten.

(6) We employed a *house* painter.

(7) The *barn* owl watched us.

(8) We left the *stable* open.

(9) The *bicycle* was parked by the wall.

(10) The *Dutch* find *English* easy to learn.

Exercise 4 Many words do have special endings to distinguish adjectives and adverbs from nouns. What is the difference between an adjective and an adverb?

(a) In each of the following, the three sentences require the noun, adjective and adverb forms respectively. For each, write down the two that have been omitted.

For example:

It was an *accident*.　　　　　(Noun)
It was an *accidental* mistake.　(Adjective)
It happened *accidentally*.　　(Adverb)

(1)　The song was a thing of great *beauty*.
　　　It was a ____ song.
　　　She sang it ____.
(2)　The *danger* was obvious.
　　　There was a ____ corner ahead.
　　　The car skidded ____.
(3)　Dad was in a ____ to go out.
　　　He ate a *hurried* tea.
　　　He ate it ____.
(4)　She was giving me her full *attention*.
　　　She was ____.
　　　She listened ____.
(5)　He ran a ____.
　　　He was a very *busy* man.
　　　He worked ____.
(6)　The child was in ____.
　　　His was ____ behaviour.
　　　He had behaved *disgracefully*.
(7)　The hero showed great ____.
　　　He was *modest*.
　　　He ____ praised his fellow soldiers.
(8)　The carpenter's ____ comes from practice.
　　　A ____ carpenter knows how to use a chisel.
　　　He uses it *skilfully*.

16

(9)   ___ was the keynote of their design.
        The *simple* design was the best one.
        The boys designed it ___.
(10) I was full of ___ for their work.
        Their work was ___.
        They had done it *admirably*.

(b) Although many adverbs are formed by adding -ly to an adjective, many words ending in -ly are *not* adverbs. Rearrange the following words in three columns, one of words that are *normally* adjectives, one of adverbs and one of nouns.

   bully, chilly, family, filly, folly, friendly, fully, ghostly, grimly, gully, purely, silly, slyly, sourly, surly.

Exercise 5 A vocabulary and spelling test: in the following, the number of dashes indicates the number of letters in the word that fits the definition, and the first letter or letters have been given to you.

   For example:
   The third day of the week (*prop. n.*): T - - - - - - - , Tuesday
(a)   The country of the Belgians (*prop. n.*): B - - - - - -
(b)   Of unknown authorship (*adj.*): an - - - - - - - -
(c)   In a confident way, with certainty (*adv.*): de - - - - - - - - -
(d)   In an awkward or clumsy way (*adv.*): c - - - - - - - -
(e)   Opposite of guilty (*adj.*): in - - - - - -
(f)   Full of knowledge, well-informed (*adj.*): k - - - - - - - - - - - -
(g)   In so obvious a way as to be noticed (*adv.*): no - - - - - - - -
(h)   An inhabitant of Norway (*prop. n.*): N - - - - - - - -
(i)   In a stealthy or cautious manner (*adv.*): st - - - - - - - -
(j)   The fourth day of the week (*prop. n.*): W - - - - - - - -
(k)   Any means of land transport on wheels (*n.*): v - - - - - -
(l)   Full of virtue (*adj.*): v - - - - - - -
(m)   Male equivalent of spinster (*masc. n.*): b - - - - - - -
(n)   In a way that can be heard (*adv.*): au - - - - -
(o)   The opposite of guilt (*abstract n.*): i - - - - - - - -

For your own writing

1 Most people have entered private property without permission at some time, either by accident or on purpose: perhaps when fishing, or when retrieving a lost ball. Most of us know the tense, slightly guilty feelings we have if we think we hear the owner or anyone in authority approaching. Can you remember clearly some occasion when *you* were trespassing, defying rules or doing something wrong? Try to relive in your mind the nervous tension (perhaps the way the slightest sound would make you jump), and describe the experience as vividly as you can in your own words. If you can honestly say you have never had such an experience, then try to imagine what it would be like.

Choose your words carefully. Use adverbs (words such as "frantically", "silently", "desperately" are effectively used in the extract), as well as adjectives and nouns. Lively verbs ("tore", "flitted", "scrambled", "careered") give the extract a great

sense of excitement. Use some comparisons also, such as "like a bat" in the extract, and "chrysanthemums ... like accusers" and "plunging and tossing like horses" in the poem.

Choose a title to suit your own composition, such as:

THE DAY I WENT TRESPASSING

or

CAUGHT IN THE ACT.

2 Write a **free verse poem** (i.e. one not restricted by rhyme or a strict rhythm pattern) about a dramatic or frightening experience like that of the child on top of the greenhouse. Make notes and work on them until you are left with a very "streamlined" version of the story, with just the vivid central ideas emphasised, as in the poem by Theodore Roethke.

For talk and action

1(a) Find out what you can about the law on trespass. What other laws about property affect our ordinary daily lives?

Can you be prosecuted just for being on private land? What is a right of way? If you see a path marked on an Ordnance Survey map, can you claim the right to follow that route?

What happens if a person your age is charged by the police?

What is the difference between a judge, a stipendiary magistrate and an ordinary magistrate or J.P.? What is meant by "the bench", a juvenile court, a probation officer, magistrates' courts and crown courts?

Are cyclists allowed on *all* main roads, even if there is a special cycle track? Does a cyclist have to observe traffic signals when he is wheeling his cycle? Is a cyclist allowed (a) to park his cycle where there are "no waiting" restrictions, (b) to carry a passenger, and (c) to ride without brakes?

How are parking meters used?

What is a parking ticket?

Can a dog owner *ever* legally allow his or her dog off a lead in a place where dogs have to be kept on a lead?

(b) What is the difference between rectangular, round and triangular traffic signs?

black on white,
with black border

black on white with
red border

white on blue,
with white border

What do the following traffic signs mean?

1 *red circle and
cross on blue*

2 & 3 *white on
blue*

4 *black on white with
red bar and circle*

5 & 6 *black on white
with red borders*

2 Work out a mime of the incident in the extract or of that in the poem. In either case you will probably want to extend and elaborate the story. Different members of the class take particular parts and try to work out the character and mannerisms of that person. Then the incident has to be rehearsed, with each character working out his or her movements and timing to fit in with the others. The mime could then form the basis of an improvised play. No script should be necessary if actors are prepared to rehearse and work out the action together.

20

For further reading

The Otterbury Incident by C. DAY LEWIS (Bodley Head; Heinemann; Puffin)
Unlike the events described in the extract, most of the adventures of Ted, Toppy and their followers are narrated by one of the boys. These adventures really started when a school window was broken by a football and the boys clubbed together to raise the money to replace it.

The Mystery of the Cross-Eyed Man by PAUL BERNA (translated by J. Buchanan-Brown) (Puffin)
A fast-moving detective story by the author of **A Hundred Million Francs**, in which Daniel and his younger brother find themselves stranded in Paris and forced to hitch-hike without money across France, followed by a sinister, cross-eyed stranger.

Forgers by LANCE GALWAY (Kestrel)
This book, which is illustrated with prints, drawings and photographs, tells the absorbing stories of many astonishing characters who used forgery to fool the public and experts alike. (Classified as 364.1.)

A Wicked Pack of Cards by ROSEMARY HARRIS (Faber)
This gripping thriller revolves round the death of an old fortune-teller and the capacity of nine-year-old Cuthbertson Halliford to spy out the truth – and the problems twenty-five-year-old Aunt Jane has in deciding whom to marry!

The Tattooed Potato and Other Clues by ELLEN RASKIN (Macmillan; Peacock; Puffin)
Forgery, blackmail and murder are just some of the problems that Dickory Dock faces when she becomes assistant to portrait painter and super-sleuth Garson. How she finally uncovers the mystery behind the mystery provides an unexpected climax to a collection of amusing adventures.

Part 1: One of the first things Tom wants to learn at Rugby School is how to play their kind of football (from which modern Rugby football has developed). As played in the first half of the nineteenth century, it was quite a challenge to an eleven-year-old new boy …

"Oh, but do show me where they play. And tell me about it. I love football so and I've played all my life. Won't Brooke let me play?"

"Not he," said East, with some indignation; "why, you don't know the rules – you'll be a month learning them. And then it's no joke playing-up in a match, I can tell you. Quite another thing from your private school games. Why, there's been two collar-bones broken this half, and a dozen fellows lamed. And last year a fellow had his leg broken."

Tom listened with the profoundest respect to this chapter of accidents, and followed East across the level ground till they came

to a sort of gigantic gallows of two poles eighteen feet high, fixed upright in the ground some fourteen feet apart, with a crossbar running from one to the other at the height of ten feet or thereabouts.

"This is one of the goals," said East, "and you see the other, across there, right opposite, under the Doctor's wall. Well, the match is for the best of three goals; whichever side kicks two goals wins: and it won't do, you see, just to kick the ball through these posts, it must go over the crossbar; any height'll do, so long as it's between the posts. You'll have to stay in goal to touch the ball when it rolls behind the posts, because if the other side touch it they have a try at goal. Then we fellows in quarters, we play just about in front of goal here, and have to turn the ball and kick it back, before the big fellows on the other side can follow it up. And in front of us all the big fellows play, and that's where the scrummages are mostly."

Tom's respect increased as he struggled to make out his friend's technicalities, and the other set to work to explain the mysteries of "off your side", "drop-kicks", "punts", "places", and the other intricacies of the great science of football.

"But how do you keep the ball between the goals?" said he; "I can't see why it mightn't go right down to the chapel."

"Why, that's out of play," answered East. "You see this gravel walk running down all along this side of the playing-ground, and the line of elms opposite on the other? Well, they're the bounds. As soon as the ball gets past them, it's in touch, and out of play. And then whoever first touches it, has to knock it straight out amongst the players-up, who make two lines with a space between them, every fellow going on his own side. Ain't there just fine scrummages then! and the three trees you see there which come out into the play, that's a tremendous place when the ball hangs there, for you get thrown against the trees, and that's worse than any hack."

Tom's chance to take part in the School-house match (their challenge to the rest of the school) comes almost immediately after his arrival . . .

And now the last minutes are come, and the School gather for their last rush every boy of the hundred and twenty who has a run left in him. Reckless of the defence of their own goal, on they come across the level big-side ground, the ball well down amongst them, straight for our goal, like the column of the old guard up the slope at Waterloo. All former charges have been child's play to this. Warner and Hedge have met them, but still on they come. The bulldogs rush in for the last time; they are hurled over or carried back, striving hand, foot, and eyelids. Old Brooke comes sweeping round the skirts of the play, and turning short round, picks out the very heart of the scrummage, and plunges in. It wavers for a moment – he has the ball! No, it has passed him, and his voice rings out clear over. the advancing tide, "Look out in goal!" Crab Jones catches it for a moment; but before he can kick, the rush is upon him and passes over him; and he picks himself up behind them with his straw in his mouth, a little dirtier, but as cool as ever.

The ball rolls slowly in behind the School-house goal, not three yards in front of a dozen of the biggest School players-up.

There stand the School-house praepostor, safest of goal-keepers, and Tom Brown by his side, who has learned his trade by this time. Now is your time, Tom. The blood of all the Browns is up, and the two rush in together, and throw themselves on the ball, under the very feet of the advancing column; the praepostor on his hands and knees arching his back, and Tom all along on his face. Over them topple the leaders of the rush, shooting over the back of the prae-postor, but falling flat on Tom, and knocking all the wind out of his small carcase. "Our ball," says the praepostor, rising with his prize, " but get up there, there's a little fellow under you." They are hauled and roll off him, and Tom is discovered a motionless body.

Old Brooke picks him up. "Stand back, give him air," he says; and then feeling his limbs, adds, "No bones broken. How do you feel, young 'un?"

"Hah-hah," gasps Tom as his wind comes back, "pretty well, thank you – all right."

"Who is he?" says Brooke.

"Oh, it's Brown, he's a new boy; I know him," says East, coming up.

"Well, he is a plucky youngster, and will make a player," says Brooke.

And five o'clock strikes. "No side" is called, and the first day of the School-house match is over.

(from **Tom Brown's Schooldays** by THOMAS HUGHES)

25

For discussion – part 1

1 How does East, who is Tom's age but has been at the school about six months, try to impress Tom (who is new to Rugby)?

2 Rugby football involved virtually all the boys in School-house. What different parts were played by those of different ages (or size or experience)?

3(a) There is an explanation here of the modern term "in touch". How did the word "touch" come to mean "beyond the side-line(s)"?

(b) A "scrummage" (or "scrimmage") meant a skirmish, scuffle or struggle. What does it (or a "scrum") mean in modern Rugby football?

4 The term "hack" is used here, and whether "hacking" should be permitted was hotly debated in the later history of Rugby Union – what did it mean? Is "hacking" allowed today?

5(a) Crab Jones is an imperturbable forward (or "player-up"). How is his habit of chewing a straw used to emphasise this?

(b) A "praepostor" was a senior pupil given some responsibility in the school. What additional responsibility did the School-house praepostor have in this game?

6 In the earlier part of Tom's first match, School-house had scored. What, then, do you think "No side" means? Under what circumstances do you think a match might have to be continued to a second day?

7 What exactly does Tom do, to earn the congratulations of Old Brooke, the Head Boy and Captain of School-house?

8 In what various ways does this description compare the game to a military battle?

For written answers – part 1

1 What formed the boundary lines for this game at Rugby?

2 What effect did "the three trees" have on the game as played at Rugby?

3 Which players took part in the "scrummages"? What form does

the modern scrummage take?

4 How many players were there on the School side? Contrast this with the numbers on each side in Rugby Union and Rugby League today (both of which developed from the game described in the extracts).

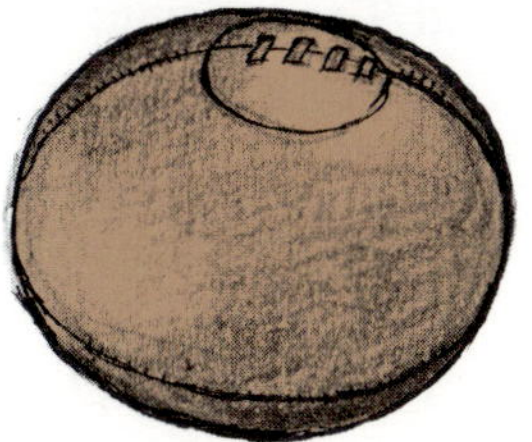

Part 2: At the end of the book, Tom is captaining the school cricket team against the visiting Marylebone eleven from Lord's. Rugby are batting, and Tom and his friend Arthur (who is a finer scholar than Tom) are talking to one of their teachers. The teacher knows as little about cricket as Tom does about classical Greek . . .

"There now," struck in the master, "you see that's just what I have been preaching this half-hour. The delicate play is the true thing. I don't understand cricket, so I don't enjoy those fine draws which you tell me are the best play, though when you or Raggles hit a ball hard away for six I am as delighted as any one. Don't you see the analogy?"

"Yes, sir," answered Tom, looking up roguishly, "I see; only the question remains whether I should have got most good by understanding Greek particles or cricket thoroughly. I'm such a thick, I never should have had time for both."

"I see you are an incorrigible," said the master with a chuckle, "but I refute you by an example. Arthur there has taken in Greek and cricket too."

"Yes, but no thanks to him; Greek came natural to him. Why, when he first came I remember he used to read Herodotus for pleasure as I did Don Quixote, and couldn't have made a false concord if he'd tried ever so hard – and then I looked after his cricket."

"Out! Bailey has given him out – do you see, Tom!" cries Arthur. "How foolish of them to run so hard."

"Well, it can't be helped, he has played very well. Whose turn is it to go in?"

"I don't know; they've got your list in the tent."

"Let's go and see," said Tom, rising; but at this moment Jack Raggles and two or three more come running to the island moat.

"Oh, Brown, mayn't I go in next?" shouts the Swiper.

"Whose name is next on the list?" says the Captain.

"Winter's, and then Arthur's," answers the boy who carries it; "but there are only twenty-six runs to get, and no time to lose. I heard Mr Aislebie say that the stumps must be drawn at a quarter-past eight exactly."

"Oh, do let the Swiper go in," chorus the boys; so Tom yields against his better judgement.

"I daresay now I've lost the match by this nonsense," he says as he sits down again; "they'll be sure to get Jack's wicket in three or four minutes; however, you'll have the chance, sir, of seeing a hard hit or two," adds he, smiling and turning to the master.

"Come, none of your irony, Brown," answers the master. "I'm beginning to understand the game scientifically. What a noble game it is too!"

"Isn't it? But it's more than a game. It's an institution," said Tom.

"Yes," said Arthur, "the birthright of British boys old and young, as *habeas corpus* and trial by jury are of British men."

"The discipline and reliance on one another which it teaches is so valuable, I think," went on the master, "it ought to be such an unselfish game. It merges the individual in the eleven; he doesn't play that he may win, but that his side may."

"That's very true," said Tom. "And that's why football and cricket, now one comes to think of it, are such much better games than fives or hare-and-hounds, or any others where the object is to come in first or to win for oneself, and not that one's side may win."

"And then the Captain of the eleven!" said the master, "what a post is his in our School-world! almost as hard as the Doctor's; requiring skill and gentleness and firmness, and I know not what other rare qualities."

"Which don't he wish he may get?" said Tom laughing; "at any rate he hasn't got them yet, or he wouldn't have been such a flat tonight as to let Jack Raggles go in out of his turn."

"Ah! the Doctor never would have done that," said Arthur, demurely. "Tom, you've a great deal to learn yet in the art of ruling."

(from **Tom Brown's Schooldays** by THOMAS HUGHES)

For discussion – part 2

9(a) What kind of batting does the master enjoy best?
(b) The "fine draw" referred to was when the batsman "drew" a tricky ball "away to leg for a safe one". Is this an example of "delicate play"?

(c) Can you explain what "irony" is? Can you think of any simple examples of irony? In what way is Tom's remark "You'll have the chance, sir, of seeing a hard hit or two" ironic?

10 Why are the boys urging Tom to alter the batting order, and what is Tom's "better judgement" on this matter?

11 The master has been drawing a parallel (an "analogy") between mastery of skill and weapons in appreciating cricket, and mastery of language in appreciating literature. How does Tom explain *his* failure to do well at Greek translation?

12 What do you think is the contrast between "Herodotus" (which Arthur read) and "Don Quixote"? Can you guess what a "false concord" might be?

13 What are "habeas corpus" and "trial by jury", and in what ways are they the "birthright" of British men? Is there any real comparison between these and cricket as the birthright of British boys?

14 Does it remain true today that cricket and football are "unselfish" games? Do you accept the contrast between these and non-team games (such as fives and cross-country running)?

15 What qualities do you think are required *today* in a captain of an amateur team? Would you add to or alter the master's list?

16 The Doctor is Dr Arnold, the famous headmaster who reformed Rugby School and laid down a new philosophy of public school education which was to be widely followed in Victorian England. What is Arthur's attitude to the Doctor?

For written answers – part 2

5 How, apparently, was the batsman out?

6 What is Jack Raggles's nickname, and what kind of reputation has he got as a cricketer?

7 Explain in your own words the contrast between cricket and football on the one hand, and fives and hare-and-hounds on the other.

8 In what ways is Tom dissatisfied with his own captaincy?

THE BALLAD OF BILLY ROSE

Outside Bristol Rovers Football Ground –
The date has gone from me, but not the day,
Nor how the dissenting flags in stiff array
Struck bravely out against the sky's grey round –

Near the Car Park then past Austin and Ford,
Lagonda, Bentley, and a colourful patch
Of country coaches come in for the match
Was where I walked, having travelled the road

From Fishponds to watch Portsmouth in the Cup.
The Third Round, I believe. And I was filled
With the old excitement which had thrilled
Me so completely when, while growing up,

I went on Saturdays to match or fight.
Not only me; for thousands of us there
Strode forward eagerly, each man aware
Of vigorous memory, anticipating delight.

We all moved forward, all, except one man.
I saw him because he was paradoxically still,
A stone against the flood, face upright against us all,
Head bare, hoarse voice aloft. Blind as a stone.

I knew him at once despite his pathetic clothes –
Something in his stance, or his sturdy frame
Perhaps. I could even remember his name
Before I saw it on his blind-man's tray. Billy Rose.

And twenty forgetful years fell away at the sight.
Bare-kneed, dismayed, memory fled to the hub
Of Saturday violence, with friends to the Labour Club,
Watching the boxing on a sawdust summer night.

The boys' enclosure close to the shabby ring
Was where we stood, clenched in a resin world,
Spoke in cool voices, lounged, were artificially bored
During minor bouts. We paid threepence to go in.

Billy Rose fought there. He was top of the bill.
So brisk a fighter, so gallant, so precise!
Trim as a tree he stood for the ceremonies,
Then turned to meet George Morgan of Triphil.

He had no chance. Courage was not enough,
Nor tight defence. Donald Davies was sick
And we threatened his cowardice with an embarrassed ki
Ripped across both his eyes was Rose, but we were tou

And clapped him as they wrapped his blindness up
In busy towels, applauded the wave
He gave his executioners, cheered the brave
Blind man as he cleared with a jaunty hop

The top rope. I had forgotten that day
As if it were dead forever, yet now I saw
Again the flowers of blood on the ring floor
As bright as his name. I cannot say

How long I stood with ghosts of the wild fists
And the cries of shaken boys long dead around me,
For struck to act at last, in terror and pity
I threw some frantic money, three treacherous pence –

And I cry at the memory – into his tray, and ran,
Entering the waves of the stadium like a drowning man.
Poor Billy Rose. God, he could fight
Before my three sharp coins knocked out his sight.

LESLIE NOR

Discussing the poem

1 What do you think the poet and his friends enjoyed about the boxing at the Labour Club when they were boys? Why was Donald Davies sick and what did the others think of him for it? Was the poet's attitude any different twenty years later, when he saw Billy Rose again?

2 Look carefully at the words the poet chooses and the comparisons he makes. In what two places is the crowd compared to a tide or river? Discuss what the poet means by: " the dissenting flags in stiff array", "the hub of Saturday violence", "a sawdust summer night", "clenched in a resin world", "the flowers of blood on the ring floor".

3 Consider the last line: could three pennies ever be used literally to blind someone? In what *indirect* way had the poet paid three pence to make Billy Rose blind?

For learning about language

You will remember from Book 1 that **verbs** are used in different **tenses** to indicate whether the actions took place in the past, are taking place in the present, or will take place in the future.

Much of the writing in the extracts at the beginning of this chapter is in the past tense:

"Tom *listened* with the profoundest respect to this chapter of accidents, and *followed* East across the level ground till they *came* to a sort of gigantic gallows..."

Some of the conversation anticipates the future:

"You *will be* a month learning the rules."

"You *will have to stay* in goal ..."

Verbs often consist of several words, forming a **verb phrase**:

"I *have played* football all my life."

"You *do* not *know* the rules."

This is true also of present tenses, when they are "present continuous" or "present perfect", as well as of past and future tenses.

For example: "Tom *is learning* the rules of rugby although he *has played* football for years."

Exercise 1(a) In the following sentences, the fifteen verbs have been printed in italics. Write out each verb and state its tense (past, present or future).

(1) I *love* football.
(2) You *will need* a month to learn the rules.
(3) One of the goals *was* by the Doctor's wall.
(4) If one side *kicks* two goals, that team *wins*.
(5) How *do* you *keep* the ball between the goals?
(6) Old Brooke *is sweeping* round the edge of the play.
(7) The ball *has passed* him and his voice *rings out*.
(8) The ball *was* slowly *rolling* behind the School-house goal.
(9) Tom *has* already *learned* his job.
(10) The leaders of the pack *were falling* on top of Tom, and he *was gasping* for breath.
(11) He *is* a plucky youngster and *will make* a good player.

(b) Each of those verbs in **(a)** has a **subject** – a noun or pronoun which limits it in person (first, second or third person) and number (singular or plural). Thus the subject of the verb "love" in (1) is:

   I – 1st person singular;

the subject of the verb "will need" in (2) is:

   You – 2nd person singular;

and the subject of the verb "was" in (3) is:

   One of the goals – 3rd person singular.

Copy these down to set the pattern; then give the subjects of the remaining twelve verbs in (4) to (11) in a similar form.

Exercise 2 As we saw above, verbs often appear as **verb phrases** of several words, one of which will be the root-word or **head-word** of the verb:

   have *play*ed . . . do not *know* . . . is *learn*ing.

Study the following, in which the head-word of the verb has been printed in italics:

   They *throw* the ball.
   They have *throw*n the ball.
   They will be *throw*ing the ball.

They should have been *throw*ing the ball.

They will go on *throw*ing the ball.

They ought to *throw* the ball.

Write out the complete verb phrase in each of the following sentences and then underline the head-word of the verb.

Example: He was always playing games.

Answer: was . . . playing.

(Note that "always" is an adverb – saying *when* he was playing – and not part of the verb.)

(a) He has been playing all day.

(b) We shall be playing soon.

(c) I still have to do my homework.

(d) She has already done hers.

(e) Mother had cooked some more mince pies.

(f) The mince pies ought to be cooked by now.

(g) The sweep did not mince his words.

(h) He was going to sweep the chimney.

(i) Sweep the room, please.

(j) Will you be sweeping for long?

Exercise 3 In the following nine sentences made-up subjects and verbs have been used. Can you again recognise and write out the verb phrases and underline the head-words?

Example: A dib was solemnly bangling.

Answer: was . . . bangling.

(a) Dibs bangle.

(b) Dibs have bangled.

(c) Dibs will be bangling.

(d) Dibs may have been bangling.

(e) Bangle all dibs.

(f) Have you been bangling the dibs?

(g) Can you dib a bangle?

(h) He certainly dibs bangles.

(i) Dibs might still be bangling, or bangles might want to dib.

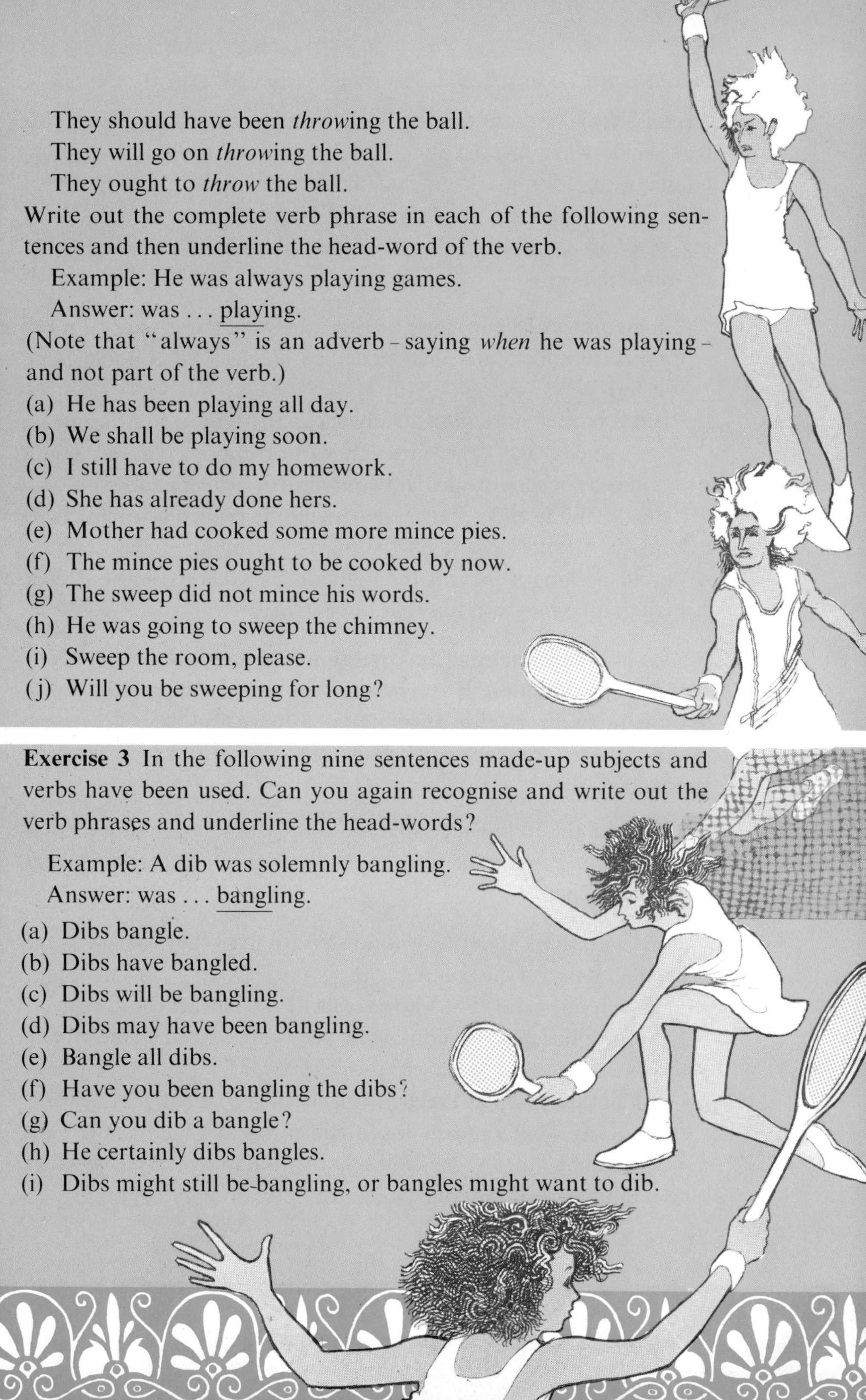

Exercise 4(a) Without turning back to look at the extract, see if you can decide what further punctuation (capital letters, full stops or commas, question marks or exclamation marks, or apostrophes) is necessary to represent the following conversation correctly in writing. (Do *not* write in this book – write out your own version, with the punctuation.)

> "come none of your irony brown" answers the master "im beginning to understand the game scientifically what a noble game it is too"
>
> "isnt it but its more than a game its an institution" said tom
>
> "yes" said arthur "the birthright of british boys old and young as 'habeas corpus' and trial by jury are of british men"
>
> "the discipline and reliance on one another which it teaches is so valuable i think" went on the master "it ought to be such an unselfish game it merges the individual in the eleven he doesnt play that he may win but that his side may"

Notice how exclamations and questions are handled with the conversation punctuation. If you have disagreed with the printed punctuation on page 28 (for example, in using a full stop "... went on the master."), discuss whether there is justification for your version.

(b) Rewrite the following conversation putting in all the punctuation (including one apostrophe). Paragraphing and capital letters are already correct.

> Do you think that one will do said Joyce as they looked at the croquet balls on the counter
>
> Which one asked Pat The red one or the blue or the green
>
> Silly replied Joyce I didnt mean any particular one I meant one as opposed to two or three
>
> Oh in that case Pat laughed you should say what you mean
>
> I did say what I meant Joyce said firmly If I had meant what you thought I meant she continued I would have asked whether you thought that *that* one would do

36

Exercise 5 In Book 1 you looked at **abstract nouns**: the names of qualities, feelings, states, such as courage, anxiety, efficiency, generosity. Many of these nouns have corresponding adjectives:

anger – angry, honesty – honest, patience – patient.

(a) In the following, substitute the corresponding adjective for each abstract noun, as in this example:

Tom's bravery – brave Tom

(1) a rival's envy
(2) Sam's restlessness
(3) the captain's gentleness
(4) a night's discomfort
(5) the young prince's hope
(6) a miser's meanness
(7) old men's miserliness
(8) a shopkeeper's annoyance
(9) the boy's misery
(10) the villain's cowardice

(b) In the remaining ten, you have to make up the phrase using the abstract noun. This will mean using an **apostrophe** to show possession, since the quality belongs to some person(s) (or animal). To revise the correct use of the apostrophe, turn to page 76.

For example:

those strong elephants – those elephants' *strength*

(1) the skilful players
(2) energetic children
(3) this lively photographer
(4) these beautiful women
(5) a proud tigress
(6) a lovely princess
(7) her humble suitors
(8) this punctual patient
(9) the impatient fans
(10) the two confident reporters

For your own writing

1 Write an account of a particular sporting event or match you have watched recently as a spectator, or seen on television, or one you yourself have taken part in. For this you could choose any sport, game or competition, not necessarily one of the popular team-games such as football or cricket.

If possible, prepare for this in advance by refreshing yourself about rules, previous records, progress of the individuals or teams concerned, and other background information. Try to make notes at the time on the main stages and turning-points in the contest. Then try to arrange your material in an interesting shape or pattern, perhaps leading up to a climax, and rounding off with a section on future prospects. Remember to write in paragraphs.

2 Write about your own favourite sport, pastime or hobby in a form that could be an article for a class or school magazine. This means that you have to try to interest readers who know little about the sport, as well as those who may share your enthusiasm. You may need to spend time in a library first, collecting information. At this stage, make rough notes, and remember to write down the title, author and page numbers (or chapter) of each book from which you take information, so that you can quickly refer back to check any details. Also, make rough sketches of any maps, drawings or diagrams you are going to include. The next stage will be to write up the complete article in full, paying careful attention to spelling, to writing in sentences, and to dividing the article into paragraphs.

For talk and action

1 The class could be divided into groups to discuss the following topics (one each or one by one). Each group should appoint a spokesman or spokeswoman to record their views and report back to the whole class.

(a) What differences are there between team games (rugby, cricket, soccer, hockey, netball etc.) in the public school traditions of the nineteenth century, and team games played by professionals in this century? Have today's players lost the ideals or the enjoyment of playing their best as a team? Give examples, past or present, of good team-play or sportsmanship, including any from games you have seen on television or as a spectator yourself.

(b) Which games do you like best (1) to play, (2) to watch? Contrast the enjoyment to be found in playing or taking part with the pleasure of watching. Is there a third kind of excitement to be derived from supporting a team? Do you approve of betting on results?

(c) The skills and rules of all sports have developed and been fixed (on an inter-club and international basis) since the early days of free-for-all football and Rugby football. Have all the changes, with the setting of higher standards of skill and fitness, been of benefit to ordinary people like you? Are you pleased that you live in a society where sports (and all the facilities for them) are so highly developed and widely available?

(d) If girls want to play soccer or rugby at school, should they be encouraged to do so? Which sports and games do you regard as mainly for boys, mainly for girls, or equally for both? Are there real differences between these sports? Are the attitudes that girls have to sport usually different from boys' attitudes, or is this just another relic of a male-dominated tradition in our history? What examples are there of real physical or mental differences between men and women that dictate different levels of performance or attitude?

(e) How important are schools (past or present, in Britain or elsewhere) in fostering sports and competitive games? Is being keen on sport something you learn, or something everyone is born with, or something that depends on a high standard of living with time and money to spare? Can Britain claim to be the greatest (or most enthusiastic) sporting nation?

(f) Who have been the greatest players and athletes of all time? Support the claim for certain sportsmen and sportswomen (past or present) to receive the title of "superstars" in sport. Who would you select, and why?

2 See if the class can be organised to produce their own form magazine or newspaper. Producing one issue a week may involve too much time and effort, but at least you could aim at one complete edition to be produced during the term.

How you reproduce your magazine will depend on the facilities available. Probably your school will have a duplicator, and if it and the paper are available, you can print pages and staple them together. Find out what the machine will do, whether it can reproduce illustrations or photographs, and whether you have to type articles on special stencils or with special carbons. If no form of duplicator is available, then at least the magazine could be typed or written out with carbon copies, say four or five copies in all, to be passed round the class and to friends. Alternatively the whole magazine could be neatly written out (on single sides) and pinned up on the noticeboard.

To organise the magazine, it is a good idea to elect an editorial committee to select and arrange the material for each edition. One committee member can be editor and write the editorial. Other members of the class will be feature-writers, reporters, interviewers, science, sports and social correspondents, reviewers of books, radio and television programmes, and so on. Illustrations will probably be best done or chosen by those who wrote the articles.

The class must also decide on a suitable name for the magazine, on whether (and how much) to charge for copies and where the best market is likely to be. School occasions (speech day, exhibition evening, or when there is a concert or play or parents' evening) are often good times to go round selling copies to parents and friends of the school, especially if the profits are going to some charity chosen by the class.

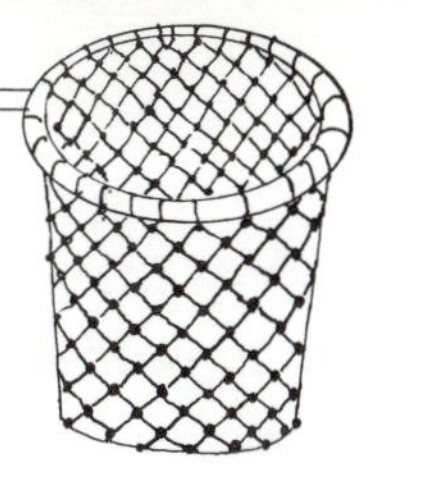

For further reading

Tom Brown's Schooldays by THOMAS HUGHES (various publishers including Puffin)
This enduring classic amongst school stories has never been out of print since it was first published in 1857. Based on the tough and demanding life at Rugby School when Dr Arnold first became Head, this is a story packed with adventure and feeling, describing the experiences of a boy who has a lot to learn about himself and other people.

The Puffin Book of Athletics by NEIL ALLEN (Puffin)
This wide-ranging book covers both track and field athletics – their history, the big events and the record-breakers. As well as a list of world records and gold medal winners, there is a practical guide for young athletes on "Athletics for You". (Classified as 796.4.)

The Oxford Companion to Sports and Games edited by JOHN ARLOTT (O.U.P.)
This is more than a reference book – it is a key to understanding and therefore enjoying most of the physical sports and games played nationally or internationally. (796.4)

Only a Game? Diary of a Professional Footballer by EAMON DUNPHY, edited by Peter Ball (Peacock; Penguin)
This is the diary of an adult professional footballer, funny, painful, tough and very convincing as an account of the modern world of soccer. (796.33)

The Olympic Games by MICHAEL GRANT (Kestrel)
The account concentrates on the origins of the modern Games in Greece, from the eighth to the third century B.C., with the careful training, strict rules and curious religious and social customs of the ancient festivals. (796.4)

3 Mystery and Magic

Tom is staying with his uncle and aunt in their flat in a large old house. In the hall stands a grandfather clock, which keeps good time but often strikes the wrong hours. One night Tom is convinced that the clock has struck thirteen, and he goes down to investigate . . .

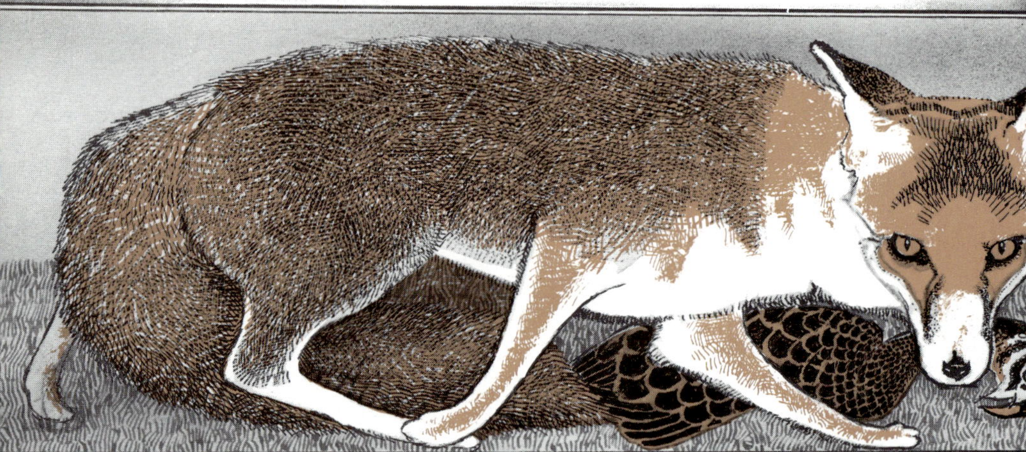

The grandfather clock was still there, anyway, and must tell him the true time. It must be either twelve or one: there was no hour between. There is no thirteenth hour.

Tom never reached the clock with his inquiry, and may be excused for forgetting, on this occasion, to check its truthfulness. His attention was distracted by the opening of a door down the hall – the door of the ground-floor front flat. A maid trotted out.

Tom had seen housemaids only in pictures, but he recognised the white apron, cap and cuffs, and the black stockings. (He was not expert in fashions, but the dress seemed to him to be rather long for her.) She was carrying paper, kindling wood and a box of matches.

He had only a second in which to observe these things. Then he realised that he ought to take cover at once; and there was no cover to take. Since he must be seen, Tom determined to be the first to speak – to explain himself.

He did not feel afraid of the maid: as she came nearer, he saw that

42

she was only a girl. To warn her of his presence without startling her, Tom gave a cough; but she did not seem to hear it. She came on. Tom moved forward into her line of vision; she looked at him, but looked through him, too, as though he were not there. Tom's heart jumped in a way he did not understand. She was passing him.

"I say!" he protested loudly; but she paid not the slightest attention. She passed him, reached the front door of the ground-floor back flat, turned the door-handle and went in. There was no bell-ringing or unlocking of the door.

Tom was left gaping; and, meanwhile, his senses began to insist upon telling him of experiences even stranger than this encounter. His one bare foot was on cold flagstone, he knew; yet there was a contradictory softness and warmth to this flagstone. He looked down and saw that he was standing on a rug – a tiger-skin rug. There were other rugs down the hall. His eyes now took in the whole of the hall – a hall that was different. No laundry box, no milk bottles,

43

no travel posters on the walls. The walls were decorated with a rich variety of other objects instead: a tall Gothic barometer, a fan of peacock feathers, a huge engraving of a battle (hussars and horses and shot-riddled banners) and many other pictures. There was a big dinner gong, with its wash-leathered gong-stick hanging beside it. There was a large umbrella-stand holding umbrellas and walking-sticks and a parasol and an airgun and what looked like the parts of a fishing-rod. Along the wall projected a series of bracket-shelves, each table-high. They were of oak, except for one towards the middle of the hall, by the grandfather clock. That was of white marble, and it was piled high with glass cases of stuffed birds and animals. Enacted on its chilly surface were scenes of hot bloodshed: an owl clutched a mouse in its claws; a ferret looked up from the killing of its rabbit; in a case in the middle a red fox slunk along with a gamefowl hanging from its jaws.

In all that crowded hall, the only object that Tom recognised was the grandfather clock. He moved towards it, not to read its face, but simply to touch it – to reassure himself that this at least was as he knew it.

His hand was nearly upon it, when he heard a little breath behind him that was the maid passing back the way she had come. For some reason, she did not seem to make as much sound as before. He heard her call only faintly: " I've lit the fire in the parlour."

She was making for the door through which she had first come, and, as Tom followed her with his eyes, he received a curious impression: she reached the door, her hand was upon the knob, and then she seemed to go. That was it exactly: she went, but not through the door. She simply thinned out, and went.

Even as he stared at where she had been, Tom became aware of something going on furtively and silently about him. He looked round sharply, and caught the hall in the act of emptying itself of furniture and rugs and pictures. They were not positively going, perhaps, but rather beginning to fail to be there. The Gothic barometer, for instance, was there, before he turned to look at the red fox; when he turned back, the barometer was still there, but it had the appearance of something only sketched against the wall, and the wall was visible through it; meanwhile the fox had slunk into nothingness, and all the other creatures were going with him; and, turning back again swiftly to the barometer, Tom found that gone already.

(from **Tom's Midnight Garden** by A. PHILIPPA PEARCE)

For discussion

1 Why did Tom feel he ought to take cover when the maid appeared? Why, in fact, was it not necessary?

2 Why do you think Tom's heart jumped?

3 Why would Tom expect the maid to ring the bell or unlock the door when she first passed out of the hall?

4 What words here indicate that Tom had only one slipper on? (He had left the other in the door of his uncle's flat, to stop it from closing.)

5 Why do *you* think the maid made less noise on her second journey through the hall?

6 What is the difference between "positively going" and "beginning to fail to be there" (in the last paragraph)?

7 What are, or were, the following?

"a Gothic barometer" "a parasol"
"an engraving" "a ferret"
"a wash-leathered gong-stick" "a gamefowl"

8 What do you think had happened in the hall when Tom went down at "thirteen o'clock"?

9 If you find the idea of these stuffed animals unpleasant, explain how the author has given you this impression.

10 Discuss how the author gives this extract a sense of mystery and strangeness. Is Tom really frightened? Would you have been frightened?

11 Do you believe in ghosts? Do you think it is possible to travel back (or forwards) in time? Could there be any reasonable explanation of Tom's experience?

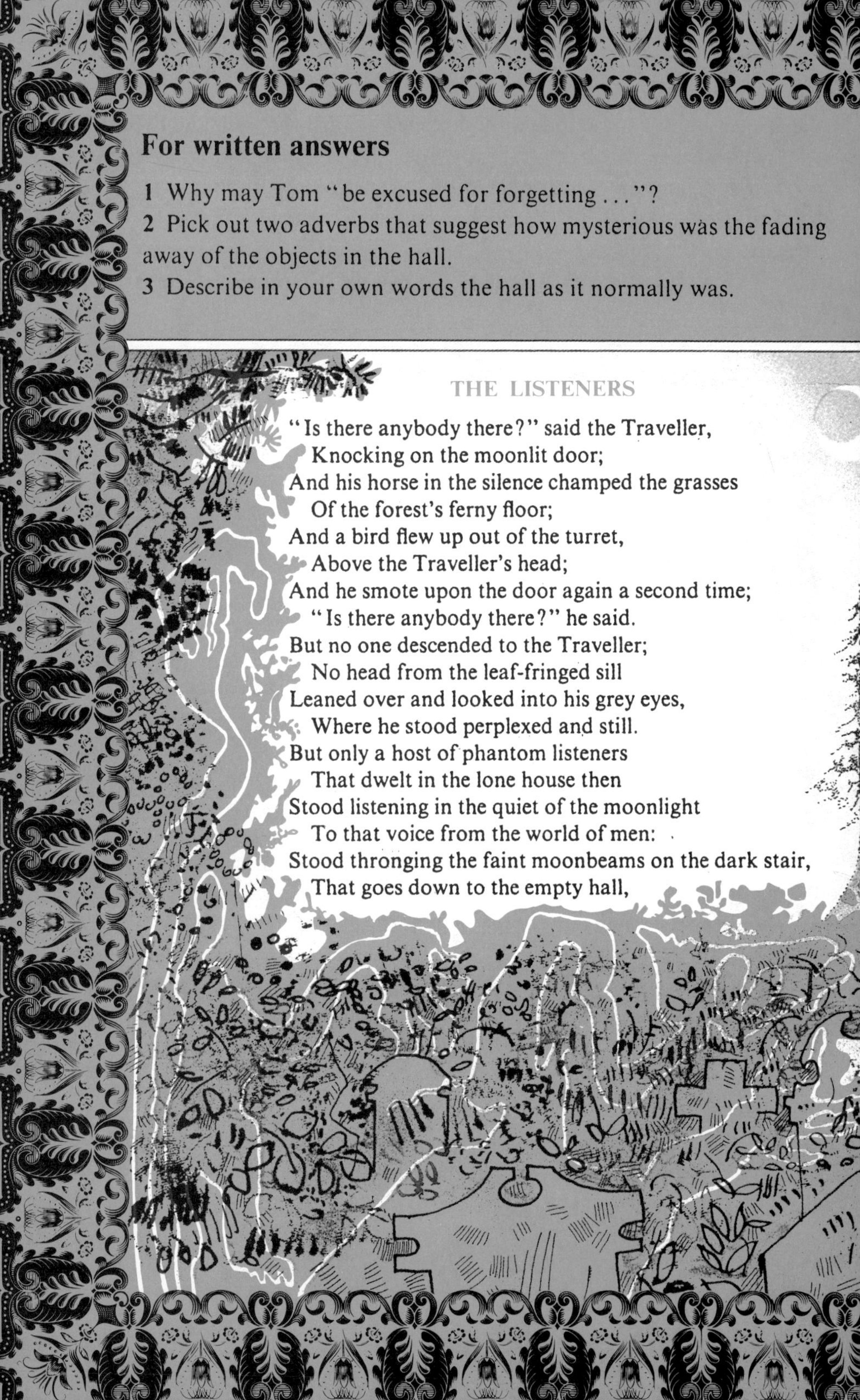

THE LISTENERS

"Is there anybody there?" said the Traveller,
   Knocking on the moonlit door;
And his horse in the silence champed the grasses
   Of the forest's ferny floor;
And a bird flew up out of the turret,
   Above the Traveller's head;
And he smote upon the door again a second time;
   "Is there anybody there?" he said.
But no one descended to the Traveller;
   No head from the leaf-fringed sill
Leaned over and looked into his grey eyes,
   Where he stood perplexed and still.
But only a host of phantom listeners
   That dwelt in the lone house then
Stood listening in the quiet of the moonlight
   To that voice from the world of men:
Stood thronging the faint moonbeams on the dark stair,
   That goes down to the empty hall,

Hearkening in an air stirred and shaken
   By the lonely Traveller's call.
And he felt in his heart their strangeness,
   Their stillness answering his cry,
While his horse moved, cropping the dark turf,
   'Neath the starred and leafy sky;
For he suddenly smote on the door, even
   Louder, and lifted his head: –
"Tell them I came, and no one answered,
   That I kept my word," he said.
Never the least stir made the listeners,
   Though every word he spake
Fell echoing through the shadowiness of the still house
   From the one man left awake:
Ay, they heard his foot upon the stirrup,
   And the sound of iron on stone,
And how the silence surged softly backward,
   When the plunging hoofs were gone.

WALTER DE LA MARE

Discussing the poem

1 Can you tell why the Traveller was calling at this place at this time? Can you guess what his business might have been?

2 Which details in the poem seem particularly effective in suggesting (a) the silence and solitude of the spot, (b) the dark night, and (c) the frightening air of mystery?

3 Do you think there was really anyone listening?

For learning about language

In Book 1 we learnt that a full statement sentence requires at least a subject (the person, place or thing that we are talking about) and a verb (a doing or being word) to tell us what is happening. A statement may contain much more, but we expect at least a noun (or pronoun) and a verb. Consider, for example, these two sentences:

(1) Corks pop.
(2) The corks of champagne bottles usually pop when pushed up with the thumb.

In both, the subject is the noun "corks" and the verb is "pop".

Exercise 1 In the following lists you will find fifteen nouns and fifteen verbs. The nouns are people, animals or things which make the noises represented by the verbs, but these are not in the corresponding order.

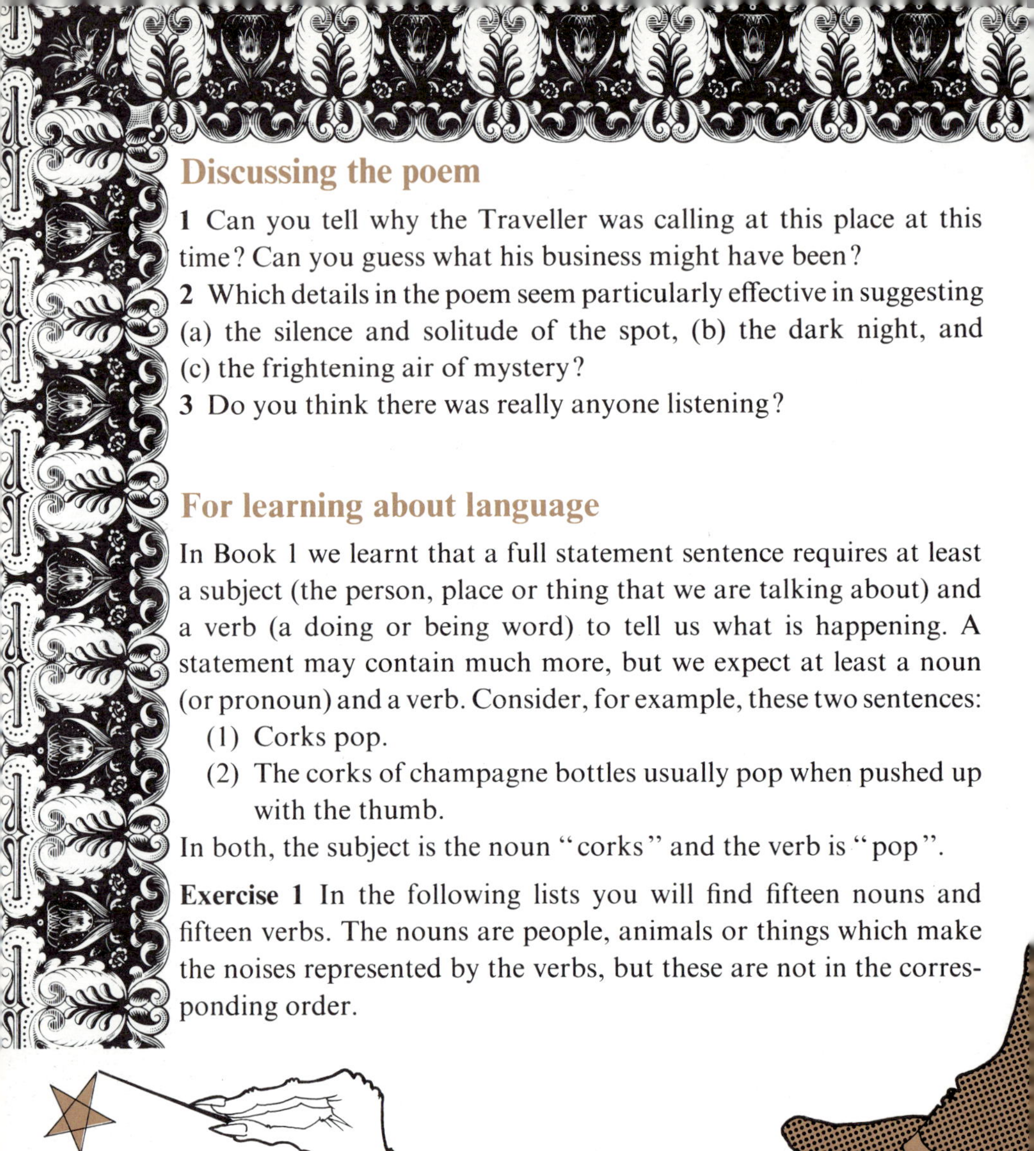

Pair off the nouns and verbs, and construct *two* sentences for each pair, like the examples (1) and (2) above; one a very short sentence, the other a longer sentence that still uses the same subject and verb.

NOUNS: babies, bells, brakes, clocks, dogs, doors, guns, (rusty) hinges, horses, monks, pistols, sleepers, streams, tom-cats, trumpets

VERBS: babble, blare, boom, caterwaul, chant, crack, cry, grate, peal, screech, slam, snore, tick, whine, whinny

As you have probably noticed in working out answers to Exercise 1, there is no rule in English to say that the subject must come first in the sentence. You may even find the subject after the verb. Consider these examples from the extract:

Along the wall projected a series of bracket-shelves, each table-high.

What projected, the wall or the shelves?

Enacted on its chilly surface were scenes of hot bloodshed.

What were enacted, the surface, the scenes, or the bloodshed?

Exercise 2(a) What are the subjects of the verbs in the following sentences, all of which have been adapted from the extract? To help you, the verbs have been put in italics.

(1) Tom never *reached* the clock.
(2) His attention *was distracted* by the opening of a door.
(3) Tom *had seen* housemaids only in pictures.
(4) "I *say*," he *protests* loudly.
(5) The walls *were decorated* with a rich variety of other objects.
(6) In a case in the middle a red fox *is slinking* along.
(7) "I*'ll light* the fire in the parlour."
(8) The Gothic barometer, for instance, *was* there at first.
(9) Meanwhile the fox *had slunk* into nothingness.
(10) All the other creatures *will be going* with him.

(b) Remembering what you learnt in Book 1, and revised in the last chapter, can you state the **tense** of each of the verbs printed in italics in **(a)**, above?

Exercise 3 It is usually easy to pick out the subject word of a statement sentence, but more difficult to spot the subject of a question, command or exclamation sentence. Consider these examples:

All last night the dog was howling.
What kind of a noise was the dog making all last night?
What a noise the dog was making all last night!
Make no noise during the night.

Is the subject of the question and the exclamation the noise or the dog? In order to find the grammatical subject, turn the sentences into the equivalent statement sentence:

The dog was making a noise all last night.

– or the question can be turned into the simplest of replies:

The dog was making a great noise last night.

The command is more complicated, because we do not usually name the subject at all – it is just "you", that is, whoever we happen to be talking to. It means:

You must make no noise. . . .

The subject is therefore "*you* understood", or the name of the person (or animal) commanded.

Write out the subject of each of the following sentences. Write them in full, with all the adjectives etc., and then underline the subject word, or **head-word**, of the subject.

For example:

During the last dance, did any young lady in the hall lose a shoe?

subject: any young <u>lady</u> in the hall

(a) Has the general's daughter got her shoe back?
(b) How utterly lost the poor travellers felt that night!
(c) George, watch your step with all those parcels!
(d) After a long, delicious meal of soup, roast beef, apple tart, cheese and coffee, the members of the committee no longer felt like discussing their problems.
(e) What is Her Majesty's Government doing about the roads?

(f) Will the main system of motorways be linked to adequate ring roads?

(g) My dear friend, please imagine yourself in my position.

(h) What hope has a football club like that?

(i) What did the last lot of tenants pay for their flats?

(j) What a long while the children had to wait!

Exercise 4(a) Without looking back at the extract, discuss where commas are necessary in these sentences, and why:

> No laundry box no milk bottles no travel posters on the walls. The walls were decorated with a rich variety of other objects instead: a tall Gothic barometer a fan of peacock feathers a huge engraving of a battle (hussars and horses and shot-riddled banners) and many other pictures. There was a big dinner gong with its wash-leathered gong-stick hanging beside it.

Turn back to see if commas were in fact used where you would have put them, and revise the rule represented by each case. Are there other uses of the comma that do not appear here but were covered in Book 1?

(b) Rewrite the following passage, inserting the twenty commas that are required.

> Fog rolled in from the sea twirling twisting creeping oozing round the buildings on the sea front. Its cold fingers felt the window panes and poked into cracks chinks and crevices through every open window down every chimney under every door. Wet coarse cold choking it breathed into our lungs hung damply on our eyebrows soaked chilly into our garments. Through the dark blank mysterious wall of fog could be heard muffled echoes: a cough footsteps on the stone the distant hoot of ships' sirens. Even the sea seemed cold subdued forlorn.

Exercise 5(a) Here are five *nouns* to do with fear or mystery. What different feelings do they suggest? Can you add at least five more nouns?

> shudder   terror   palpitation   qualm   alarm

(b) Here are five *verbs* to do with fear or mystery. What is the difference between the feelings they represent? Can you add at least five more?

shrink   haunt   horrify   torment   blench

(c) Here are five *adjectives* describing frightening experiences or frightened people. Again, give the meanings and add five more.

hideous   nervous   aghast   eerie   sinister

(d) Here are five *phrases* to do with fear. Again, give the meanings and add five others if you can.

to have cold feet   to turn white as a sheet
to make someone's flesh creep   to make one's teeth chatter
to make the blood run cold

(e) Make up five short, vivid descriptions of different terrifying experiences, using some of the words given above, or those that you have collected yourself.

For example:

As I saw the mutilated body lying in the road by the car, my blood ran cold and I blenched, aghast at what had happened. The chill terror seemed to be urging me to turn and run.

1 Study the extract from **Tom's Midnight Garden** again, noting how the author uses detail and a careful choice of words and phrases to build up a description full of mystery and wonder. The situation is incredible, but the way she tells the story makes it seem real.

There is an art in conveying suspense or mystery in words. Part of the secret is economy: you must not explain too much too soon, but keep the reader uncertain about what is going to happen. Even more important is your choice of descriptive words: those that are always being used ("he was terrified", "it was awful", "you could have knocked him down with a feather") have no real effect on the reader, so you need to find fresh and original words and comparisons. But perhaps most important is your ability to imagine exactly what it would be like, exactly how someone would feel at the terrifying moment, and then to make the reader share these feelings.

Write a ghost story or a short thriller of your own, remembering to try to make it credible, so that anything weird or frightening does seem real and convincing. If you have no good ideas of your own for a plot, then you could continue the story of Tom in the extract, bringing it to a conclusion of your own invention.

2 Write a free verse poem, expressing strong feelings of terror, horror, disgust or mystery. It will probably be better not to tell a story, but to imagine some vivid incident and concentrate on your feelings and reactions. What flashed through your mind's eye? What did you want to do? What did you feel like, in your stomach, or the palms of your hands, or the roots of your hair? Write simply and directly, going from one word-picture to the next as swiftly and simply as the words will let you. This is much more important than worrying about rhyme or rhythm.

On the opposite page is an example written by a boy of about your age.

The best poems could be selected for publication in the class magazine, possibly with accompanying illustrations.

For talk and action

1 Tom's midnight adventures took him back in time about 75 years. Imagine you are able to travel back in time, and prepare, for the class or for the class magazine, an account of a visit to any past age. Use all the reference books you can to help get details correct. The section 942 in most libraries is devoted to British history, and you should look for books such as: **London Through the Ages** by Dorothy M. Stuart (Methuen), 942.1; **Growing up in the 13th Century** by Alfred Duggan (Faber), 942.035; **Illustrated English Social History**, 4 volumes, by G. M. Trevelyan (Longmans), 942.

2 Prepare for a debate on the proposal "That it is foolish to believe in ghosts". You will need a chairman to conduct the discussion in an orderly fashion, and a proposer and a seconder to prepare speeches (to be given first and third respectively) on one side, and an opposer and a seconder for the opposition (to speak second and fourth respectively) on the other. The two seconders prepare shorter speeches, since part of their task is to give answers to the arguments that the proposer or opposer has just put forward. The debate is then thrown open to the rest of the audience to speak (one at a time!), and three minutes before the end the proposer (only) has the right to make a *short final speech*. Then two tellers (or counters of votes), appointed beforehand, count the votes for and the votes against, and the chairman declares the proposal carried or defeated, and adjourns the debate.

For further reading

Tom's Midnight Garden by A. PHILIPPA PEARCE (O.U.P.; Heinemann; Puffin)

Tom's midnight excursions take him back in time to make friends with a girl called Hattie who had been lonely in that house years before. He finds that he is visiting the house and its beautiful garden at different stages in her life, and only on the last day of his stay does he discover the secret of his mysterious adventures.

Philippa Pearce has written several other stories (published O.U.P.; Puffin); **Minnow on the Say** is particularly good. The "Minnow" is a canoe which David finds swept down by floodwaters to the landing-stage at the bottom of his garden. It leads him to his friendship with Adam and into a most unusual treasure-hunt.

Ghostly Gallery and **Witch's Brew** by ALFRED HITCHCOCK (Puffin)
These collections offer spooky and weird horrors, ancient and modern, for those who like uncanny tales of the supernatural.

A Wrinkle in Time by MADELINE L'ENGLE (Longman; Kestrel; Puffin)
Mrs Whatsit, the strange visitor in a man's felt hat, a shocking-pink stole, rough overcoat and black rubber boots, arrives mysteriously one dark, stormy night and sets the Murrays on the track of their father – an eminent physicist who was lost on a government mission.

A Traveller in Time by ALISON UTTLEY (Faber; Puffin)
Penelope, visiting her uncle and aunt at the sixteenth-century farm-house, Thackers, strays through a door and finds herself talking to an Elizabethan aunt kneading dough in an Elizabethan kitchen. The Babingtons are supposed to have lived at Thackers, and through her dreams Penelope becomes increasingly involved with the family and with the fate of Mary, Queen of Scots.

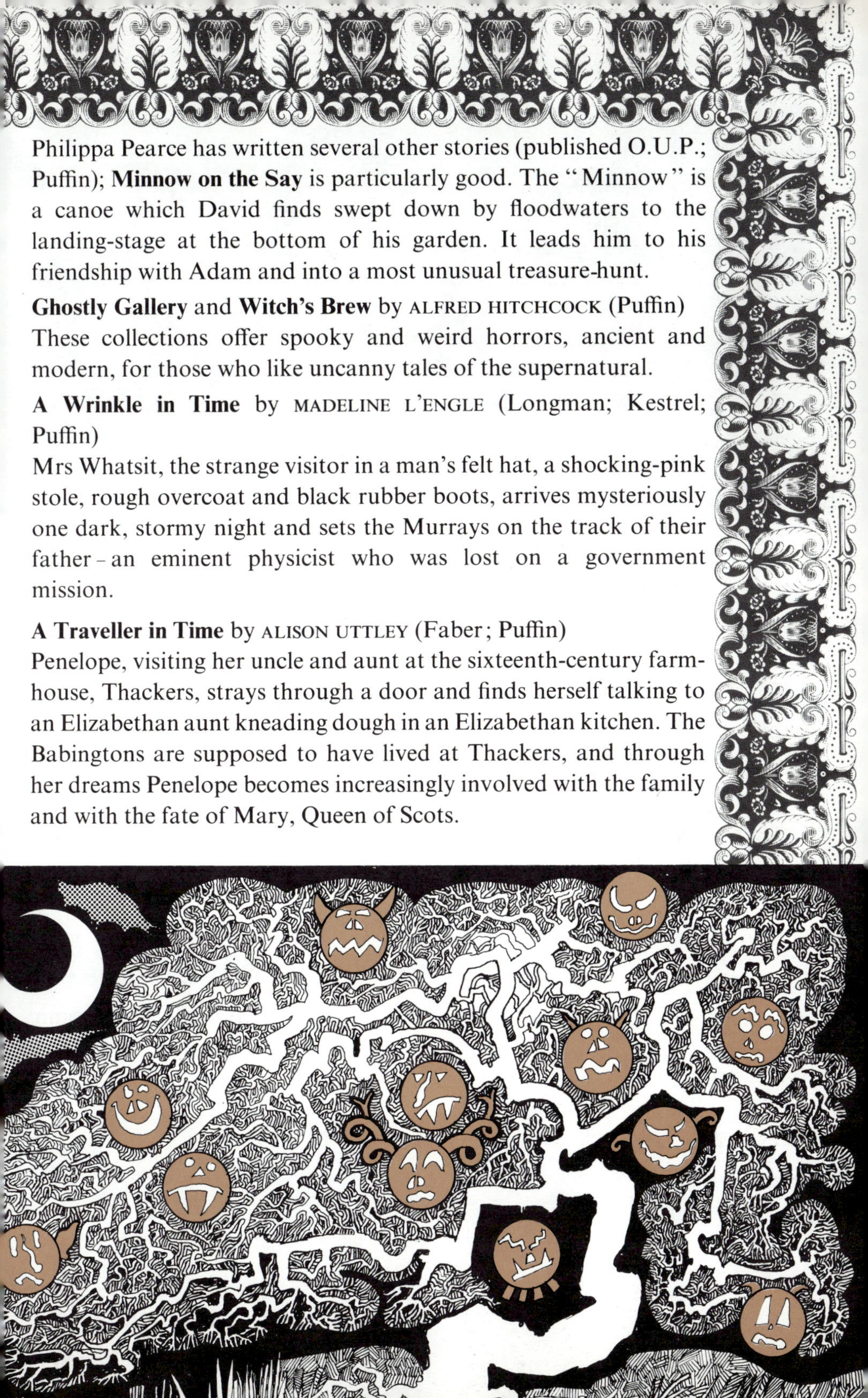

4   **Trapped**

*Jake, Martin and their grandfather are trapped without light in a
disused drift-mine (a tunnel into the cliff-face) alongside the deeper
Annerton Pit. Both sets of workings have been abandoned since the
disaster of 1837. Jake, 15, the youngest, has been blind from birth;
it is therefore Jake who is best able to explore further into the
darkness of the tunnel . . .*

Twenty yards up the tunnel Jake paused. He wished he had his stick.
The floor was mostly smooth clay, slippery on the surface and
slightly rubbery below, but here and there chunks of rock – or was
it coal? – had fallen from the roof and were half embedded in the
clay. He listened to the drips around him, tuning out the metallic
tock of the can he'd placed under a more rapid drip a few yards
back. He clicked his tongue against his palate to set up more echoes –
yes, there was what Granpa had called a monks-working cell on his
left, the third he'd passed, but the other two had been as drippy as
the main tunnel. He moved to the entrance and clapped his hands.
The echo came straight back at him, a curt denial, as though to say
"Not this way, buster." A couple of claps more and he knew that
the chamber broadened from the entrance till it was about five feet
wide and three or four times as long. It was empty, and felt no drier
than anywhere else.

As he moved on up the tunnel he began to worry about Granpa's
last words. If you have any trouble breathing . . . What had old Mr
Smith said about Annerton Pit? Never any trouble with gas. Never
any explosions . . . But this wasn't Annerton Pit. Jake had done the
Industrial Revolution in last year's history. He had never somehow
got hold of it, and finished with poor marks, but he remembered
strongly a description of the man dressed in layer on layer of damp
rags who crawled round the mine with a flame on the end of a long
stick, setting off little explosions in the pockets of gas that had built

57

up near the roof, so they couldn't grow big enough to cause a real bang. There was choke-damp and firedamp. You had to keep the air moving. But the air in here was as still as the grave.

Close at hand the hill hooted. Now, *that* was moving air. And moving water too, rippling beneath the hoot. Jake moved more carefully forward, concentrating on the sound, tuning out the surrounding drips and echoes. Now more than ever it seemed to come out of the rocks all round him, until he was actually standing at what seemed to be its centre, but still without being able to feel the slightest movement in the dead air of the mine.

He shrugged and was moving on when he realised that the nature of the floor had changed. It was as slimy as ever on the surface, but underneath was unyielding. A pace on and a pace back he found the familiar squidge of clay, but in the middle was this hard level patch. He stamped his foot on it, producing a thud that was barely a sound, more a resonance that travelled up the bones of his other leg. But yes, here the floor was hollow, and through the hollow place water was chuckling and air hooting. At the acid touch of reason the ghost melted into nothing.

Granpa and Martin were arguing as he came back, arguing about the ghost in Annerton Pit ...

"... looked up the records," Granpa was saying, "before I left Newcastle. It was a very wet spring and summer, just right for a rock-slip, with the water-table rising and lubricating strata that are normally dry. Both shafts blocked, cutting off ventilation. And, you see, the rock-slip might release a big pocket of gas. Candles everywhere ... So there was an explosion."

"Nobody heard one," said Martin, unable to prevent himself scoring the point, even though he must have known that Granpa had to get through the argument before he could rest.

"It could have been blanketed by the sound of the rock-slip," said Granpa. "Or they didn't hear it at the surface through the blocked shafts. Or they did hear it and the owners suppressed the fact, because they hadn't been using safety lamps ... after a big explosion you get a rush of choke-damp – carbon dioxide mixed

58

with coal-dust. They could all have been gathered at the bottom of the shaft and suffocated there, without a mark on them."

"They let it out of the rock," said Jake. He had dissolved his own ghost, but was still glad to help Granpa do the same to Mr Smith's. "He meant the gas," he added.

"Well, you got that off your chest, Granpa," Martin said. "Find anything, Jake?"

"I don't know, I didn't go right to the end. Everywhere's just as damp as everywhere else. There's one place where the floor's hollow. You can hear the wind hooting through, and water running."

"Wind?" said Martin. "That's got to come from somewhere. Are you sure?"

(from Annerton Pit by PETER DICKINSON)

For discussion

1 Jake "wished he had his stick". How would it have been useful? Without it, what method did he use to "see" the size and shape of the drift-mine?

2 Explain what Jake was doing when "tuning out" the "metallic tock" (first paragraph) and later the "surrounding drips and echoes" (third paragraph).

3 Which kind of gas ("choke-damp" or "firedamp") do you think the man in damp rags ignited? Why was he dressed in damp rags and why did he crawl, do you think?

4 What kind of noise do you imagine from the words "the hill hooted"? What different noise is represented by "rippling", "chuckling", "running" water?

5 What do you think is the distinction between a "sound" and a "resonance"?

6 What do you think lay under the "hard level patch" that Jake found? What use do you think Granpa, Martin and Jake might make of this discovery?

7 Why is Martin excited about Jake's news that he could hear the wind "hooting through"?

8 What hints are there in this extract that Granpa had set out to investigate the "ghost" of Annerton Pit? Do you think Granpa believed in ghosts?

9 The story that came down through "old Mr Smith" and his family was that the miners had "let a ghost out" in 1837. What was Granpa's theory as to how the miners might have died?

10(a) What do you think is meant by: "At the acid touch of reason the ghost melted into nothing"?

(b) Martin says to Granpa, "You got that off your chest." What does he mean? Do you think Granpa felt any better afterwards?

11 Explain, if you can, what these phrases mean:

"a curt denial"

"the . . . squidge of clay"

"just right for a rock-slip, with the water-table rising and lubricating strata that are normally dry".

For written answers

1(a) What, according to the extract, was "choke-damp"?

(b) What do you think "firedamp" is?

(c) Is either of these explosive?

(d) Under what circumstances do you think "firedamp" might cause a pit disaster?

2 What was mysterious about the corpses found after the Annerton Pit disaster?

3 What did this mystery have to do with the story of the ghost?

4 Granpa offers three possible reasons for thinking there was an explosion, even though the disaster was not afterwards recorded as a pit explosion. What were these reasons? (Write them in your own words.)

CALIBAN IN THE COAL MINES

God, we don't like to complain –
We know that the mine is no lark –
But – there's the pools from the rain;
But – there's the cold and the dark.

God, You don't know what it is –
You in Your well-lighted sky,
Watching the meteors whizz;
Warm, with the sun always by.

God, if You had but the moon
Stuck in Your cap for a lamp,
Even You'd tire of it soon,
Down in the dark and the damp.

Nothing but blackness above,
And nothing that moves but the cars –
God, if You wish for our love
Fling us a handful of stars.

LOUIS UNTERMEYER

Discussing the poem

1 Find out who Caliban was (in Shakespeare's play **The Tempest**), and try to explain the title of this poem.

2 What features of working in a mine does the poem describe? What, for instance, are "the cars"?

3 Why are the miners addressing God? Is the poem suggesting that life in a mine is "God-forsaken"?

For learning about language

Certain verbs need (or can have) an **object**, as well as a **subject**, to make complete sense. Jake said to Granpa:

He meant the gas.

The subject of that sentence is "he" (old Mr Smith), the verb is "meant", and "the gas" is the **object**, *what* he meant.

Exercise 1 In the following examples, the objects (i.e. the things meant, explored, lost, placed etc.) have been printed *in italics*. In each case, identify the subject and the verb, like this:

subject – he; verb – meant.

(a) Jake explored *the tunnel*.

(b) He had lost *his precious stick*.

(c) He had placed *a can* under one of the drips.

(d) He clapped *his hands*.

(e) Jake had studied *the Industrial Revolution*.

(f) A man, dressed in rags, sets off *little explosions*.

(g) Jake stamped *his foot* on the level path.

(h) His stamp produced *a thud*.

(i) Nobody heard *an explosion*.

(j) You can hear *the wind*.

Exercise 2 Think of suitable objects to complete the following sentences, and rewrite them completed.

(a) At Waterloo, Wellington defeated ...

(b) Britain, Russia and America fought ... in the Second World War.

(c) A wheelwright makes and repairs ...

(d) George Stephenson built ...

(e) In the play by Shakespeare, Romeo loved ...

(f) Fog often holds up ...

(g) In 1492 Columbus discovered ...

(h) Florence Nightingale founded ...

(i) Elizabeth Fry used to visit ...

(j) Charles Dickens wrote ...

62

Exercise 3 In the following sentences, exchange the subjects for the objects. For example: The chairman selected the committee.

The committee selected the chairman.

(a) The hero shot the villain through the shoulder.
(b) Every nice girl loves a sailor.
(c) A well-known young offender has just attacked an old lady.
(d) You may like your best friend, but I prefer mine. (*N.B. 2 verbs*)
(e) Workers need the new factories.
(f) They used to know us.
(g) Battling Bill defeated Slim Jim in the ring.
(h) You can take your friends home after the party.
(i) The cavalry attacked the troops on the left flank first.

Exercise 4(a) Look carefully at the paragraphing of the extract from **Annerton Pit**. What is each paragraph about and why did the author go on to a new paragraph in each case? Discuss also the way in which each paragraph is linked to the next. A paragraph is, of course, a series of sentences about one subject or one aspect of a subject, but a good writer ensures that each paragraph leads logically on to the next. Thus, at the end of the second paragraph, the mention of the need to keep air moving in a mine leads on to the beginning of the next paragraph where Jake is puzzled to hear air (and water) on the move somewhere close at hand. Examine the other paragraphs to see how one is linked to the next in each case, and how paragraphing is also used in setting out conversation.

(b) The following account should be divided into five paragraphs. Indicate where you would divide the passage either by writing it out in full or by writing down the first three and last three words of each paragraph. Be prepared to discuss your reasons for these divisions.

Caves were used as shelters or homes from the earliest times, but for Old Stone Age man many caves seem to have had a further importance. In these caves we find the most remarkable evidence of their skill with painting and sculpture. And the caves containing this evidence are often long distances into the hillside, where there is no daylight and no easy access. Clearly they were not caves to be lived in. On the walls of these caves the primitive artists scratched or painted pictures of the animals they knew and hunted. But they were not painting for the pleasure of decorating the walls. The animals are often shown with arrows piercing them, and it is quite clear that the artists believed that by painting them they were gaining power over them, so that the animals would really appear to be hunted, killed and eaten. This helps explain the great care the artists took to record the animals they hunted, the bulls, horses, deer, reindeer and buffalo. Artists must have worked by the flickering light of torches made of branches or the feeble flames of rough stone lamps burning animal fat. The caves, then, deep in the heart of the hills, were temples for the magic ceremonies of the hunters, and the artists were in the first place magicians seeking power over their prey.

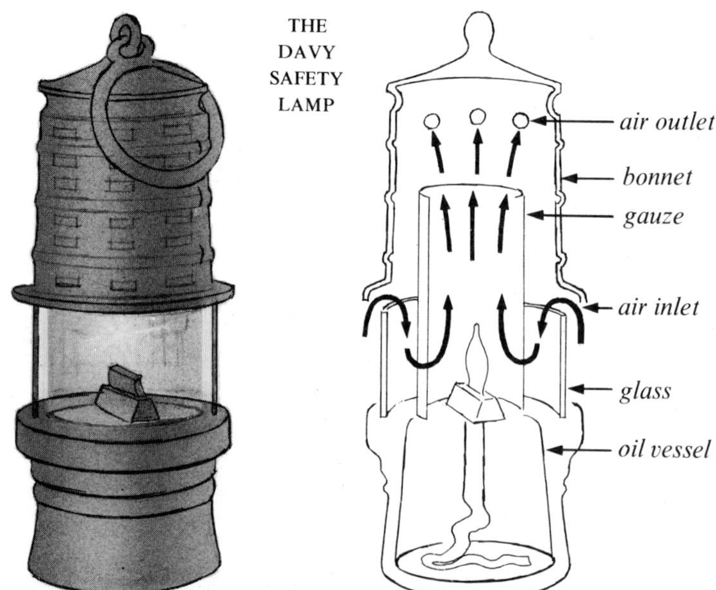

Exercise 5 Here is a list of nouns representing the dwelling-places of various people or animals.

barracks	den	igloo	vicarage
byre	drey	kennel	warren
cave	earth	manse	wigwam
chalet	eyrie	palace	
coop	hive	stable	
cote	hutch	sty	

The people or animals appear in a similar list below. Write twenty sentences, pairing them, like this: A king lives in a palace.

American Indian	Eskimo	bees	squirrel
troglodyte	fox	cow	Swiss villager
parish priest	hen	dog	wild rabbit
pet rabbit	horse	dove	
Scottish minister	king	eagle	
soldier	lion	pig	

For your own writing

1 In the extract from **Annerton Pit**, the author describes the sounds and the feel of the dark drift-mine through Jake's impressions. In the following description, George Orwell relied on his personal experience of a visit to a coal-mine in about 1935. Again, the emphasis is on what the author heard and felt, on movement and noise, as well as on what he could see.

> When you go down a coal-mine it is important to try and get to the coal-face when the "fillers" are at work ...
>
> The time to go there is when the machines are roaring and the air is black with coal-dust, and when you can actually see what the miners have to do. At those times the place is like hell, or at any rate like my own mental picture of hell. Most of the things one imagines in hell are there – heat, noise, confusion, darkness, foul air, and, above all, unbearably cramped space. Everything except the fire, for there is no fire down there except the feeble beams of Davy lamps and electric torches which scarcely penetrate the clouds of coal-dust.
>
> When you have finally got there – and getting there is a job in

itself: I will explain that in a moment – you crawl through the last line of pit-props and see opposite you a shiny black wall three or four feet high. This is the coal-face. Overhead is the smooth ceiling made by the rock from which the coal has been cut; underneath is the rock again, so that the gallery you are in is only as high as the ledge of coal itself, probably not much more than a yard. The first impression of all, overmastering everything else for a while, is the frightful, deafening din from the conveyor belt which carries the coal away. You cannot see very far, because the fog of coal-dust throws back the beam of your lamp, but you can see on either side of you the line of half-naked kneeling men, one to every four or five yards, driving their shovels under the fallen coal and flinging it swiftly over their left shoulders. They are feeding it on to the conveyor belt, a moving rubber belt a couple of feet wide which runs a yard or two behind them. Down this belt a glittering river of coal races constantly. In a big mine it is carrying away several tons of coal every minute. It bears it off to some place in the main roads where it is shot into tubs holding half a ton, and thence dragged to the cages and hoisted to the outer air.

(from: **The Road to Wigan Pier**)

As in the extract at the beginning of the chapter, this is an older mine-working. Can anyone in the class compare these with modern pits (perhaps seen on a visit or on film), or with other caves or underground passages that are open to the public (such as those at Cheddar or in Derbyshire)?

Write a short story or a description involving any kind of pit, cave, tunnel or passage underground, whether past or present. One possibility would be to imagine an accident or an explosion in a mine; another would be to describe a rescue from a cave, or an incident when cave explorers find themselves cut off by rising water.

Make sure that your story or description is carefully planned in paragraphs, and leads up to a climax. Try to make the situation as realistic as possible.

2 Using the diagram on page 64, write (in words only) as exact and clear a description of the famous Davy safety lamp as you can. The fine wire mesh (or gauze) in the lamp allows air to reach the flame, but prevents the heat from escaping in sufficient quantities to set fire to any firedamp (methane) present in the mine.

For talk and action

1(a) If you, as an individual or as a class, have a chance to visit a mine or any underground caves (officially and in safety, of course), then take it. Accounts of such a visit, or poems about the world underground, should make excellent material for the class magazine, or for a folder or wall-display.

One former mine that now caters entirely for visitors interested in mining history is Chatterley Whitfield Mine near Stoke-on-Trent. There are also museums of mining, mines or quarries open to the public in Blaenau Ffestiniog (Llechwedd Slate Caverns), in Llanberis (North Wales Quarrying Museum), in Salford (The Museum of Mining), near Port Talbot (The Afan Avgoed Miners' Museum) and in Cornwall (The Wendron Forge and Poldark Mining Museum).

(b) Collect information, poems, ballads and stories about mining disasters of the past. One of the worst in Canadian history, in 1958, inspired a ballad by Ewan MacColl and Peggy Seeger which begins like this:

> In the town of Spring Hill, Nova Scotia,
> Down in the dark of the Cumberland Mine,
> There's blood on the coal, and the miners lie
> On roads that never saw sun nor sky,
> Roads that never saw sun nor sky.
>
> In the town of Spring Hill you don't sleep easy,
> Often the earth will tremble and roll;
> When the earth is restless miners die,
> Bone and blood is the price of coal,
> Bone and blood is the price of coal.

See if you can find recordings of this and other songs and ballads about the dangers and difficulties of life in the mines.

2(a) Take one of the following as a topic for library research.

Coal-mining – in the eighteenth and nineteenth centuries (942.07).

Coal-mining – today (622.33).

Salt-mining (664.4), or copper-mining, or tin-mining (622.3).

Tunnelling: the eighteenth- and nineteenth-century pioneers (942), or tunnelling today (624.19).
Caving and pot-holing as a pastime (551.44).
Great natural caves (551.44), or cave-men (573), or cave-paintings (571.7).
Beautiful caves and rock-formations (551.44).
How coal has been formed, and why it burns (622).
Smelting iron ore (672).
Mining rare minerals (622.33).
Tapping underground supplies of oil and natural gas (665).
Oil refining (665).
Careers in mining (371.425).

Use reference books and books in the sections whose numbers are given.

(b) In connection with these topics, write business letters to the following organisations, asking for information and free pamphlets. (Only *one* letter should be sent to each address, on behalf of the class.)

The Public Relations Department,
The National Coal Board,
Hobart House,
Grosvenor Place,
London,
SW1X 7AE.

Shell Education Service,
Shell International Petroleum Co. Ltd.,
Shell Centre,
London,
SE1 7NA.

The Public Relations Officer,
British Waterways Board,
Melbury House,
Melbury Terrace,
London,
NW1 6JX.

For further reading

Annerton Pit by PETER DICKINSON (Gollancz; Heinemann; Puffin)
Jake's adventures began when he and Martin went looking for their grandfather, who was following his pastime of hunting (and explaining) ghosts. But the story ends in mine-workings that are both haunted by memories of disaster and used for their own ends by modern terrorists, who will stop at nothing to make their protest. Peter Dickinson has written several other stories published as Puffins:

The Weathermonger is the first of three science-fiction books, about a time of conflict between monstrous machines and superstitious men. In this one, a young boy discovers that he has extraordinary power to control the weather. **The Devil's Children** and **Heartsease** are the other titles.

In **The Blue Hawk** and **The Dancing Bear** Peter Dickinson takes you back in time, to find exciting but thought-provoking adventures.

The Cave by RICHARD CHURCH (Heinemann; Pan)
The five boys of the Tomahawk Club secretly plan an expedition to explore a cave near their home on the River Severn. Their exciting adventure turns into a stern test of endurance for each member of the gang. In **Down River** (Heinemann) the Club continues the investigation the following summer, against sinister opposition.

Caving Manual by JAMES LOVELOCK (Batsford)
Caving is an exciting but dangerous and demanding sport, *never* to be undertaken alone, or without preparation and training. Here is a clear, well-informed book by an experienced caver offering an insight into the fascination and the techniques of an increasingly popular pastime. (Classified as 796.5.)

The Fox Hole by IVAN SOUTHALL (Methuen)
Ken is trapped in a disused gold-mine with a sinister history. This is a powerful early story by this Australian author, about a city boy who finds unexpected adventure when he goes to stay in the country.

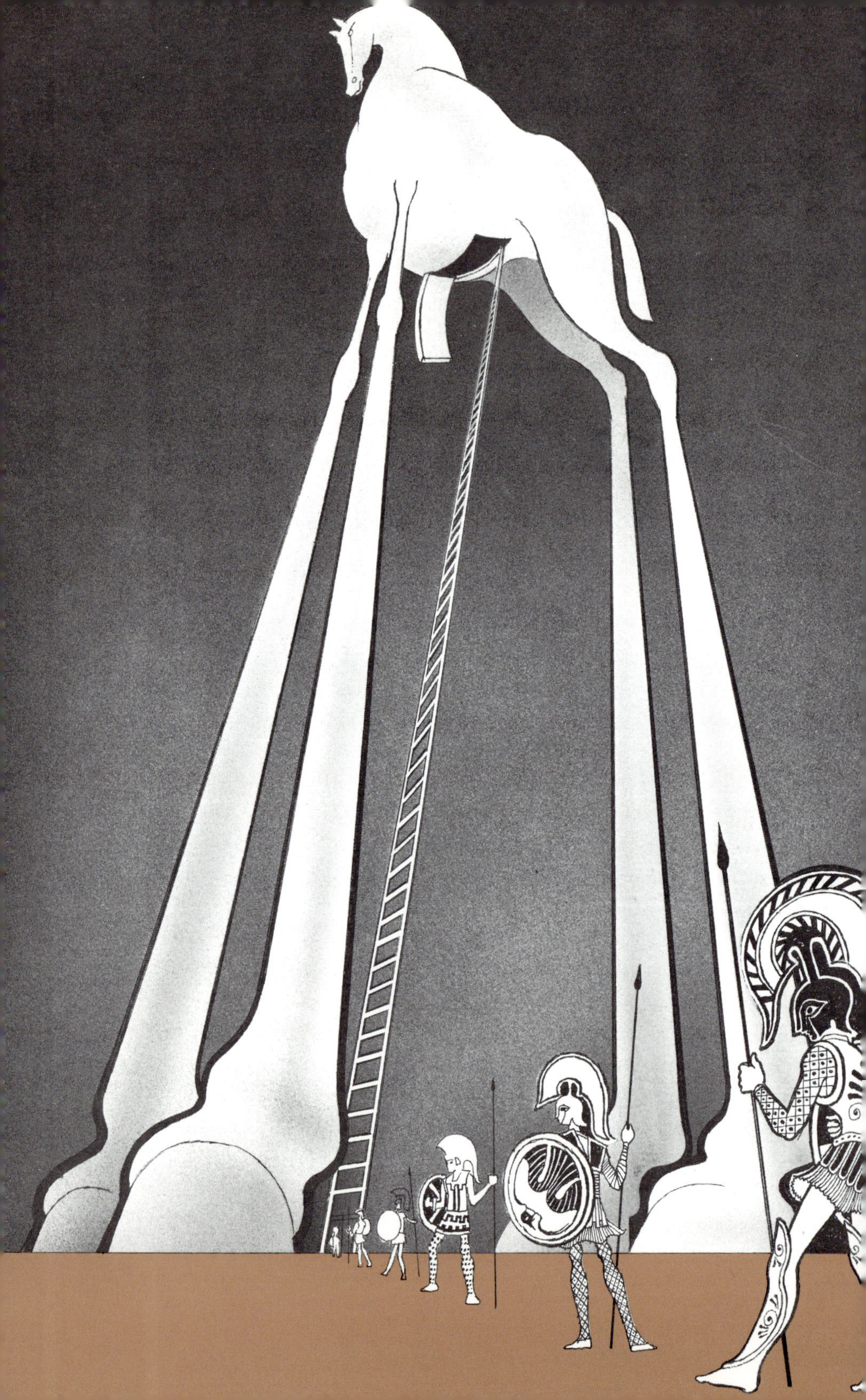

5 Modern Versions

"Greeks and Trojans" is an adaptation by Rex Warner of Homer's "Iliad" and other ancient stories about the Trojan War. When the extract opens, the city of Troy has already been besieged by the Greeks for ten years and many of the greatest warriors on both sides are dead; the war itself seems no nearer a conclusion than when it began. But the Greeks have a plan ...

It was Odysseus who made the plan which was to lead to the fall of Troy. Under his orders the Greeks made out of wood the figure of a huge horse. The face and nostrils of the horse, its feet and hooves were beautifully carved. Its body was hollow and was of such a size that twenty armed men could hide within it. And this is what they did. Odysseus himself with Diomedes, Menelaus, Neoptolemus and others of the best of the Greeks climbed inside the wooden framework of the horse's gigantic body and there they waited fully armed, knowing that this desperate venture would end either in their own deaths or in the destruction of Troy.

For while these great warriors lay hidden inside the horse, Agamemnon, with the rest of the Greek army, had embarked on their ships by night and sailed away. They sailed just as far as the shelter of the island of Tenedos, which lies some twelve miles distant from the Trojan coast. There the fleet was out of sight, and when the dawn came and the Trojan sentries reported that the Greek camp was deserted, all the Trojans believed that their enemies, exhausted and dispirited by their sufferings, had sailed back to Greece, abandoning finally the purpose of their great expedition. It was a day of joy and gratitude in Troy. The people came out of the city, singing and dancing and offering thanks to the gods for what they imagined was their deliverance ...

When the Greeks had sailed away, they left behind them one man, named Sinon, promising him a great reward and instructing him to tell a false story so that the Trojans would take the horse inside their walls. Now this man Sinon, who had given himself up to a patrol of Trojan soldiers, was brought by them, with his hands tied behind his back, in front of the chief men of Troy. Sinon told his story well. He pretended that he was an enemy of Odysseus and that Odysseus had planned to take his life. Therefore, he said, he had been forced to hide from the Greeks and to throw himself on the mercy of the Trojans. As he spoke of his pretended sufferings, he wept what seemed to be real tears, and there were few who did not believe what he said. As for the horse, he told them that it was an offering which the Greeks had been commanded to make to the goddess Athene. If the Trojans were to destroy it, that would mean certain destruction for their city; but if they took it inside their walls, they would always have the protection of Athene and, in course of time, they would invade Greece itself and conquer the sons or the grandsons of those who had fought against them for so long . . .

So the horse was brought within the walls of Troy and all day the Trojans gave themselves up to feasting and rejoicing. Far into the night their feast continued; no sentries were posted on the walls or along the coast. Confident in their security and tired out from their exertions and their rejoicings, at length they slept in a city that was already almost in their enemies' hands.

For as soon as all was quiet, Sinon made his way to the place where the horse stood. He undid the cunningly contrived bolts, and pulled the timbers apart. Moonlight shone on the eager and expectant faces of the Greeks within, who now gripped their arms, descended from their place of concealment and went quietly through the sleeping city to the gates.

Meanwhile Agamemnon with the whole fleet had set sail from Tenedos. In the silent moonlight they had drawn their ships up on the beach that they knew so well. Silently they had crossed the plain, and now, when Odysseus, Diomedes and the rest opened the city gates to them, they joined forces together and swept into Troy, killing and burning as they went. Almost before the Trojans could arm themselves and long before they could make any plans for defence, the city was lost, high towers were crumbling in ruin and tall flames shooting upwards to the sky. In the moment of their triumph the Greeks showed mercy neither to young nor old. Small children and white-haired men were butchered in the streets and in their very beds. So great was the hatred that this long war had provoked, so bitter and outrageous the feelings of those who were at last victorious.

(from **The Fatal Horse** in **Greeks and Trojans** by REX WARNER)

For discussion

1 Why was the story that the horse was an offering to Athene a good one? What made the Trojans believe it?

2 In what ways was Sinon vital to the Greek plan?

3 In what various ways might "this desperate venture" have ended in the deaths of the Greeks inside the horse?

4 What convinced the Trojans of the truth of Sinon's story? Were they very stupid to believe it?

5 Why was the city "already almost in their enemies' hands" as the Trojans went to sleep?

6 Why was it particularly easy for the Greek fleet to return unseen and for the men from the horse to open the gates unnoticed?

7 Why do you think the Greeks knew the beach so well?

8 What explanation does the author give for the merciless destruction of Troy by the Greeks? Was such cruelty really justified?

9 Does the fact that the Trojans had been feasting and rejoicing make the effect of the end of the story any different?

10 Discuss what the class know of the causes and course of the famous Siege of Troy, and of Homer, who recorded it.

For written answers

1 Explain in what respects and why the horse was beautifully carved.

2 Explain why the bolts and timbers had to be cunningly contrived.

3 Give the Trojan explanation for the desertion of the Greek camp, in your own words.

4 Describe the city of Troy in your own words, as you imagine it after reading this extract.

5 Describe the scene of destruction as the Greeks swept into Troy, again in your own words.

THE DAVID JAZZ

David was a Young Blood, David was a striplin',
Looked like the Jungle Boy, yarned about by Kiplin' –
Looked like a Jungle Boy, sang like a bird,
Fought like a tiger when his temper got stirred.

David was a-tendin' the sheep for his Pa,
Somebody hollered to him – that was his Ma –
"Run down to camp with this little bitta snack,
Give it to your brothers, an' hurry right back."

David took the luncheon, and off he hurried,
There he saw the Isra'lites lookin' right worried.
Asked 'em what's the matter – they pointed to the prairie –
There he saw a sight to make a elephant scary!
There he saw Goliath,
Champion o' Gath,
Howlin' in his anger,
Roarin' in his wrath;
Stronger than a lion,
Taller than a tree –
David had to tiptoe to reach to his knee!
"Come on," says the giant, a-ragin' and a-stridin' –
"Drag out your champions from the holes where they're hidin',
Drag out your strong men from underneath their bunks,
And I'll give 'em to the buzzards, an' the lizards, an' the
   skunks."

David heard him braggin', and he said, "I declare,
The great big lummox got 'em buffaloed for fair."
Goes to the brook, and he picks him out a pebble,
Smooth as a goose-egg an' hard as the debbil.
Starts for the giant, dancin' on his toes,
Whirlin' his sling-shot and singin' as he goes –
"Better get organised, for here I come a-hoppin',
Time's gettin' short, and hell am a-poppin',
Hell am a-poppin' and trouble am a-brewin',
Nothin's going to save you from Big Red Ruin.
Trouble am a-brewin' and Death am distillin' –
Look out, you Philistine – there's gwine ter be a killin'!"

Giant looks at David an' he lets out a laugh –
Acts like a tiger bein' sassed by a calf;
Laughs like a hyena, grins from ear to ear,
Rattles on his armor with his ten-foot spear,
Starts out for David, bangin' and a-clankin' –
"Come on, l'il infant, you're a-goin' to get a spankin'!"
David takes his sling-shot, swings it round his head,
Lets fly a pebble – and the gi'nt drops dead!

Moral

Big men, little men, houses and cars,
Widders and winders and porcelain jars –
Nothin' ain't safe from damage an' shocks,
When the neighbourhood chillen gets to slingin' rocks!

EDWIN MEADE ROBINSON

Discussing the poem

1 Find and read the Bible version of this story (I Samuel 17: 4–11,
17–27 and 38–51).
2 Discuss any words or phrases in this poem (or in the Bible
version) that you do not understand.
3 Consider the ways in which details have been changed in the
poem. Why is there talk of "the prairie", "bunks" and "skunks"?
What other similar changes of scene have been made, and why?
4 Discuss the title of the poem and the "Moral". What effect do
these have on the reader? Is this meant to be a funny story?

For learning about language

Exercise 1(a) A large number of **apostrophes** have been used in E. M. Robinson's poem to represent the American Negro dialect of English. Nearly all of them are examples of the first rule for the apostrophe in Book 1: they indicate a letter or letters left out (and not pronounced). Write out in full the more usual forms of:

striplin'	o' Gath	Time's	l'il
an'	they're	Nothin's	gi'nt
Isra'lites	hidin'	there's	ain't.
'em	I'll	bein'	

(b) In **The Fatal Horse** we find examples of the second rule for the apostrophe, to indicate possession:

the horse's body – the body of the horse

their enemies' hands – the hands of their enemies.

Can you remember from Book 1 this rule for deciding where to put the apostrophe? If not, refer to the footnote at the end of Exercise 5.

What would be the difference in meaning between the following?

the landlady's prices

the landladies' prices

How would the following phrases (all adapted from the extract) be rewritten with an apostrophe (as in the examples above)?

the destruction of Troy	the mercy of the Trojans
the shelter of the island	the protection of Athene
the chief men of Troy	the sons of their enemies
the story of Sinon	the expectant faces of the Greeks
the enemy of Odysseus	the feelings of the victors

Exercise 2 Rewrite the following passage, inserting the twenty apostrophes that are required.

"Its uncertain," said the princesss press secretary, "whether her Highnesss engagements will permit her appearance at the St Pauls Charity Societys Jubilee. In its fifty years history its always enjoyed a royal persons patronage, and its her Majestys wish to continue her familys association with the Societys childrens homes. Shell be delighted," he added, turning to the journalists cameras with a smile, "to see the Presss interest in the St Pauls homes. The babies happiness depends on the publics generous support and the publics always been most generous in past years."

Exercise 3 We have already seen that in English we do not necessarily begin every sentence with its subject. Good writers vary their sentences as much as possible. Look at the third paragraph of **The Fatal Horse** extract: the main subject and verb of the first sentence is "they left"; of the second "this man was brought"; of the third "Sinon told".

Each of the following sentences has several main points. In this example they are numbered:

They^1 went^2 out, but their^3 parents disapproved^4.

This might be rewritten:

Although their^3 parents disapproved^4, they^1 still went^2 out.

Or, in another version:

In spite of their^{3+4} parents' disapproval, they^1 still went^2 out.

Without leaving points out, rearrange the following sentences, beginning with the opening word or words suggested:

(a) They all spent a day by the sea but the rain ruined it.
  Their day ...

(b) The match was postponed and the club did not offer any money back.
  In spite of ...

(c) The stretcher party descended with great care so as not to jolt the injured climber.
  To avoid ...

(d) He loved to hunt; he loved to ride; he loved to fish; he loved to shoot: these were his chief pleasures.
  Hunting ...

(e) He sacrificed everything so that his daughter might be healthy.
For the sake of . . .

(f) He did not wait for the order to charge, but thundered down the slope alone.
Without . . .

(g) They knew that this desperate venture might end in death, but they climbed inside the horse.
Knowing . . .

(h) The governors were pleased by the school's success and this led them to declare a half holiday.
The governors' . . .

(i) Some people live in glass houses and those people should not throw stones.
People who . . .

(j) The leader said something to his men and this fired them with new enthusiasm.
What the leader . . .

Exercise 4 We have noticed before that writers frequently use comparisons to describe people, things and actions. Find comparisons

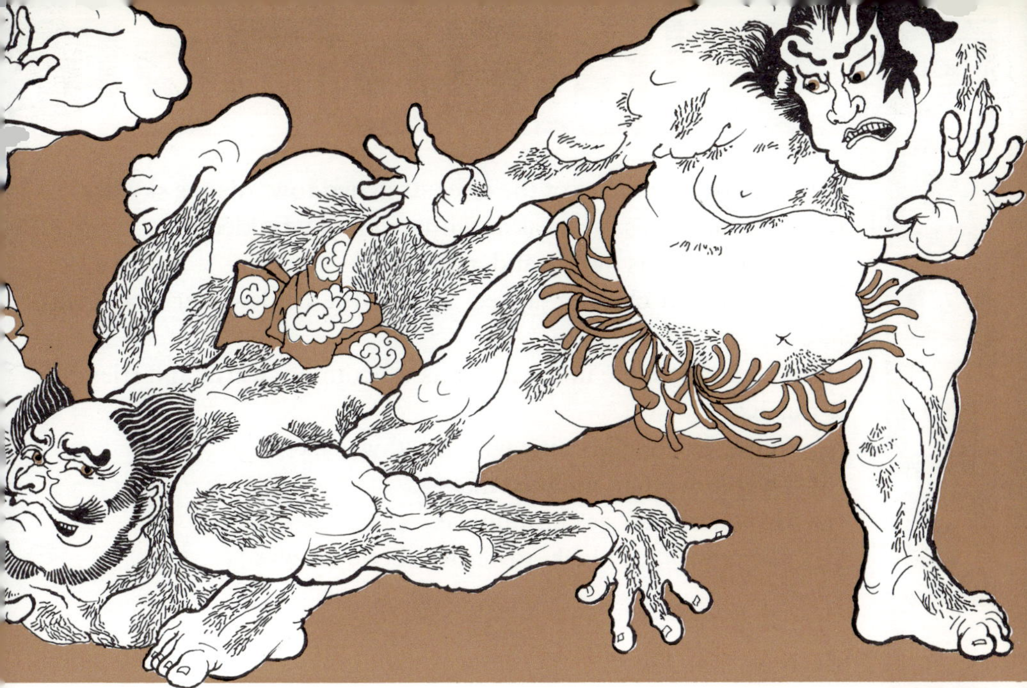

in THE DAVID JAZZ to tell us how David fought, how smooth and hard the pebble was, and how the giant acted when faced with David. These comparisons, using the words *like* and *as*, are called **similes**. (Make sure you learn to pronounce this word correctly.) The writer's aim is to use something familiar in order to describe something that is strange, unusual or special. On the other hand, if the comparison itself becomes too familiar, we accept it without thinking, and it does not really add to the description at all.

Thus:
Johnny was as good as gold.
no longer helps describe how good he was. And:
He ran as fast as anything.
is almost meaningless!
But to talk of:
"A line of elms plunging and tossing like horses"
is lively, vivid, unusual and yet extremely appropriate.

Complete the following sentences with the most original, interesting and appropriate similes you can think of.
(a) The angry Greeks fell on their enemies like . . .

(b) The bare branches of the trees stretched towards the sky like . . .

(c) The old man's face was as withered and wrinkled as . . .

(d) She danced as lightly and gaily as . . .

(e) The ruined church, jagged against the cold winter's sky, was like . . .

(f) The atmosphere in the hall was welcoming, warm and friendly: it was like . . .

(g) The cobweb, glistening with frost, was like . . .

(h) The old woman moaned like . . .

(i) He was always as charming as . . .

(j) The new office block, towering above us, was . . .

Exercise 5(a) On the left below you will find a list of nouns and a list of adjectives. Pair them off so that they are all suitably matched. On the right are lists of verbs and adverbs: again, pair them off.

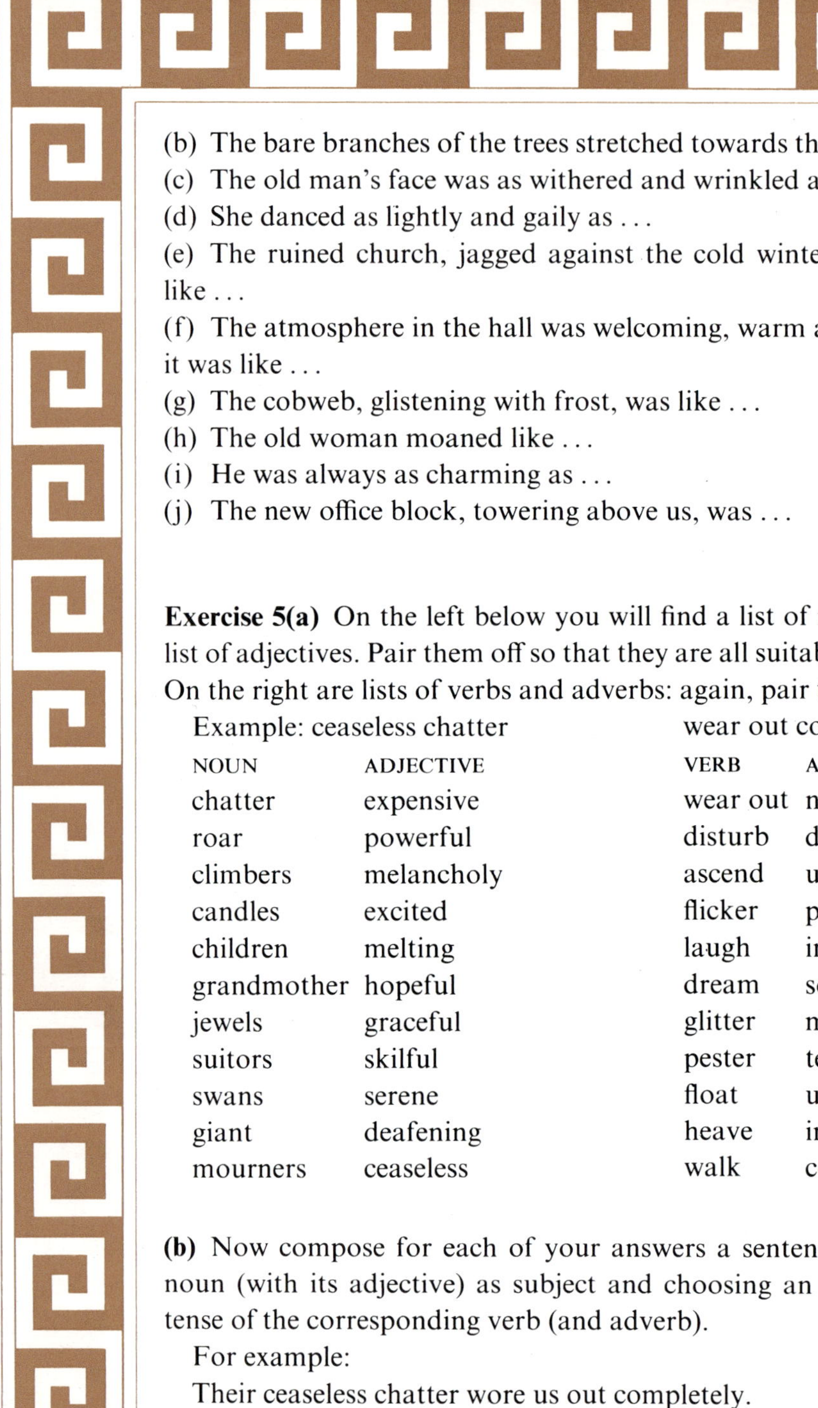

Example: ceaseless chatter   wear out completely

NOUN	ADJECTIVE		VERB	ADVERB
chatter	expensive		wear out	noiselessly
roar	powerful		disturb	deftly
climbers	melancholy		ascend	uproariously
candles	excited		flicker	peacefully
children	melting		laugh	insufferably
grandmother	hopeful		dream	solemnly
jewels	graceful		glitter	mightily
suitors	skilful		pester	temptingly
swans	serene		float	uncertainly
giant	deafening		heave	increasingly
mourners	ceaseless		walk	completely

(b) Now compose for each of your answers a sentence using the noun (with its adjective) as subject and choosing an appropriate tense of the corresponding verb (and adverb).

For example:

Their ceaseless chatter wore us out completely.

Footnote: The rule for using the apostrophe to show possession is as follows:

Add an apostrophe to the noun naming the owner of some thing or quality; then add an s, unless the noun already ends in a *single* -s.

For example:

men's suits; girls' shoes; the boss's car; the foreman's office.

This rule works with only a few exceptions, such as "bus's" and proper names such as "St Thomas's".

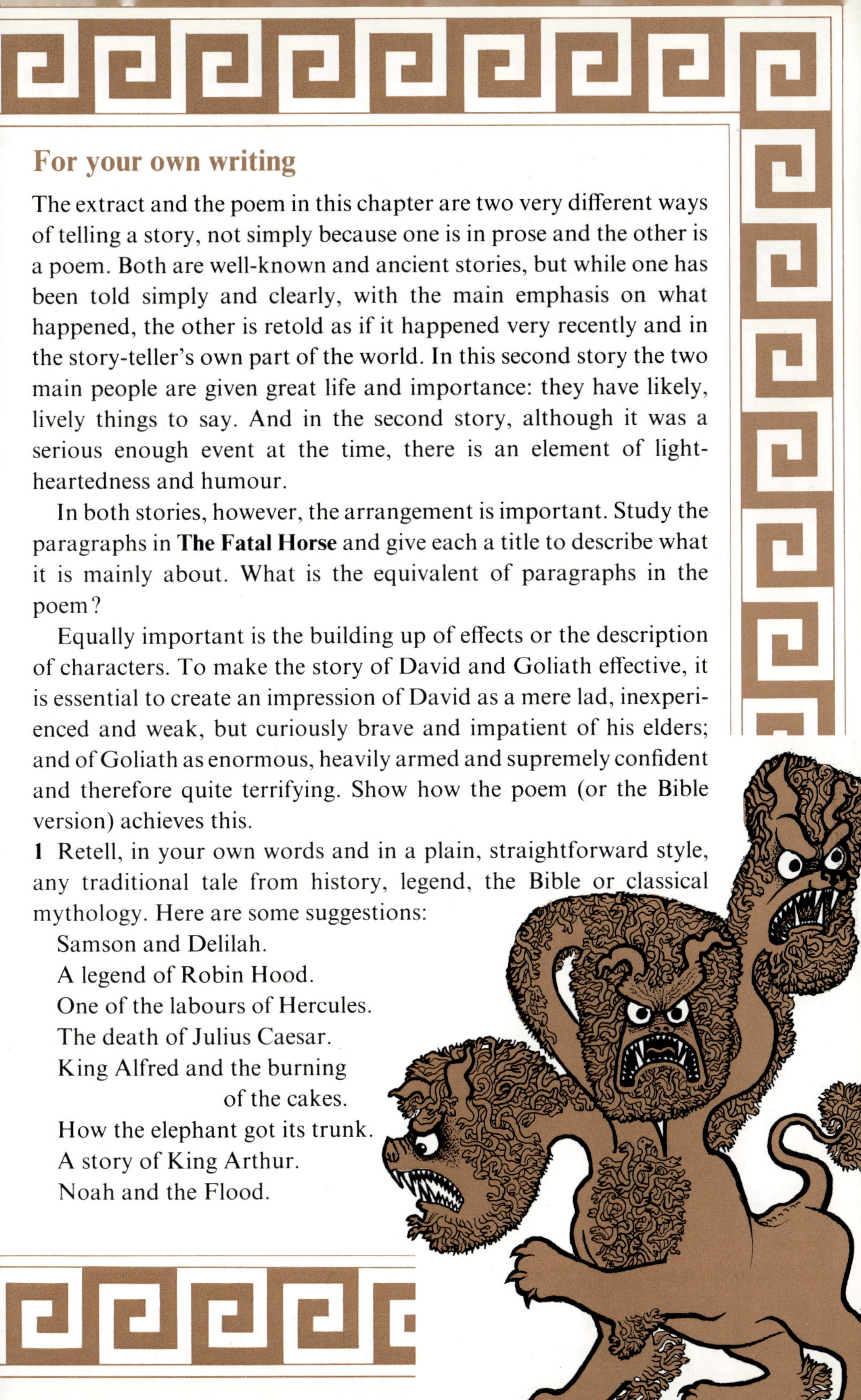

For your own writing

The extract and the poem in this chapter are two very different ways of telling a story, not simply because one is in prose and the other is a poem. Both are well-known and ancient stories, but while one has been told simply and clearly, with the main emphasis on what happened, the other is retold as if it happened very recently and in the story-teller's own part of the world. In this second story the two main people are given great life and importance: they have likely, lively things to say. And in the second story, although it was a serious enough event at the time, there is an element of light-heartedness and humour.

In both stories, however, the arrangement is important. Study the paragraphs in **The Fatal Horse** and give each a title to describe what it is mainly about. What is the equivalent of paragraphs in the poem?

Equally important is the building up of effects or the description of characters. To make the story of David and Goliath effective, it is essential to create an impression of David as a mere lad, inexperienced and weak, but curiously brave and impatient of his elders; and of Goliath as enormous, heavily armed and supremely confident and therefore quite terrifying. Show how the poem (or the Bible version) achieves this.

1 Retell, in your own words and in a plain, straightforward style, any traditional tale from history, legend, the Bible or classical mythology. Here are some suggestions:

Samson and Delilah.

A legend of Robin Hood.

One of the labours of Hercules.

The death of Julius Caesar.

King Alfred and the burning
            of the cakes.

How the elephant got its trunk.

A story of King Arthur.

Noah and the Flood.

2 Take any traditional character, plot or situation, and write your own version of the story in one of the following ways.

(a) You could modernise an old story, translating it into modern terms.

(b) You could retell the story from an unusual view – Noah's wife's view of the Flood and that absurd plan to build an ark, for instance.

(c) You could dramatise a scene from a well-known story, setting it out in play-form.

(d) You could write a poem, describing events or representing the feelings of one or more characters involved in the story.

For talk and action

1 Find out what you can about the characters mentioned in the extract (Odysseus, Menelaus etc.), and about Homer, his **Iliad** and **Odyssey**. Despite popular belief, the story of the Wooden Horse is to be found not in the works of Homer but in the **Aeneid** of Virgil. Use reference books such as:

> **Who's Who in Classical Mythology** by Michael Grant and John Hazel
>
> **The Oxford Companion to Classical Literature**
>
> **Lemprière's Classical Dictionary**
>
> **The Oxford Junior Encyclopaedia, Vol. I: Mankind**
>
> **A Classical and Biblical Reference Book** by H. A. Treble.

You will need to understand the meaning of *q.v.*, and be prepared to look up the information under various headings.

2 Work out a mime or an impromptu dramatisation of either **The Fatal Horse** or THE DAVID JAZZ. The story of the Wooden Horse should offer a wide variety of very different characters to act, and you will have to be ingenious to work out an effective way of showing the horse itself, and the men inside – perhaps some construction of desks and chairs would do.

3 Some of the short stories written by the class should be useful contributions to the class magazine. As a variation on short stories, an individual or a group could work on a serial story in several parts. Careful planning will be necessary, and it is important to end each episode at an exciting point so that readers will be eager to buy the following issue to read what happens next.

For further reading

Greeks and Trojans by REX WARNER (Heinemann)
The author retells the story of all the main episodes of the Trojan War in a clear and exciting modern English version, from the founding of Troy and the judgement of Paris to the deaths of Hector and Achilles and the sack of the city.

Rex Warner is well known for his modern versions of classical Greek stories. These include **Stories of the Greeks** (MacGibbon & Kee), **Athens at War** (Heinemann; Bodley Head), **Men and Gods** (Heinemann) and **Vengeance of the Gods** (Heinemann).

A Book of Myths by ROGER LANCELYN GREEN (Dent; Dutton)
This is a book of stories from the ancient civilisations of the Middle East, not retold before: strange tales of gods, creation, war and adventures in life and after death. This author has rewritten a number of other mythical tales, many published by Puffin Books.

The Gorgon's Head (O.U.P.; Heinemann) and **The Way of Danger** by IAN SERRAILLIER (O.U.P.; Heinemann; Puffin)
These are both books about Greek heroes. The first is the story of Perseus, and of the head of Medusa that turned all things to stone. The second is the life of Theseus, from his adventurous journey to find his father, King of Athens, to his death by treachery. **The Ivory Horn** (O.U.P.; Heinemann) by the same author retells the story of Roland, nephew to the Emperor Charlemagne, who fought and died heroically in the struggle against the pagan armies in Spain in the eighth century.

6　Christmas is Coming

Among Laurie Lee's memories of childhood in a Gloucestershire village in the 1920s is the following story of Christmas. There is fun and magic in the air when he and the other boys go carol-singing . . .

The week before Christmas, when snow seemed to lie thickest, was the moment for carol-singing; and when I think back to those nights it is to the crunch of snow and to the lights of the lanterns on it. Carol-singing in my village was a special tithe for the boys, the girls had little to do with it. Like haymaking, blackberrying, stone-clearing, and wishing-people-a-happy-Easter, it was one of our seasonal perks.

By instinct we knew just when to begin it; a day too soon and we should have been unwelcome, a day too late and we should have received lean looks from people whose bounty was already exhausted. When the true moment came, exactly balanced, we recognised it and were ready . . .

Eight of us set out that night. There was Sixpence the Tanner,

84

who had never sung in his life (he just worked his mouth in church);
the brothers Horace and Boney, who were always fighting everybody and always getting the worst of it; Clergy Green, the preaching
maniac; Walt the bully, and my two brothers. As we went down the
lane other boys, from other villages, were already about the hills,
bawling "Kingwenslush", and shouting through keyholes "Knock
on the knocker! Ring at the Bell! Give us a penny for singing so
well!" They weren't an approved charity as we were, the Choir; but
competition was in the air.

Our first call as usual was the house of the Squire, and we trouped
nervously down his drive. For light we had candles in marmalade-
jars suspended on loops of string, and they threw pale gleams on
the towering snowdrifts that stood on each side of the drive. A
blizzard was blowing, but we were well wrapped up, with Army
puttees on our legs, woollen hats on our heads, and several scarves
around our ears.

As we approached the Big House across its white silent lawns, we
too grew respectfully silent. The lake near by was stiff and black,
the waterfall frozen and still. We arranged ourselves shuffling
around the big front door, then knocked and announced the
Choir . . .

85

This huge stone house, with its ivied walls, was always a mystery to us. What were those gables, those rooms and attics, those narrow windows veiled by the cedar trees? As we sang "Wild Shepherds" we craned our necks, gaping into that lamplit hall which we had never entered; staring at the muskets and untenanted chairs, the great tapestries furred by dust – until suddenly, on the stairs, we saw the old Squire himself standing and listening with his head on one side.

He didn't move until we'd finished; then slowly he tottered towards us, dropped two coins in our box with a trembling hand, scratched his name in the book we carried, gave us each a long look with his moist blind eyes, then turned away in silence.

As though released from a spell, we took a few sedate steps, then broke into a run for the gate. We didn't stop till we were out of the grounds. Impatient, at last, to discover the extent of his bounty, we squatted by the cowsheds, held our lanterns over the book, and saw that he had written "Two Shillings". This was quite a good start. No one of any worth in the district would dare to give us less than the Squire ...

Steadily we worked through the length of the valley, going from house to house, visiting the lesser and the greater gentry – the farmers, the doctors, the merchants, the majors, and other exalted persons. It was freezing hard and blowing too; yet not for a moment did we feel the cold. The snow blew into our faces, into our eyes and mouths, soaked through our puttees, got into our boots, and dripped from our woollen caps. But we did not care. The collecting-box grew heavier, and the list of names in the book longer and more extravagant, each trying to outdo the other.

Mile after mile we went, fighting against the wind, falling into snowdrifts, and navigating by the lights of the houses. And yet we never saw our audience. We called at house after house; we sang in courtyards and porches, outside windows, or in the damp gloom of hallways; we heard voices from hidden rooms; we smelt rich clothes and strange hot food; we saw maids bearing in dishes or carrying away coffee-cups; we received nuts, cakes, figs, preserved ginger, dates, cough-drops, and money; but we never once saw our patrons. We sang as it were at the castle walls, and apart from the Squire, who had shown himself to prove that he was still alive, we never expected it otherwise . . .

Crossing, at last, the frozen mill-stream – whose wheel in summer still turned a barren mechanism – we climbed up to Joseph's farm. Sheltered by trees, warm on its bed of snow, it seemed always to be like this. As always it was late; as always this was our final call. The snow had a fine crust upon it, and the old trees sparkled like tinsel.

We grouped ourselves round the farmhouse porch. The sky cleared, and broad streams of stars ran down over the valley and away to Wales. On Slad's white slopes, seen through the black sticks of its woods, some red lamps still burned in the windows.

Everything was quiet; everywhere there was the faint crackling silence of the winter night. We started singing, and we were all moved by the words and the sudden trueness of our voices. Pure, very clear, and breathless we sang:

> As Joseph was a-walking
> He heard an angel sing;
> "This night shall be the birth-time
> Of Christ the Heavenly King.
>
> He neither shall be bornèd
> In Housen nor in hall,
> Nor in a place of paradise
> But in an ox's stall . . ."

And two thousand Christmases became real to us then; the houses, the halls, the places of paradise had all been visited; the stars were bright to guide the Kings through the snow; and across the farmyard we could hear the beasts in their stalls. We were given roast apples and hot mince pies, in our nostrils were spices like myrrh, and in our wooden box, as we headed back for the village, there were golden gifts for all.

(from **Cider with Rosie** by LAURIE LEE)

For discussion

1 What is a "tithe"? In what sense was the carol-singing "a special tithe for the boys"?

2 What is a "perk"? This word is a common abbreviation: what is it short for? With what various times of the year were the other "seasonal perks" connected?

3 What carol can you identify in "Kingwenslush"? What is clear about the quality of the carol-singing of the "other boys" from this spelling and from the word "bawling"?

4 What are "Army puttees", and where do you think they had originally come from?

5(a) How did the boys show their nervousness as they visited the Squire?

(b) Why do you think they were nervous?

6 Why are the words "Squire" and "Big House" printed with capital initial letters? What feelings do you think the boys had about the Squire?

7 What details in the description emphasise the Squire's age and state of health?

8 What seems to have driven the boys on, despite the cold and discomfort?

9(a) Can you explain the following words and phrases?

"bounty"   "gables"   "our patrons"

"maniac"   "sedate steps"   "a barren mechanism"

"ivied walls"   "no one of any worth" "myrrh"

(b) "We trouped … down his drive." What is the difference in meaning between this spelling of "trouped" and "trooped"?

10 Discuss the effectiveness of examples of repetition in this extract such as:

"we called … we sang … we heard … we smelt …

we saw … we received … but we never once saw …".

11 Point out any parallels you can see in the last paragraph of this extract (a) with the traditional stories of the first Christmas, (b) with the words they have just sung.

12 If you have been out carol-singing yourself, what contrasts (and comparisons) were there with Laurie Lee's experience?

For written answers

1 What did Laurie Lee and his friends use as "lanterns"?

2 What do you think Laurie Lee means by "an approved charity"?

3 Explain in your own words why the timing for beginning the carol-singing season was so important.

4 Why did the boys go to the Squire's house first? How well did they know him?

5 What gave the snow "a fine crust" and made the trees "sparkle like tinsel"?

6 What does the author mean when he writes: "the frozen mill-stream – whose wheel in summer still turned a barren mechanism"?

THE COMPUTER'S FIRST CHRISTMAS CARD

jollymerry
hollyberry
jollyberry
merryholly
happyjolly
jollyjelly
jellybelly
bellymerry
hollyheppy
jollyMolly
marryJerry
merryHarry
hoppyBarry
heppyJarry
boppyheppy
berryjorry
jorryjelly
moppyjelly
Mollymerry
Jerryjolly
bellyboppy
jorryhoppy
hollymoppy
Barrymerry
Jarryhappy
happyboppy
boppyjolly
jollymerry
merrymerry
merrymerry
merryChris
asmerryasa
Chrismerry
asMERRYCHR
YSANTHEMUM

EDWIN MORGAN

Discussing the poem

1 Does the computer seem to have any pattern at all in the combination of letters and words it experiments with? Do you feel that the made-up words (such as "bellymerry") might in fact mean something? What instructions do you think were given to the computer?

2 Can you see any significance in the use of capital letters in this poem?

3 In fact, we can assume that Edwin Morgan wrote this poem, rather than programing a computer to write a Christmas message for him. Has he conveyed some of the spirit of Christmas fun?

For learning about language

Examine these **adjectives**, in contexts taken from the extract:

When snow seemed to lie *thickest* . . .

No one . . . would dare to give us *less*.

The collecting-box grew *heavier*, and the list of names in the book *longer* and *more extravagant*.

What is the significance of the endings -er and -est? Discuss these and the following variations on basic adjectives:

thick – thicker – thickest   heavy – heavier – heaviest

little – less   – least   long   – longer   – longest

extravagant – more extravagant – most extravagant.

In each case, the first form is called the **positive** form of the adjective, the second the **comparative** and the third the **superlative.** Can you explain these names? Comparatives are used when comparing *two* people, things etc. The superlative is used for picking out the most extreme of three *or* more.

For example:

Tonight it is *cold,* but yesterday night was *colder* and last Thursday was the *coldest* night of the winter so far.

With a few exceptions, most short adjectives add -er and -est to form the comparative and superlative, but if these would be clumsy to pronounce, we can use the separate words *more* and *most* instead.

Exercise 1(a) Write out the positive, comparative and superlative of these adjectives:

tall	sad	beautiful	late	bad
large	grimy	hopeless	good	rugged.

(b) In the following sentences decide which form of the adjective would sound most correct in standard English, and rewrite each sentence using it.

(1) This must be the (lonely, lonelier, loneliest) lighthouse of all on that coast.

(2) The (handsome, handsomer, handsomest) of the two brothers was home on leave.

(3) I earned (few, fewer, fewest) penalties than all the other competitors.

(4) Indeed I had the (promising, more promising, most promising) round of all.

(5) The (much, more, most) money you have, the (big, bigger, biggest) your contribution should be.

(6) Who is the (heavy, heavier, heaviest), Pat or Joan?

(7) Has Pat, Joan or Paula the (long, longer, longest) hair?

(8) That is a (clever, cleverer, cleverest) way to make a toboggan, but I know a(n) (ingenious, more ingenious, most ingenious) one than that.

Exercise 2(a) Discuss the following five differently punctuated versions of the same nine words. How should each be pronounced when read aloud? What differences in meaning are there between them?

(1) "What! Do you think he replied with a smile?"

(2) "What do you think?" he replied with a smile.

(3) "What do you think! He replied with a smile."

(4) "What do you think?"
   He replied with a smile.

(5) "What? Do you think?" he replied with a smile.

(b) See how many different versions you can make of the following sentences, simply by altering the punctuation (do not add or omit any words). When every member of the class has made his or her

92

own attempt, pool all the different suggestions, checking that they all make sense.

(1) why did he go to discover the truth
(2) how do you know he answered frankly
(3) he said I said it was not true
(4) I know he thought too much
(5) what she said was the reply they suggested

Exercise 3 Study this extract, adapted from a dictionary.

slight   *a.* slim, slender, frail-looking;
                 not substantial; trifling.
         v. to disregard; to neglect.
         n. indifference; an act of discourtesy.
         slightly *adv.* not greatly, to a slight degree.
slim   *a.* thin, slight; crafty. (-ly, *adv.*; -ness, *n.*)
         v. to make (oneself) thin.
slime   *n.* sticky mud; sticky fluid.
         slimy *a.* covered with slime; slippery. (-ily, *adv.*; -iness, *n.*)

What do the abbreviations *a., n., v., adv.* stand for? Why are some of the words in **bold type** not against the left-hand margin? Why is there a comma after "slender", but semicolons after "frail-looking" and "not substantial"?

(a) Using the dictionary extract above, identify the exact meaning and use of the words in italics in the following sentences.

For example, the first one is:

"slight" – adjective (describing "man") meaning "frail-looking"
Number the others 1 to 10.

The father was a *slight* man, old, careworn, with a *slight* stammer. I knew him *slightly*, but when his *slim* figure appeared on the balcony, and he did not greet me, I felt sure it was a deliberate *slight* or snub. Indeed, the whole family *had slighted* us at every *slight* opportunity. My sister might have been something that had crawled out of the *slime* to them. When she slipped once on the *slimy* jetty by their boat-house, John, the tall, *slim* one, turned his head *slightly* and then walked away.

(b) Answer the following questions about the dictionary extract:

(1) Is there an adverb formed *directly* from "slime"?

(2) What are the abstract nouns formed from "slight", "slimy" and "slim"?

(3) What is the less common meaning of "slim"?

(c) Compose one sentence using *slim* as a verb and another using *slime* in its second meaning.

Exercise 4(a) Study this short business letter. George wants the catalogue of model kits so that he can choose some suitable ones to give as Christmas presents.

110 Goldings Road,
NAPEBURY,
Leicestershire,
LE5 3AT.
4th December, 19—

Stickwell Models Ltd.,
Borough Road,
Ealing,
London,
W13 2FD.

Dear Sirs,

Would you please send me a free catalogue and price-list of all your model kits, both Series A and Series B?

I am particularly interested in your special Christmas offer of Double-one kits, as advertised in the " Young Modeller" last week.

Yours faithfully,
George Weekly.

It is usual to put both addresses at the top of a business letter. Can you think of any good reasons for this? Why did George start the letter "Dear Sirs," instead of "Dear Sir" or "Dear Stickwell Models" or "Dear Mr Stickwell"? Why did George add his

94

second paragraph? How will Stickwell Models know where to send the catalogue? Notice how the addresses and the date are set out and punctuated, and also the correct way to end a business letter.
(b) Set out the following business letter correctly, with all the necessary punctuation. (Jean is going to spend a week in London after Christmas.)

14 hob lane cressingford gloucestershire gl8 7qz 30th november 19— the public relations officer london transport 55 broadway london sw1h 0bd dear sir please could you send me a copy of the booklet visitors london together with a set of free london transport maps I enclose a postal order for 75p and trust that this will cover the cost and postage yours faithfully jean cousins

Exercise 5 Study the comparisons that Laurie Lee uses to enrich his description. Which ones would you call **similes**? Many of the comparisons are **metaphors**, comparisons in which one thing is described as if it *is* something else, rather than *like* something else.

For example:

" those narrow windows veiled by the cedar trees"

This one is a metaphor in which the pattern made by the windows is compared to a face and the trees are compared to a veil that covers the face, partly obscuring what the observer can see, and suggesting that the house is " shy" or mysterious.

(a) Discuss the following, making a similar analysis of the comparison (i.e. what is compared to what, and in what respects?).

(1) The great tapestries furred by dust. (metaphor)

(2) As though released from a spell we ... broke into a run. (simile)

(3) We sang as it were at the castle walls. (simile)

(4) Joseph's farm ... warm on its bed of snow. (metaphor)

(5) Broad streams of stars ran down over the valley and away to Wales. (metaphor)

(6) Everywhere there was the faint crackling silence of the winter night.

(What does this metaphor suggest to you about what the boys " heard" in the silence?)

(b) Try to make up your own comparisons, completing each of the following as vividly and interestingly as you can.

(1) The group of trees on the hill stood like …

(2) The skaters sped across the ice as …

(3) We watched the car headlights in the distance, like …

(4) It was a clear, crisp, starlit night, as if …

(5) The old squire tottered towards the boy, like …

(6) Where the traffic had churned up the snow, it was …

(7) On the last Saturday before Christmas, the market was …

(8) She stood amongst those brightly coloured wrapping papers, like …

(9) Warm in bed on Christmas Eve, he felt like …

(10) The toboggans raced down the steep hillside …

For your own writing

1 What seem to you the most exciting and satisfying aspects of Christmas? Do you enjoy the shops, overflowing with light and piled high with good things for sale, or the decorations at home and in public places, bright and glowing in the cold December evenings? Or are you more interested in the active preparations for the festival, in all the cooking, making cards and presents, putting up decorations, preparing for parties, and so on? Or is it the religious plays and carol services, the warm sense of beauty and goodwill and holiness that you can experience at Christmas? Or pantomimes and shows in the theatre or on television? Or perhaps Christmas simply means to you what you can get out of it – rich food and drink, and

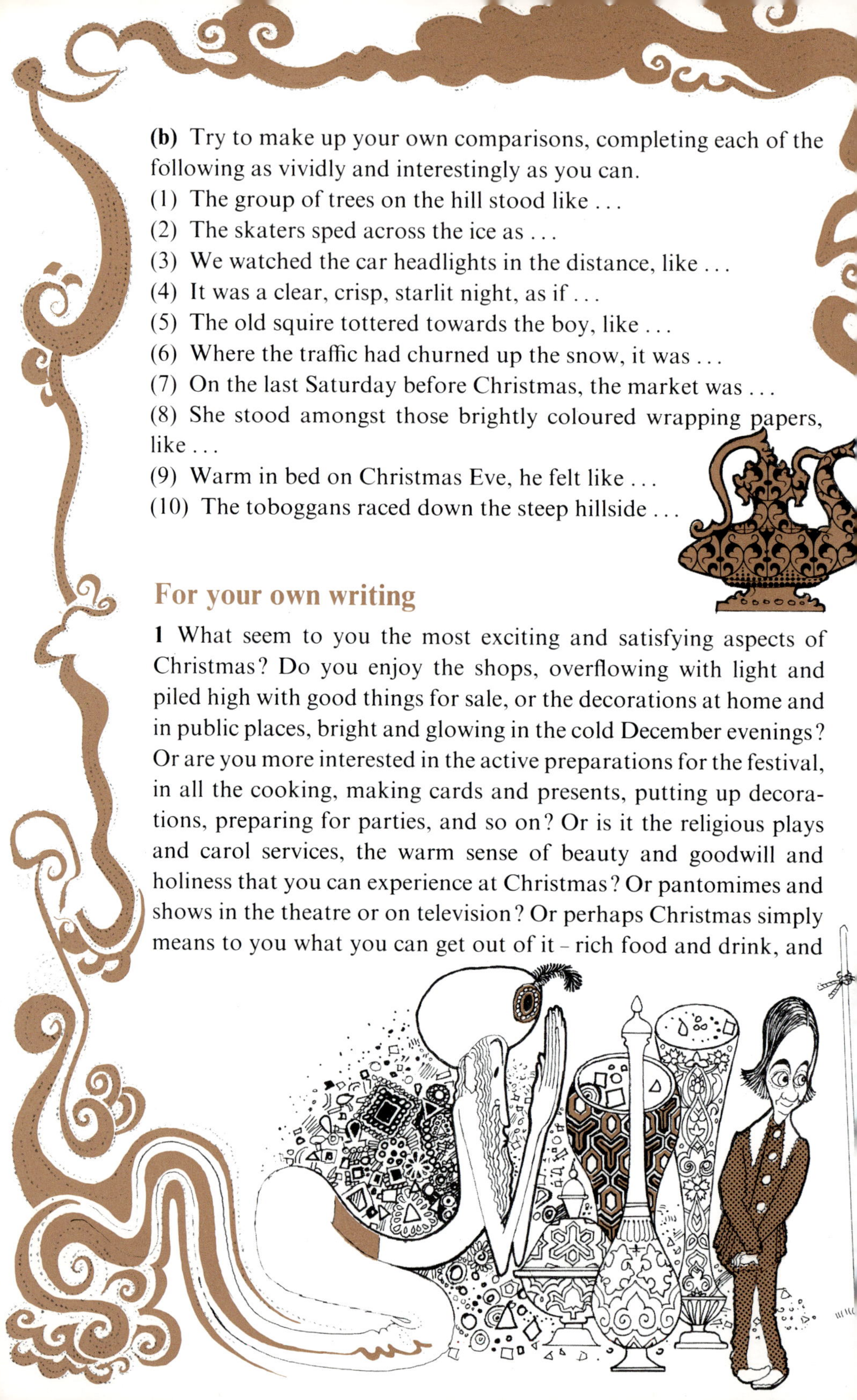

plenty of presents – and you are cynical about the whole business. Whatever your view, try to express it fully, with detail and description, in a composition entitled:

WHAT CHRISTMAS MEANS TO ME.

2 Write ONE of the following business letters, using the example on page 94 as a model.

(a) An answer to the following imaginary advertisement:

HELP FIGHT POVERTY WHEN YOU BUY

CHRISTMAS CARDS THIS YEAR –

FOR A FREE CATALOGUE OF DELIGHTFUL CARDS,

SPECIALLY DRAWN FOR THE CAMPAIGN

BY WORLD-FAMOUS ARTISTS,

WRITE TO

WORLD CAMPAIGN AGAINST POVERTY,

35 MARTIAN ROW, GLASGOW, G22 3AW.

HELP THE POOR TO HELP THEMSELVES THIS CHRISTMAS.

(b) A covering letter to accompany a cheque for a sum of money which your class has raised by selling its class magazine, to the St Boniface Home for Handicapped Children, St Boniface House, East Lane, Troon, Ayrshire, KA10 8LF. The class have unanimously voted to give the money to this home.

(c) A request to a store in your nearest large town to deliver a particular article which you want to give as a present. Find the address in a telephone book. Describe the article very clearly by its correct trade name, with any necessary details about size, and, of course, say you enclose a postal order to cover cost and delivery or postage.

For talk and action

1 Do you have candles at home at Christmas? Either at home or at school, study a burning candle: an ordinary, cheap white candle will do, and it is not difficult to arrange to burn a dozen of these round the class-room on saucers. Study the flame and the wax closely: does the flame reach to the bottom of the wick? Is the flame the same colour throughout? How does it react to a draught or a vibration of the desk? What shapes does the flame take? What happens to the melting wax? Is there smoke or shimmering air above the candle? What happens when you put out the flame? Make notes first, and then work these into a poem or a piece of descriptive writing, like the example above by a pupil.

2 A Christmas edition of the class magazine will be an excellent way of raising money for some charity this Christmas. The class could suggest possible good causes and vote on which to choose.

The magazine should have a special Christmas cover, and the contents should have a Christmas flavour: plenty of light-hearted material, puzzles and games suitable for the season, articles and stories on Christmas themes (for instance, hints on Christmas parties, and so on).

A school play, concert, exhibition or parents' party would be an excellent opportunity to sell copies to parents and friends of the school.

3 Make a selection of Christmas poems and unusual carols. Include some of your own original verse and illustrations. This could be a class anthology, brought together and bound in a folder; or an individual one, representing your own taste and skill.

4 Try to write a Christmas carol or poem of your own, either to a tune of your own composition or using some well-known tune that you think suitable, and fitting words to it. Several people might co-operate to compose a carol between them.

For further reading

Cider with Rosie by LAURIE LEE (Hogarth; Longman; Penguin)
Laurie Lee remembers his childhood vividly, as if it were yesterday – his sisters, his mother, Chad village school, eccentric old grannies, the seasons, outings and pastimes of a vanished world. His sequel, **As I Walked Out One Midsummer Morning**, is an equally lively first-hand impression, of Spain just before the Civil War (Heinemann; Deutsch; Penguin).

An Old Fashioned Christmas by IRIS GRENDER (Hutchinson)
This book is full of fascinating information about Christmas, with anecdotes and explanations about the past, and ideas (including recipes and carols) for today. (Classified at 394.2, as is other non-fiction about Christmas.)

The Thirteen Days of Christmas by JENNY OVERTON (Faber; Puffin)
This is one explanation of the origin of the well-known carol about the twelve days of Christmas. It is also a highly amusing tale, full of the flavour of an old-fashioned family Christmas.

London Snow by PAUL THEROUX (Hamish Hamilton; Puffin)
This is a twentieth-century London Christmas story, thought-provoking and interesting, and with a thoroughly Dickensian atmosphere.

7 Keeping a Record

Somehow the sheltered valley in which the Burden family lived had survived the nuclear disaster a year before. Now, sixteen-year-old Ann Burden is the only one left there – the rest of her family having failed to return from a search for other survivors. For four months, Ann has kept a diary, convinced that she must be the last person alive on earth. Then one day from her cave she notices smoke from a fire over the far horizon . . .

May 24th

It is a man, one man alone.

This morning I went as I planned. I put on my good slacks, took the .22 and hung the binoculars around my neck. I climbed a tree and saw him coming up the road. I could not really see what he looks like, because he is dressed, entirely covered, in a sort of greenish plastic-looking suit. It even covers his head, and there is a glass mask for his eyes – like the wet suits skin-divers wear in cold

100

water, only looser and bulkier. Like skin-divers, too, he has an air-tank on his back. But I could tell it was a man, even though I could not see his face, by his size and the way he moves.

The reason he is coming so slowly is that he is pulling a wagon, a thing about the size of a big trunk mounted on two bicycle wheels. It is covered with the same green plastic as his suit. It is heavy, and he was having a hard time pulling it up Burden Hill. He stopped to rest every few minutes. He still has about a mile to go to reach the top.

I have to decide what to do.

Still May 24th
Now it is night.

He is in my house.

Or possibly not in it, but just outside it, in a small plastic tent he put up. I cannot be sure, because it is too dark to see clearly. I am watching from the cave, but the fire he built – outside the house, in the garden – has burned down. He built it with my wood.

He came over the top of Burden Hill this afternoon. I had come up to watch, having eaten some lunch and changed back to my blue jeans. I decided not to show myself. I can always change my mind later.

I wondered what he would do when he reached the top. He must have been pretty sure, but not quite, that he was coming to a place where things were living. As I said, you can see it from the ridge, but not too well – it is a long way. And maybe he had been fooled before; maybe he thought it was a mirage.

There is a flat place where the road first reaches the top of the hill – a stretch of about a hundred yards or so before it starts descending again, into the valley. When you get just past the middle of this you can see it all, the river, the house, the barn, the trees, pasture, everything. It has always been my favourite sight, maybe because when I saw it I was always coming home. Being spring, today it is all a new fresh green.

When he got to that place he stopped. He dropped the shaft of the wagon and just stared for about a minute. Then he ran forward down the road, very clumsy in his plastic suit, waving his arms. He ran to a tree by the roadside and pulled a branch, tearing off the leaves and holding them close to his glass face mask. You could tell he was thinking: Are they real?

I was watching from a place only a little way up the hillside, a

path in the woods. I had my gun beside me. I did not know whether he could hear or not with that mask on, but I did not move or make a sound.

All at once he pulled at the mask, at a fastening at the neck of it, as if he were going to take it off. So far I could not see his face at all, but only the glass plate, so I was staring. Then he stopped, and instead ran back to the wagon. He unsnapped the plastic cover at one end and pulled it open. He reached inside and took out a glass thing – a sort of tube with a metal rod in it, like a big thermometer. It had some kind of a dial or gauge on it to read – I couldn't see from where I was, but he held it in front of his mask and turned it slowly, studying it. He walked back down the road to the tree, looking at the rod. He held it down close to the road, then up high in the air. Then back to the wagon again.

He took out another machine, something like the first one but bigger; after that he pulled out a black, round thing: it was an earphone, with a wire dangling from it. He plugged the wire into the machine and put the earphone up beside his mask, next to his ear. I could tell what he was doing: using one machine to check against the other. And I knew what they must be; I had read about them but never seen one: radiation counters, Geiger counters they call them. He walked down the road, a long way this time – half a mile at least, watching one counter, listening to the other.

Then he took off the mask, and shouted.

It startled me so that I jumped back. I started to run – then I stopped. He was not shouting at me. He was cheering – a long

"*Haaay*" sound, the kind they make at football games. He didn't hear me (luckily); the shout went echoing down the valley, and I stood absolutely still again, though my heart was still thumping – it was so long since I had heard a voice except my own, when I sing sometimes.

Then silence. He put his hands beside his mouth and shouted again, aiming down the hill. This time he called, very loudly:

"Anybody here?" . . .

Now I think he is asleep. He could have slept in the house, but I suppose he didn't trust it. I think that green plastic stuff – the suit, the tent, the wagon cover – is something that stops radiation.

I will go into the cave now and sleep. I am still afraid. And yet it is – what is the word I mean? – *companionable* to know there is someone else in the valley.

May 25th

It may be that he has made a mistake. I am not sure. And if it was a mistake, I don't know how bad. It worries me, because I suppose I could have stopped him, though I don't know how. Not without showing myself.

When I came out of the cave this morning, very carefully, on hands and knees, keeping my head down, he was already awake, though the sun was barely up. He was folding his tent; he put it back into the wagon, and then several things happened very quickly.

First, somewhere out behind the chicken yard one of the hens cackled. It had laid an egg, of course. Almost immediately a rooster crowed. And from the distance, as if it were answering, one of the cows *mooed*, a real bellow, long and loud. He dropped a pan he was

holding and jumped up, listening. He looked amazed, as if he could not believe it. He probably had not heard an animal sound for more than a year . . .

He saw the cows right away, as soon as he got past the barn and the fence. They were off by the pond, in the far field . . .

He started to follow them, then changed his mind and walked to the edge of the pond. He stared into the water, first from a few feet away then, obviously very interested, kneeling down with his face close to the surface. I could tell. He was looking at the minnows – there are always some up near the edge. He took his glass counter and held it close to the water; finally he stuck one end of it *in* the water. He put out his hand, cupped some and tasted it. It tastes fine; I know, I drink it all the time, though I get it from the brook at the other end. You could tell he felt like cheering . . .

It was now nearly eleven o'clock; the sun was high and bright and the day had turned warm. And that was why, when he got back to the house, he made the mistake. He went swimming, and took a bath, in the dead stream, Burden Creek . . .

I can see how he did it. He thought, not knowing the geography of the valley very well, that it was all the same stream. He did not know that there were two streams, and he had seen the fish. Being so hot – and, maybe, not having had a bath in a long time – he picked up the soap and ran across the road. There he took off his coverall and jumped in with a splash. If he had been a little less eager he might have noticed that there were no fish there, and that all the grass and weeds have died back for about two feet along both the banks. Quite a few of the trees along there are dying, too. But he didn't. He stayed in quite a long time with his piece of soap.

(from **Z for Zachariah** by ROBERT O'BRIEN)

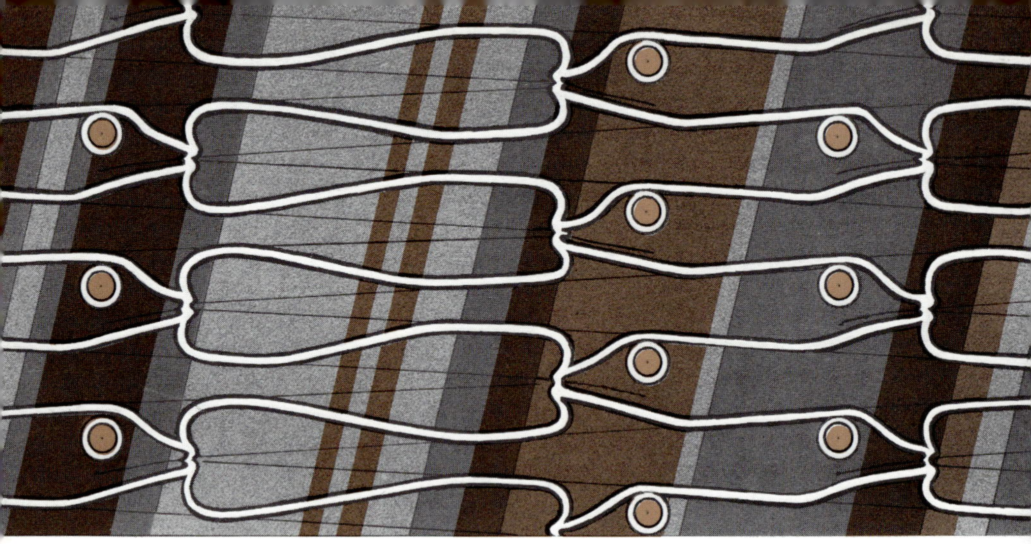

For discussion

1 Ann had planned to go from her cave up the hill to watch the stranger. Why, at this point, did she put on her "good slacks"? Why did she then (in the afternoon) change back into plainer "blue jeans"?

2 What is a ".22", and why was Ann so careful to take it with her, and keep it beside her?

3 Why did Ann find it so difficult at first to describe the stranger? How did she conclude it was a man, not a woman?

4 From reading the extract what sort of things do we know that the man carried on his wagon? What other things would you guess he had on it?

5(a) Why was Ann so cautious and so easily startled and frightened by this man?

(b) Do you think Ann would have been less suspicious if a large, mixed group of refugees had reached her valley?

6 Ann had scattered the animals on her smallholding and removed obvious signs of recent habitation from the farmhouse. How did the stranger find out about some of the farm animals, and what effect did this have on him?

7(a) How did the stranger come to the conclusion that the water was safe to drink and to bathe in? **(b)** How far was he right? **(c)** How did he make his "mistake"? **(d)** What consequences do you think this mistake could have?

106

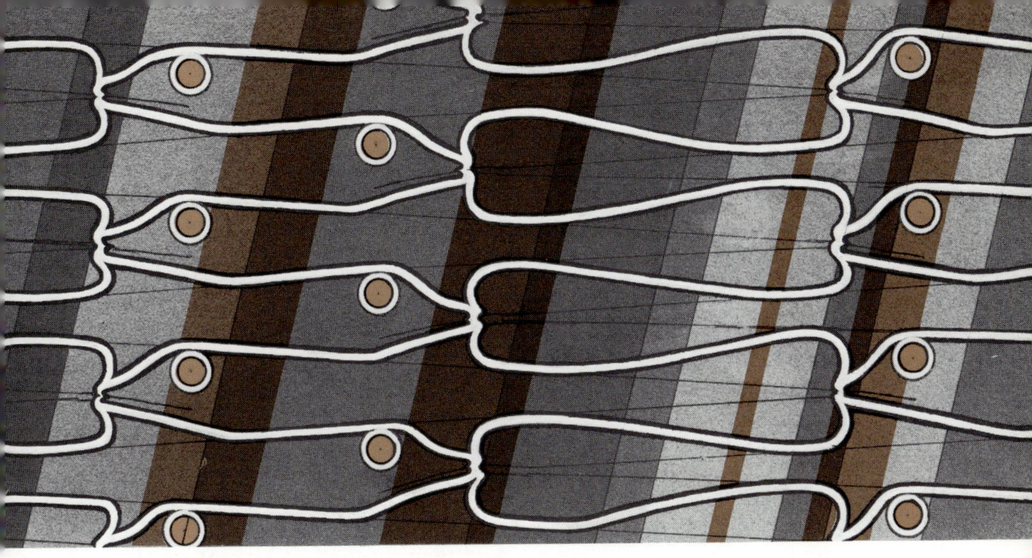

8 What picture do you get from this extract of the advantages Ann had whilst she was living on her own in this valley?

9 What do you know about radiation counters and about the dangers of atomic radiation (or "radioactive fall-out")?

10 Ann has mixed feelings towards the stranger – she is not only afraid and cautious. What other feelings are in evidence?

11 What do you think is likely to happen in this story? Do you think Ann was wise not to reply when the stranger called: "Anybody here?" What would *you* have done?

For written answers

1 What precaution does Ann take to prevent the stranger from seeing or hearing her?

2 Why had the man been wearing his green suit and mask? What made him decide to remove them?

3 Where did the man sleep on his first night in Ann's valley? Where was Ann that night?

4 Twice the man cheered or shouted with excitement. What discoveries brought this reaction from him?

5 What made the man so eager to swim?

6 Why was Ann so worried about his mistake in swimming?

7 What were the important differences between the water in the brook and pond, and the water in Burden Creek?

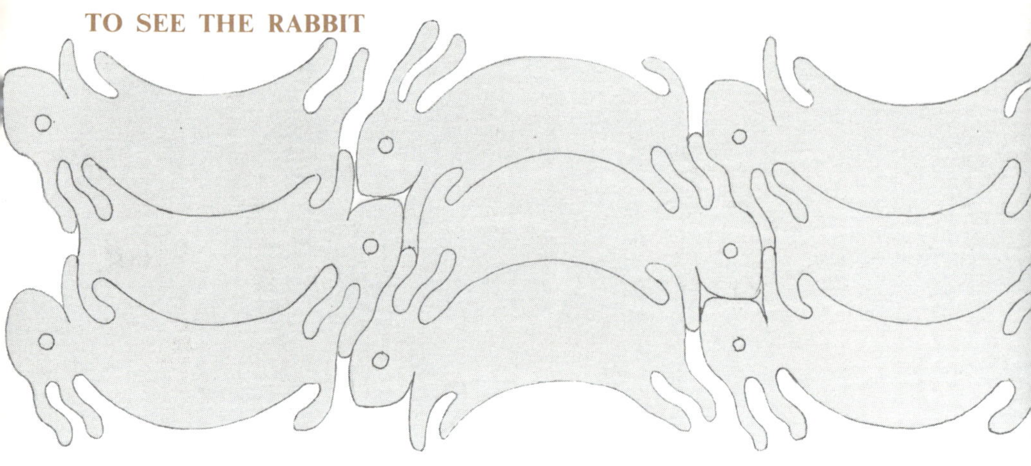

We are going to see the rabbit.
We are going to see the rabbit.
Which rabbit, people say?
Which rabbit, ask the children?
Which rabbit?
The only rabbit,
The only rabbit in England,
Sitting behind a barbed-wire fence
Under the floodlights, neon lights,
Sodium lights,
Nibbling grass
On the only patch of grass
In England, in England
(Except the grass by the hoardings
Which doesn't count).
We are going to see the rabbit
And we must be there on time.

First we shall go by escalator,
Then we shall go by underground,
And then we shall go by motorway,
And then by helicopterway,
And the last ten yards we shall have to go
On foot.

And now we are going
All the way to see the rabbit,
We are nearly there,
We are longing to see it,
And so is the crowd
Which is here in thousands
With mounted policemen
And big loudspeakers
And bands and banners,
And everyone has come a long way.

But soon we shall see it
Sitting and nibbling
The blades of grass
On the only patch of grass
In – but something has gone wrong!

Discussing the poem

1 What view of the future (in contrast with the nuclear disaster in the story of Ann Burden) does this poem take as a starting-point? In what ways have both Robert O'Brien and Alan Brownjohn imagined present dangers taken to a future extreme?

Why is everyone so angry,
Why is everyone jostling
And slanging and complaining?

The rabbit has gone,
Yes, the rabbit has gone.
He had actually burrowed down into the earth
And made himself a warren, under the earth,
Despite all these people,
And what shall we do?
What *can* we do?

It is all a pity, you must be disappointed,
Go home and do something else for today,
Go home again, go home for today.
For you cannot hear the rabbit, under the earth,
Remarking rather sadly to himself, by himself,
As he rests in his warren, under the earth:
"It won't be long, they are bound to come,
They are bound to come and find me, even here."

ALAN BROWNJOHN

2 What "message" does the poem convey to you? Is it about our responsibility for the natural world?

3 Discuss the ways in which the poem uses repetition.

4 Try dividing the poem up into "parts" for four or more different voices, so that it can be recited aloud by four people (or four groups of people).

For learning about language

Everyone has come a long way.
But soon *we* shall see *it*.
Do *something* else for today.
They are bound to come and find *me*.

In these sentences (taken from the poem) the **pronouns** have been printed in italics. What person(s) or thing(s) does each pronoun stand for? Notice that some are singular and some plural, and that some have different forms for subject and object. As a reminder, here are the *personal pronouns* that were discussed in Book 1.

	SUBJECT	OBJECT
Singular	I	me
	you	you
	he	him
	she	her
	it	it
Plural	we	us
	you	you
	they	them

In addition, the following *singular* pronouns are found as subject *or* object:

each, everyone, anyone, none, no one, anybody, nobody, one, this, that, some, another, something, someone.

And the following *plural* pronouns can also be subject *or* object:

all, both, these, those, some, others.

Exercise 1 In the following passage, twenty-two pronouns are printed in italics. State whether each is subject or object, singular or plural, and what each refers to. The first two have been done for you.

   (1) I – subject, singular, refers to Ann Burden.
   (2) me – object, singular, refers to Ann Burden.

I was afraid the man would see *me*, but *he* was not expecting *anyone* to be alive. *He* came with his cart, pulling *it* by hand. *It* carried several instruments to measure radiation; *he* used *one* to

110

check *another*. When *he* realised my valley was still alive, and had tested *it* for radioactivity, *he* took off his mask and shouted *something* like, "Is *anybody* here?" Although *I* do not trust *him*, *I* am relieved to know that *someone* has survived. *We* might even find *others* and help *them*.

Exercise 2 In the dictionary extract in the last chapter (page 93), *slight* as an adjective was said to mean *slim* or *slender*. These three adjectives are very similar in meaning. Words of similar meaning are called **synonyms**. Which two synonyms did the dictionary extract give for *slim*, and which one for *slimy*? Synonyms, however, are not always identical in meaning: slippery things are not always slimy – think of an example to show this, and discuss the subtle difference in meaning.

With the help of a dictionary, find synonyms (as many close ones as you can) for:

tall, clever, small, strong, old (all adjectives);

edge, man, teacher, flag, beginning (all nouns);

plunge, jump, slip, annoy, talk (all verbs).

Exercise 3 Rewrite the following sentences, choosing the most suitable word to complete the sentence from the synonyms given in brackets.

For example:

The falling saucepans made a great

(*clatter*, roar, uproar, hubbub, blare).

(a) Joan of Arc was (inflamed, roasted, burned, singed) at the stake.

(b) The magician waved his (rod, stick, wand, staff, bar) and the rabbit appeared.

(c) His jacket was (sullied, stained, tarnished, tainted) with ink.

(d) He was inclined to (peek, peep, peer, pry) into other people's business.

(e) The old-fashioned way of making bread involves (massaging, rubbing, kneading, stroking, manipulating) the dough.

(f) The third (shake, quiver, flutter, ripple, tremor) of the earthquake was the worst.

(g) Iron-ore is smelted in a (blast-furnace, fire-box, crematorium, kiln, oven, incinerator).

(h) In the fourth round, after being severely cut over one eye, the Slogger (conceded, admitted, confessed, avowed) the victory to his opponent.

(i) First one has to remove the (peel, crust, bark, skin, rind, husk, shell) of the bananas.

(j) He tried to pass some (mock, sham, spurious, counterfeit, artificial) money over the shop counter, and was accused of (fabrication, forgery, invention, fraud, falsification).

Can you say what slightly different meanings the other synonyms in each of these lists have?

Exercise 4 In the following well-known proverbs the subjects in the left-hand column have been separated from the rest of the sentences on the right, and placed in the wrong order. Sort them out so that each subject is placed in its appropriate sentence and write out the resulting traditional proverbs.

> For example:
> Empty vessels make most sound.

Empty vessels	flock together
Little pitchers	make most sound
Possession	is believing
Pride	may look at a king
A rolling stone	goes before a fall
A bird in the hand	does not make a summer
Birds of a feather	have long ears
A stitch in time	gathers no moss
Too many cooks	are better than one
Silence	is better than no bread
Everybody's business	is worth two in the bush
A friend in need	is nine points of the law
Seeing	is as good as a feast
Two heads	run deep
A cat	is golden

Enough	never boils
Still waters	sweep clean
One swallow	saves nine
New brooms	spoil the broth
Half a loaf	is nobody's business
A watched kettle	is a friend indeed

Exercise 5 Here is a letter that Michael wrote to his uncle, Joseph Johnson, at 17 Peg Hill, Huddersfield, West Yorkshire, HD8 0NW.

12 Lace Lane,
Peckham,
London,
SE15 2EU.
9th January, 19—

Dear Uncle Joe,

Mum is going into hospital tomorrow, Friday, a bit earlier than we expected, and Dad hopes you will not mind if he does not bring Grandma and me up by car tomorrow. He wants to be in London so that he can visit Mum over the weekend. He is planning to drive us up to King's Cross and put us on the Inter-City train in the morning. We should reach Huddersfield at 3.30 in the afternoon, all being well.

Could you please meet us with the car at the station? We shall have quite a lot of luggage and, of course, Grandma's wheelchair, and would be grateful for the help.

We are both looking forward very much to our stay.

Love from us all,
Michael.

(a) Imagine that, in the rush of getting his mother ready for hospital and himself and Grandma ready for the trip to Yorkshire, Michael had time only for a brief postcard to explain the situation. Write the postcard, remembering that you can shorten the sender's address and date to save space.

(b) Imagine now that it is already early on the 10th January when they decide to go by train. Uncle Joe has no telephone. Make up a very brief telemessage to send before Michael leaves for King's Cross.

Find out how much your telemessage would cost.

For your own writing

The first purpose of a diary or log-book is to record events soon after they happen in order to aid one's own memory or leave a record for others. Shortly after beginning her diary (in **Z for Zachariah**) the author makes Ann Burden write this: "Sometimes I thought – what's the use of writing anyway, when nobody is ever going to read it? Then I would remind myself: some time, years from now, *you're* going to read it."

Here are some of the last entries in the famous diary that Captain Scott kept on his tragic last expedition in the Antarctic – he and his companions are on the return journey from the South Pole.

(*Wednesday*) *March 21* – Got within 11 miles of depot Monday night;* had to lie up all yesterday in severe blizzard. Today forlorn hope, Wilson and Bowers going to depot for fuel.

22 and 23 – Blizzard as bad as ever – Wilson and Bowers unable to start – tomorrow last chance – no fuel and only one or two (rations) of food left – must be near the end. Have decided it shall be natural – we shall march for the depot with or without our effects and die in our tracks.

(*Thursday*) *March 29* – Since the 21st we have had a continuous gale from W.S.W. and S.W. We had fuel to make two cups of tea apiece and bare food for two days on the 20th. Every day we have been ready to start for our depot 11 miles away, but outside the door of the tent it remains a scene of whirling drift. I do not think we can hope for any better things now. We shall stick it out to the end, but we are getting weaker, of course, and the end cannot be far.

It seems a pity, but I do not think I can write more.

R. Scott.

Last entry. For God's sake look after our people.

*the 60th camp from the Pole

114

What reasons do you think Scott had for keeping this diary?

1 A diary is partly a record of events and partly a way of expressing your own impressions and feelings, and your reactions to events and people. Writing a diary regularly helps you to sort out your own ideas and to find a special kind of relief in expressing just what you feel – this is especially true if you decide to keep your diary strictly private.

Whether or not you decide to keep a private diary regularly from now on, keep one for the next week at least, as a composition exercise. Try to make it as interesting as you can. If the events of the week are not in themselves very exciting, then introduce more personal comment and make the diary a record of your feelings and impressions. You may use a diary style of writing (not using "I" very often) if you wish.

2 Write at least five days in an imaginary diary of a man or woman in exciting circumstances, perhaps exploring, or on a long, difficult journey, or on an exciting holiday. Pay careful attention to accurate detail, and continuity.

For talk and action

1 Letters and diaries are important forms of communication. Find out more about the postal and telephone services available in your area, for instance:

Where is the nearest Post Office?

How much do local calls from a telephone-box cost?

How much (per minute) does it cost to make a call to Paris? How do you make such a call?

What does it cost to send the following to addresses in this country: letters (first and second class); postcards; printed papers; parcels?

What is a greetings telemessage card? How much does it cost?

How can you find out the following by telephone: the time, the local weather forecast, a telephone number you cannot find in the directory? What other services are available from British Telecom in your area?

What are the following: Registered Post, Express Letters, Recorded Delivery, Air Letters, the Business Reply Service?

You will probably find the **Post Office Guide** and the local **Telephone Directories** in your nearest public library and the Post Office.

2 Make up some other postcards and telemessages (see Exercise 5), and discuss the art of getting as much as possible into the fewest words. Also, imagine that you have to make a telephone call where accuracy is important. Suppose you have to telephone a doctor about an accident, the fire brigade giving details of a fire, or a friend to give him exact directions to reach your house (or the school) from some distant address: what would you say? Discuss how to answer the telephone correctly. All these imaginary calls should be made in front of the class, so that the rest can criticise each one for any lack of clarity, politeness or accuracy.

3 Some pocket diaries give calendar information about feasts, holidays, anniversaries and official dates. Where would you look for this kind of information in the reference section of a library? Try to find out something about each of the following – what dates they fall on, what the terms mean or the days commemorate, whether they are public holidays, and so on.

Epiphany and Hogmanay.

The Oxford and Cambridge University Terms (what they are called, how long they last).

The beginning and end of the partridge and other shooting seasons.

Candlemas, Michaelmas and Martinmas.

Quarter Days.

The main Saints' Days.

Plough Monday, Shrove Tuesday, Ash Wednesday, Maundy Thursday, Good Friday and Palm Sunday.

Equinoxes and Solstices.

Rogation Days and Ember Days.

Lady Day.

The Dog Days.

Septuagesima, Sexagesima.

For further reading

Z for Zachariah by ROBERT O'BRIEN (Gollancz; Collins; Armada; Lions)
Ann's story is compelling, convincing and terrifying. Can she trust a man who will not stop at murder in the battle to survive? If she cannot, where can she go for help?

In **The Silver Crown**, Robert O'Brien explores a rather different world of fantasy. Ellen's adventures begin when she finds a silver crown on her pillow on her tenth birthday (also Collins; Lions).

Life with Lisa by SYBIL BURR (Puffin)
Writing her diary was the only way Lisa could think of to make her "Mark in Life", for fate had given her neither wealth nor beauty nor brains. Full of telling detail, the diary is written in a distinctively individual style.

A Rag, a Bone and a Hank of Hair by NICHOLAS FISK (Kestrel)
A nuclear accident has caused the birthrate to drop drastically and twelve-year-old Brin is one of the few remaining young people. He is entrusted with the task of monitoring the artificially created children, the "Reborns", on whom the survival of the human race depends. This is not only a gripping science-fiction story, it is also a thought-provoking book about Man's desire for freedom of choice.

Scott's Last Expedition from **The Personal Journals of Capt. R. F. Scott** (Murray; Tandem)
The story of Scott's last journey to the South Pole, in close rivalry with Amundsen's Norwegian expedition, remains (as his son, Peter Scott, reminds us) "as timeless as the human spirit". Told in the words of his own diary, it is indeed exciting and inspiring.

The Time of the Kraken by JAY WILLIAMS (Gollancz; Macmillan; Topliner)
In this science-fiction fantasy of the distant future, two warring peoples are faced by the disaster threatening the whole earth – the monster of the deep. Jay Williams has also compiled a collection of science-fiction stories, **Unearthly Beasts and Other Strange People** (Macmillan; Topliner).

8 Snow

John Ridd tells his own story of his family's feud with the Doones, the outlaws of seventeenth-century Dartmoor, and his love for Lorna Doone, and its terrible consequences. The extract shows him as a young farmer on Dartmoor, facing not the Doones but the natural hardships that threaten men and animals . . .

With some trouble, and great care, lest the ancient frame should yield, I spread the lattice open; and saw at once that not a moment must be lost, to save our stock. All the earth was flat with snow, all the air

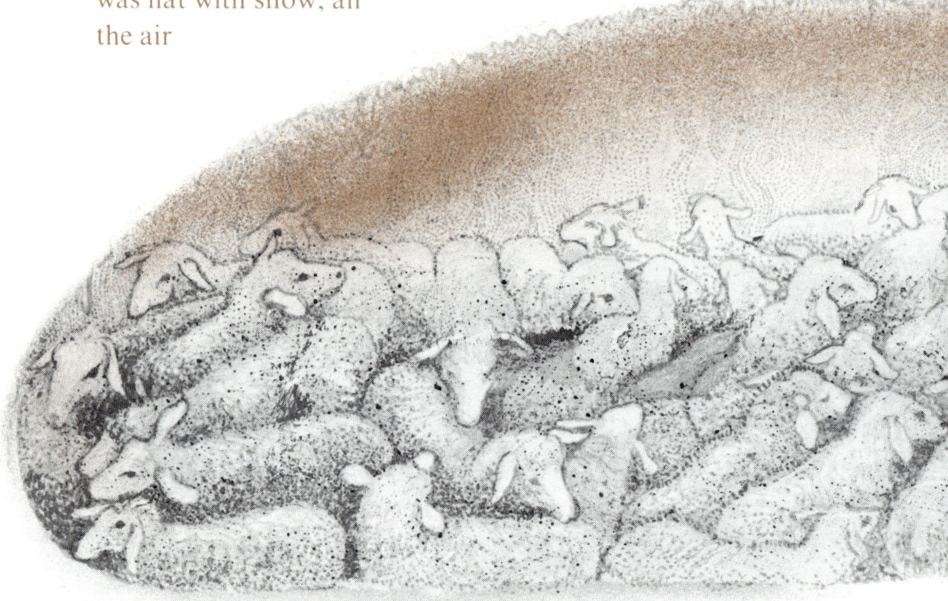

was thick with snow; more than this no man could see, for all the world was snowing.

I shut the window, and dressed in haste; and then set forth to find John Fry, Jem Slocombe, and Bill Dadds. But this was easier thought than done; for when I opened the court-yard door, I was taken up to my knees at once, and the power of the drifting cloud

prevented sight of anything.
It must have snowed most wonderfully to have
made that depth of covering in about eight hours. For one
of Master Stickles' men, who had been out all the night, said that
no snow began to fall until nearly midnight.

All this time it was snowing harder than it ever had snowed
before, so far as a man might guess at it; and the leaden depth of the
sky came down, like a mine turned upside down on us. Not that the
flakes were so very large; for I have seen much larger flakes in a
shower of March, while sowing peas; but that there was no room
between them, neither any relaxing, nor any
change of direction.

Yet after a deal of floundering, some laughter and a little swearing, we came all safe to the lower meadow, where most of our flock was hurdled.

But behold, there was no flock at all! None, I mean, to be seen anywhere; only at one corner of the field, by the eastern end, where the snow drove in, a great white billow, as high as a barn and as broad as a house. This great drift was rolling and curling beneath the violent blast, tufting and combing with rustling swirls, and carved (as in patterns of cornice) where the grooving chisel of the wind swept round.

But although, for people who had no sheep, the sight was a very fine one, yet for us, with our flock beneath it, this great mount had but little charm. We four men set to in earnest, digging with all our might and main, shovelling away at the great white pile, and fetching it into the meadow. Each man made for himself a cave, scooping at the soft cold flux, which slid upon him at every stroke, and throwing it out behind him, in piles of castled fancy. At last we drove our tunnels in (for we worked indeed for the lives of us), and all converging towards the middle, held our tools and listened.

Further in, and close under the bank, where they had huddled themselves for warmth, we found the poor sheep packed as closely as if they were in a great pie. It was strange to observe how their vapour, and breath, and the moisture exuding from their wool had scooped, as it were, a coved room for them, lined with a ribbing of deep yellow snow. Two or three of the weaklier hoggets were dead, from want of air, and from pressure; but more than three-score were as lively as ever; though cramped and stiff for a little while.

Then of the outer sheep (all now snowed and frizzled like a lawyer's wig) I took the two finest and heaviest, and with one beneath my right arm, and the other beneath my left, I went straight home to the upper sheppey, and set them inside, and fastened them. Sixty-and-six I took home in that way, two at a time on each journey; and the work grew harder and harder each time, as the drifts of the snow were deepening ...

That great snow never ceased a moment for three days and nights;

and then when all the earth was filled, and the topmost hedges were unseen, and the trees broke down with weight (wherever the wind had not lightened them), a brilliant sun broke forth and showed the loss of all our customs.

That night, such a frost ensued as we had never dreamed of, neither read in ancient books, or histories of Frobisher. The kettle by the fire froze, and the crock upon the hearth-cheeks; many men were killed, and cattle rigid in their head-ropes. Then I heard that fearful sound, which never I had heard before, neither since have heard (except during that same winter), the sharp yet solemn sound of trees, burst open by the frost-blow.

(from Lorna Doone by R. D. BLACKMORE,
abridged by Stephanie Nettell)

For discussion

1 The "lattice" was an upstairs window, with leaded panes of glass, against which there was a pile of snow. Why was it so difficult to open, and so important for John Ridd to be careful when doing so? Why did he open the window at all?

2 In the third paragraph "hurdled" means "enclosed". What was (or is) a "hurdle" on a farm, and what connection is there with "hurdles" in athletics?

3 Elsewhere, John Ridd talks of the sheep "upon the mountain" and the cattle "on the upper burrows" which they had less hope of saving. What reasons might they have had to make first for "the lower meadow"?

4 How does John Ridd describe the size and shape of the snowdrift with the sheep beneath it? What made it that particular shape?

5 The snow in the drift is called "the soft cold flux" – what does the word "flux" suggest to you?

6 A "hogget" is a sheep more than one but less than two years old. How had the weaker ones died? More than "three-score" were still alive and had to be carried home. What is "a score"? How many more than three score did John Ridd in fact carry back?

7 What made this carrying job harder and harder? What impression have you formed from this of John Ridd's physical build?

8 Is there a likely connection between the brilliant sunshine and the record-breaking frost that followed that night?

9 Why do you think the sound of the trees "burst open by the frost-blow" seemed both "fearful" and "solemn"? What do you think causes trees to "blow open" when the frost is very severe?

10 This book was published in 1869, but R. D. Blackmore was imitating the West Country language of about 1700. Discuss some of the unusual words and expressions he uses, and how easy it is to guess their meaning:

> "I was *taken* up to my knees"
>
> "This great drift was ... *tufting* and *combing* with *rustling swirls.*"
>
> "throwing (the snow) out behind ... in *piles of castled fancy.*"
>
> "all now snowed and *frizzled* like a lawyer's wig."
>
> "I went straight home to the upper *sheppey*, and set them inside."
>
> "a brilliant sun broke forth and showed the *loss of all our customs.*"
>
> "we had never ... read in ancient books, or *histories of Frobisher.*"
>
> "the *crock* (froze) upon the *hearth-cheeks.*"

11 Discuss the effectiveness of the description in this extract:

> **(a)** to emphasise the relentless volume of the snowfall;
>
> **(b)** to show the effect of the wind on the snowdrift; and
>
> **(c)** to explain how the sheep were, when the men dug through to them.

To what extent are vivid, unusual words, repetition, and interesting comparisons used in the description?

For written answers

1 At about what time was John Ridd dressed and ready to go out?

2 Which direction do you think the blizzard blew from, and why did the sheep huddle together in the particular spot they did?

3 Why did the four men hold their shovels and listen, as they neared the middle of the drift?

4 What, would you guess, made the snow near the sheep "yellow" in colour?

5 What saved the sheep under the snow from being either suffocated or frozen to death?

6 What various things made the frost seem so extraordinary to John Ridd?

SNOW

No break of wind,
No gleam of sun –
Still the white snow
Whirls softly down –
Twig and bough
And blade and thorn
All in an icy
Quiet, forlorn.

Whispering, rustling
Through the air,
On sill and stone,
Roof – everywhere,
It heaps its powdery
Crystal flakes;
Of every tree
A mountain makes;
Till pale and faint
At shut of day,
Stoops from the west
One wintry ray.
And, feathered in fire,
Where ghosts the moon,
A robin shrills
His lonely tune.

WALTER DE LA MARE

Discussing the poem

1 How does the poet emphasise that the snow covers *everything*? How can the snow be said to make a "mountain" of every tree?
2 What is the contrast between the description in the first sixteen lines of the poem, and that in the last eight? Does the robin make the scene seem more friendly and full of life?
3 Discuss the sense in which snow can be said to "whisper" or "rustle", in which "one wintry ray stoops from the west", a robin is "feathered in fire", and the moon "ghosts".

For learning about language

In English, a group of words often plays the same part in a sentence as a single word. Such a group of words, acting together as a noun, an adjective, an adverb or a verb, is called a **phrase**, or sometimes (if it includes a separate verb of its own) a **clause**.

Adverb phrases tell us how, when, where or why something happens.

For example:

1 *With some trouble, and great care*, I spread the lattice open. (adv. phrase saying *how* I spread the lattice open)
2 No snow began to fall *until nearly midnight*. (adv. phrase saying *when* the snow fell, or did not fall)
3 *All this time* it was snowing harder. (adv. phrase saying *when* it was snowing)
4 *Further in*, and *close under the bank, where they had huddled themselves for warmth*, we found the poor sheep. (two adv. phrases and one adv. clause, all three saying *where* we found them)

Exercise 1 In the following sentences, the adverb phrases have been put in italics. State what question (how? when? where? why?) each answers.

(a) I shut the window and dressed *in haste*.

(b) We four men set to *in earnest*.

(c) We were digging *with all our might and main*.

(d) *From the west* one wintry ray shines out.

(e) It heaps its powdery crystal flakes *on sill and stone and roof*.

(f) White famine had come *to the high country*.

(g) *Towards evening* a great horned owl beat *along the ridges*.

(h) *Down through the snapping air* the feathered hunter whistled.

(i) *With a savage grunt*, the wolf lay down.

Choose a single adverb that might be used instead of each phrase, from this list.

alongside	eastwards	hurriedly	there
angrily	energetically	later	
downwards	everywhere	seriously	

Exercise 2 Expand the following into fuller, more interesting sentences by substituting adverb phrases (or clauses) for the single adverbs printed in italics. You may rearrange the order of the sentence if necessary.

For example:

The snow fell *thickly*.

The snow fell in a curtain of clinging, woolly flakes.

(a) *Afterwards* the garden was knee-deep in snow.

(b) We played *there* with our sledge.

(c) We dragged our sledges *uphill*.

(d) We swept swiftly *down*.

(e) The sledges sped *smoothly* over the ice.

(f) We *then* felt hungry and trudged *wearily* home.

(g) The hungry wolf turned *angrily* on the hunters.

(h) One of the men was *very quietly* creeping up with a net.

(i) *Very swiftly* he threw the net over the beast.

(j) The wolf was *therefore* caught.

SNOW

Exercise 3(a) Both the extract and the poem included some vivid, unusual and interesting vocabulary. Consider the following instances. What makes the words in italics effective? Can you say whether each is a noun, a verb, an adjective, or an adverb?

(1) The *leaden* depth of the sky came down.

(2) The *power* of the *drifting cloud* prevented sight of anything.

(3) This great drift *was rolling* and *curling* beneath the *violent blast* ... and carved ... where the *grooving chisel* of the wind *swept* round.

(4) Still the white snow *whirls softly* down.

(5) Everywhere it *heaps* its *powdery crystal* flakes.

(b) Using vivid nouns, adjectives, verbs and adverbs wherever you can and adding words wherever necessary, rewrite the following and expand them into much more interestingly written sentences.

(1) Snow fell on everything.

(2) The car went up the hill.

(3) The car slipped dangerously on the ice.

(4) Snow made the birds hungry.

(5) Icicles were on the twigs and they caught the sunlight.

(6) The wolf ate its prey hungrily.

(7) Floodwater fell over the waterfall.

(8) Floodwater surrounded the cottages.

(9) The sun shone through the trees.

(10) The glider flew up and down in the warm air.

Exercise 4 One of the difficulties in English spelling occurs in words that contain silent letters – letters which are no longer pronounced, and which do not have any obvious function within the word. These are very often letters that *were* pronounced several hundred years

ago, and in a few cases they are still pronounced in some dialects of English; for instance, in Scotland the -gh- in "night" is sometimes still pronounced as a -ch- sound (as in "loch").

What letters would not normally be pronounced in the following examples, taken from the extract?

should	thought	knees	sight
weight	light	solemn	

Although silent letters cannot have any function in spoken English, they do differentiate on paper between words of similar sound but different meaning, as in:

knot – not	knight – night	reign – rain
wring – ring	buoy – boy	sought – sort.

Write down as many of the following words as you can, with correct spelling, using your dictionary to check any you are not sure of.

For example:

Song of praise (to God), *n.* hymn

(a) A sacred song (in the Old Testament), *n.* p ___
(b) Line (of persons etc.) waiting their turn, *n.* q ___
(c) Metre or beat of verse or music, *n.* r ___
(d) Struggle with or against, grapple, *v.* w ___
(e) Crease in the skin (usually produced by age), *n.* w ___
(f) Cover, for persons or parcels, *n.* w ___
(g) Dweller next door or nearby, *n.* n ___
(h) Draw a deep breath (expressing sadness etc.), *v.* s ___
(i) Faculty of vision; thing seen, *n.* s ___
(j) Goblin or dwarf, *n.* g ___
(k) Bite persistently, *v.* g ___

(l) Work into a dough or paste, *v*. k ____

(m) Cutting instrument with two pivoted blades, *n.pl.* s ____

(n) Place where something occurs; part of a play, *n*. s ____

(o) Light sailing vessel for racing, *n*. y ____

(p) Yellow part of an egg, *n*. y ____

(q) Promoting health; good, *a*. w ____

(r) Person entertained at one's house, *n*. g ____

(s) Sentry; official in charge of a train etc., *n*. g ____

(t) Shelved closet or cabinet, *n*. c ____

Exercise 5 As we saw in Chapter 7, synonyms are words of similar meaning, but there is often a slight difference in meaning between them, so that only one may be suitable in a particular sentence.

For example:

The door was quite (surely, securely) fastened.

"Securely" is the more suitable word. Rewrite the following sentences, using (and underlining) the more appropriate word.

(a) The young man was utterly (untrue, untruthful) in all he said to the policeman.

(b) The walls were one metre (wide, thick) but there were (wide, thick) gaps in them for doors and windows.

(c) Before the beginning of the race, each (competitor, rival) was given a number to wear.

(d) The party set out to (explore, reconnoitre) the unmapped areas of the Upper Amazon.

(e) There was a (mutiny, rebellion) among the troops sent to deal with the (mutiny, rebellion) against the island's governor.

(f) This (frail, fragile) old woman inspired a (revolution, revolt) in the treatment of prisoners.

(g) His answer was (hasty, rapid) and ill-considered.

(h) They enforced the rules (strictly, severely) and punished offenders (strictly, severely).

(i) This (famous, notorious) police chief successfully tackled the (famous, notorious) criminal gangs in the city.

(j) Your stop-watch may be working (correctly, accurately) but it is not sufficiently (correct, accurate) for timing this experiment.

128

For your own writing

1 Prepare for this composition by making full notes. Make a survey of the winter scene. Look at the trees, bushes and grass. Does winter sunshine seem different from summer sunshine? Look at the frost and ice; pick up a sheet of ice one morning and look through it, feel it, break it. Study the birds and other animal life in winter. If you have the opportunity, go out into snow while it is falling. Notice how it falls and how it lies. Is snow always white? Does it always lie evenly over every part of the landscape? Take some snow and press it; watch it melt; if you can, examine snowflakes under a microscope or magnifying glass.

Make a list of suitable adjectives, verbs or phrases (look again at Exercises 2 and 3). Explore possible comparisons to describe what you see, hear, smell, taste and feel on a winter's day (or night).

Write a description of any typical winter scene, trying to make it as vivid and exciting as John Ridd's picture of Dartmoor. Here are a few suggestions.

A park in winter, bleak and cold.
A tobogganing scene.
A skating scene.
Your garden as snow falls.
Any snow scene, in town or country.
Animal habits in winter.

2 As
a short
composition,
give full and
clear instructions
for *one* of the following.

    Building a simple toboggan.

    Learning to ice-skate.

    Making a snowman.

    Helping birds and other wild creatures in very severe weather.

    Playing ice-hockey.

    Slowing and stopping on skis.

Pay particular attention to working out the correct order for the instructions; and make your style simple and direct. You are not telling a story, only giving instructions.

For talk and action

1 Make an anthology of poems, descriptions and pictures on the theme of winter weather.

Try writing a winter poem. Study Walter de la Mare's poem before you begin, and, without necessarily trying to make your poem rhyme, write as vividly and directly as you can.

Put together the best ideas and work from the class on this theme in one or more of these ways:

(a) as a display on the notice-board

(b) as a short programme of spoken items, either performed "live" or pre-recorded on tape

(c) as material for a mid-winter issue of the class magazine.

2 Prepare a talk on some aspect of winter: for instance, any of the winter sports and pastimes (including ski-jumping, ice-yachting, figure-skating, bob-sleighing), the weather in winter (difference between frost, snow, sleet, hail, rain and dew, or the cause of winter fogs), animals or plant life in winter, winter flowers (both wild and cultivated), precautions against snow and ice on roads or railways, machines such as snow-ploughs, motor sledges, snow track-vehicles, ice-breakers, or winter in various other countries.

130

For further reading

Lorna Doone by R. D. BLACKMORE (Various publishers)
The extract in this chapter is taken from the "abridged" version by Stephanie Nettell, published as a Puffin. Cleverly shortened and slightly simplified, this romantic story of seventeenth-century love and treachery, hatred and honour, appeals directly to teenage readers.

The Wolves of Willoughby Chase by JOAN AIKEN (Cape; Puffin)
Set in an imaginary past, when wolves ravaged the frozen north of nineteenth-century England, this is a wild, fantastic story about two exceptional girls, Sylvia and Bonnie, and a grim governess.

Julie of the Wolves by JEAN GEORGE (Hamish Hamilton; Macmillan; Puffin)
A young Eskimo girl, lost in the desolate winter in Alaska, is befriended by a wolf-pack. But she is coming to terms not only with the natural world her ancestors have always understood, but also with modern Western civilisation.

Winter Holiday by ARTHUR RANSOME (Cape; Puffin)
This is one of Arthur Ransome's famous series of books set in the Lake District. This one, set in mid-winter, includes the rescue of a sheep stranded in the snow as well as an exciting race to the "north pole" on an ice-yacht across the frozen lake.

Avalanche by ANNA RUTGERS VAN DER LOEFF (Puffin)
Werner and his father save the lives of a group of Italian orphans who are on holiday in Werner's village in the snow-covered Swiss Alps. Then the avalanche strikes and Werner's father is believed to be killed.

WATOSH
HAIR RESTORER
WHAT
Piffle
COM
BLOGS
Maz
Razor
Blades

 The Customer is Always Right

The story is set in a working-class neighbourhood of an industrial town where the barber's shop is run as a part-time occupation by Rag Bob, the local rag-and-bone man, and his wife, Alice. A haircut in this place is a memorable experience . . .

It was to his shop I went one Friday afternoon to have my hair cut. My dad had been nagging me that much about it, until he got fed up and said he wouldn't give me my Friday's sixpence until it had been cut. I hated the idea of having a haircut because, apart from the ordeal of plucking and itching and keeping still, there was always something warm and matey about having long thick hair covering your neck and hanging like a fringe over your jersey collar.

There was no getting out of it, except to go without spending money, so at half-past four I went into Rag Bob's.

The saloon, as it was called, was the front room of an ordinary two-up and two-down cottage. It had no fancy equipment, and the stone floor was white from rubbing stone, and your clogs made a nice clack when walking over it. The haircutting and shaving seats were old-fashioned chairs with no sliding backs. The boys' chair was a rocking-chair with the rockers sawn off. The hot water came from a big iron kettle on the hob. The gaslight was on all the time because of the big spinning-mill just across the narrow street, from which a cool dark shadow spread over the cottages on sunny days. In fact, you could feel the floor vibrating from the machinery across the way as you sat on your chair. All in all, it was a very homely barber-shop . . .

It was six o'clock when Bob put me on the high chair, and fastened the sheet round my neck, picked up the heavy, old-fashioned clippers and began to press and drive them up the back of my head. He was a very mannerly chap, and if you hadn't been for a haircut for six months, which I hadn't, he would never make any comment about it. I was looking through the mirror, watching Alice lather this chap from the tannery who had a big Adam's apple.

The chap gave a sour grunt. "Watch what you're doing," he said.

"I'm watching what I'm doing," said Alice.

"Then what do you keep shovin' it up me nose for?"

"Shovin' what up your nose?" said Alice.

"Lather," he said. "You keep shovin' lather up me nose."

"Don't be so soft," said Alice. "Anyway, you're not too big to have a bit of soap up your nose."

At this Bob turned to Alice. "Now, that's enough, Alice," he said quietly.

"Do you mind keeping your big nose out of this?" said Alice to Bob.

"My wife wouldn't have to talk to me like that," said the man with the Adam's apple.

At once I felt Bob's grip tighten on the top of my head.

"I never knew you had a wife," said Alice.

"I haven't," said the chap in the chair. "I mean, if I 'ad one."

"You needn't worry about that," said Alice, "you never will have one so long as you've got an Adam's apple like that. It sticks out like Blackpool Tower."

"*Alice*!" hissed Bob. "Shut up!" I could feel those fingers almost crushing my head in.

"I'm not standing for it," said the chap in the chair, trying to rise. Alice just forced his head back and started rubbing all the thick, lathery soap all over his nose and eyes.

The chap shouted and squirmed, and then Bob let go of me and grabbed at Alice. But she swung free of him. "You men are all alike," she yelled out, "each rotten miserable one of you thinks he's a lord of creation." Then she snatched the shaving mug she had been using, and flung the hot, soapy water all over Bob. He let out a terrible roar. Alice flew to the door, jumping over the clogged feet

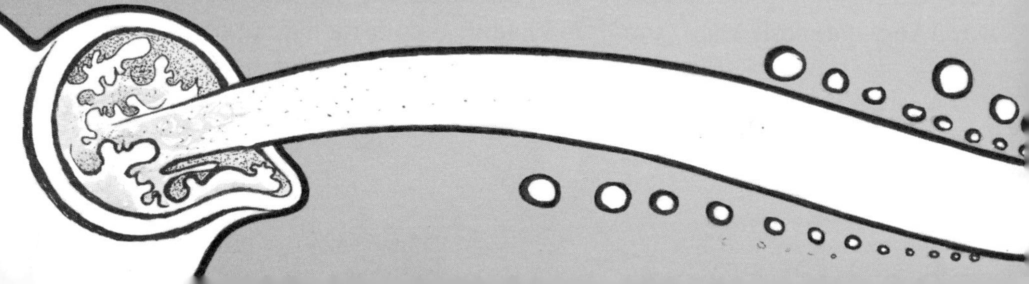

of the customers. Then she slammed it after her. Bob flung down the clippers, picked up a razor, and chased after her. Away up the street I could hear him howling as he ran after her.

(from **The Haircut** in **The Goalkeeper's Revenge** by BILL NAUGHTON)

For discussion

1 Describe a "two-up and two-down" cottage.

2 What are "sliding backs" on barbers' chairs and what are they for?

3 What would "old-fashioned clippers" be like? What else seems old-fashioned about this barber's?

4 In what ways does this extract illustrate that Bob "was a very mannerly chap"?

5 What were Alice's feelings about men in general and Bob in particular? Was she justified, do you think?

6 What indications are there in the extract that the story is set in the North of England?

7 Do you know anyone who still wears clogs in this country? Until recently, in one part of Britain clogs were the normal footwear for working. Where was this? What foreign country are they associated with?

8 What were the boy's various reasons for putting off his haircut? Do you agree with any or all of them? Do you think people should be able to wear their hair any way they please?

9 Did either Bob or Alice seem to believe that the customer is always right? Is this a good motto for a shopkeeper?

10 How do you think this story ended? After you have discussed possible endings, someone could borrow a copy of the book from a library and read the whole story to the class.

For written answers

1 Did Bob and Alice have gas or electricity? How did they heat the shaving water?

2 What effects did the mill have on the barber-shop?

3 How did Alice and Bob divide the work in the shop?

4 How did Bob show his annoyance at first?

5 What does "My wife wouldn't have to talk to me like that" mean?

Pricing an object
On the low shelf
Of a store counter
I kneel in the aisle
One leg sticking out.

A small boy who trips
Over me says
I beg your pardon.

Says the boy's mother
You don't have to beg
His pardon, he works here.

Discussing the poem

1 What do you think the poet feels about this incident? Does he agree with the attitude of the small boy or that of his mother?
2 What is the effect of dividing this poem up into lines? Are they of equal length? Would the story seem different if it was set out as an ordinary piece of writing with inverted commas and full stops?
3 What does "protocol" mean? Should we treat people differently when they are doing a particular job (as opposed to when we meet them as individuals)? Consider people who work as policemen, bank cashiers, first-division soccer players, waiters, nurses.

For learning about language

Just as phrases can do the work of a single adverb and describe a verb, so phrases can do the work of an adjective and describe a noun. In the extract we read of:

chairs *with no sliding backs*

the big spinning-mill *just across the narrow street.*

The phrases in italics describe the chairs and the mill, and distinguish them from other chairs and other mills.

What is described by the **adjective phrases** in italics in each of the following sentences, adapted from the extract?

The boys' chair was a rocking-chair *with the rockers sawn off.*

The floor vibrated from the machinery *across the way.*

He would never make any comment *about it.*

Alice lathered this chap *from the tannery.*

So said the man *with the Adam's apple.*

The chap *in the chair* tried to rise.

Alice jumped over the clogged feet *of the customers.*

In most of these cases it would be difficult to think of a single adjective that could do exactly the same work as the adjective phrase. In the following, however, the phrase and the adjective mean the same.

He was a man *of great strength.*

He was a *strong* man.

Exercise 1 Rewrite the following sentences, replacing the adjective phrases in italics by single adjectives of much the same meaning.
(a) Those hills *in the distance* are the Cotswolds.
(b) We found we had hired a horse *with a limp*.
(c) They found a pram *without any wheels*.
(d) They brought the climber *with the injury* down the mountain.
(e) We have a cottage *in the country*.
(f) The tunnel *under the ground* caved in during the floods.
(g) Joan stayed in the hotel *beside the lake*.
(h) Bill was the driver *of a bus*.
(i) Her answer was quite *out of the ordinary*.
(j) His was the only barber-shop *in that area*.

Exercise 2 Rewrite the following, replacing the adjectives in italics by adjective phrases of similar meaning.
(a) The *hilltop* castle was never captured.
(b) The *red-haired* girl was the one who fell.
(c) *Blond* film stars were very popular at that time.
(d) In such lonely country, a *roadside* inn draws a lot of business.
(e) *Farm* workers were underpaid.
(f) All the *nearby* houses were being sold.
(g) Some *Japanese* shrubs grew by the stream.
(h) The *bearded* singer then took the guitar and sang.
(i) As a Member of Parliament, he needed a *town* flat as well as a *country* house.

Exercise 3 Each of the adverb phrases printed in italics in the sentences below, could be replaced by one of the adverbs in the following list:

    dully, duly; luxuriantly, luxuriously; crudely, rudely;
    respectfully; shyly, slyly; successively, successfully; truly,
    truthfully; warily, wearily.

Use a dictionary to check the meaning of any you do not know and rewrite the sentences using the single adverb in place of the phrase.

(a) They trudged home *in a tired way.*

(b) He gave his answers *with complete honesty.*

(c) The hut was built *with rough, unfinished materials.*

(d) The speaker talked *in a boring way* of his experiences.

(e) She blushed and answered *in a timid voice.*

(f) They proceeded *with great caution* over the snake-infested rocks.

(g) He was *without any doubt* a born violinist.

(h) The young men pushed past the waiting queue *in an impolite manner.*

(i) We raised our hats *to show our deference.*

(j) They were smiling *in a cunning and mischievous way.*

(k) The King was crowned *in the proper way and at the proper time.*

(l) The operation was completed *with considerable success.*

(m) The three men each bowled *one after another.*

(n) The creeper had grown *in great profusion*, and covered the whole wall.

(o) The room was furnished *in luxury and comfort.*

Exercise 4 To give the feeling of a northern town, the conversation in the extract is written and spelt to suggest the northern accent of the speakers. People in all regions of Britain have their own accents and dialects: their own ways of pronouncing words and their own variations of "standard English". In the extract, the man with the Adam's apple says:

"You keep shovin' lather up me nose."

What words here would have to be changed to make this standard English?

In the following exercise, there is one alteration to be made in each sentence to change it into standard written English. Rewrite them accordingly.

Example: I had been there ten minutes when I seen Joan in the distance.

Answer: I had been there ten minutes when I <u>saw</u> Joan in the distance.

(a) He has bought hisself a motor cycle.

(b) I have forgotten all me fishing tackle.

(c) I been waiting here an hour or more.

(d) I found I had done the homework wrong.

(e) After tea they gave theirselves a treat and went down to the amusement arcade.

(f) Did you collect them parcels for me?

(g) I ran faster than I ever done before in my life.

(h) We managed to get fifty pence off of him for the charity.

(i) Bill, George, Ted and me all went to report the loss at the police station.

(j) My friends and I were given a form and was told to fill it in.

Exercise 5 A very large department store lists the following departments at the entrance.

antiques	haberdashery	pharmacy
confectionery	hosiery	poultry
crockery	household linen	soft furnishings
cutlery	ironmongery	sportswear
delicatessen	jewellery	stationery
electrical	millinery	travel agency
estate agency	monumental masonry	valet service
garden equipment	off-licence	
glassware	optical	

To which of these departments would you go for the following?

sweets	a duck
ointment	rye bread
an iron	a stoneware casserole
some cuphooks	curtain material
carbon paper	a Victorian gramophone
a pair of ear-rings	a pair of stockings
a lady's hat	to have a suit cleaned
a set of buttons	a pair of spectacles
to rent a country cottage	a set of pillowcases
a decanter	a pruning knife

140

for information about   ski boots
    visiting country houses   a carving knife
a headstone for a grave   a bottle of wine

For your own writing

1 Choose a shop in your area that you know well, and that has a distinctive air about it. It would be best to select a small, personal business run by a shopkeeper with a strong personality which is imprinted on the shop. Make notes before you begin to describe the shop or its owner.

First, the shop: what does it sell? Where is it? What impression does it give from the outside? Inside, has it a special smell? Are there particular sounds associated with it? What is the first impression you get as you enter? How is this built up as you look around more closely?

Secondly, the shopkeeper or assistant: make notes about his or her appearance, the voice, mannerisms, kind of clothes, the jokes he or she makes and generally how the shopkeeper treats the customers.

Thirdly, work out how the owner fits the shop. Is the shop an expression of his or her personality? Does the owner apparently enjoy running the shop? Is it a success, a friendly place where one is tempted to spend one's time and money? If so, try to show why this is so.

Now write a description (not a story) entitled:

THE SHOP ROUND THE CORNER.

2 Write a short story, or a poem, to fit the title of this chapter:

THE CUSTOMER IS ALWAYS RIGHT.

For talk and action

1 The class could make a survey of prices in local shops. First, agree on a list of *basic* items required for ordinary housekeeping, subdivided if it seems necessary (e.g. British butter and imported butter). In each case, decide on a simple quantity (500 g butter, 250 g tea, 1 kilo granulated sugar, 3 kilo potatoes etc.).

Then divide into groups to cover different shops or different areas, and different kinds of goods. When you visit the shop, note down the cheapest basic prices of the goods on your list; also take note of any concessions, such as trading stamps or free gifts, that the shop may be offering. Do *not* worry the assistants with a lot of questions.

	Co-op High St.	Brown's North Road	Hypermarket Park Ave.	Superstore High St.
250 g Danish butter				
1 kg Granul. sugar				
6 Size 3 eggs				

Back at school the information could be compiled and presented as a series of charts, something like the one begun above, with written notes to accompany them.

Finally, draw some conclusions about where to go to buy most economically in your area; but take into account the expense of time and money in travelling! What other considerations should also be taken into account when deciding where you get the best value for money?

2 Find out what the following mean or are.

an auction	a job lot
a lot	on "sale or return"
a Dutch auction	made to measure
a store detective	off the peg
a shopwalker (or floor-walker)	seconds
	C.O.D.
a buyer	a cash refund
a sale	a credit card
a bargain basement	a cash register (or till)
a remnant	a cafeteria
a shop-soiled article	a bill
price maintenance	a receipt
discount	cash and carry

3 The situation where various customers meet in a shop, a hairdresser's or a laundrette would be a good subject for an improvised play. Clearly there is room for interesting characterisation amongst staff and customers, and once each actor has firmly established the kind of person he or she is, there should be no need for a complete script: work the conversation out as the play goes on.

For further reading

The Goalkeeper's Revenge by BILL NAUGHTON (Heinemann; Macmillan; Puffin)
This collection of short stories is about extraordinary boys in ordinary situations – boys fishing, fighting, playing football, in hospital, or going for a job. Most of the stories are both convincing and funny.
Bill Naughton was born in Ireland but brought up in Lancashire, and he uses his own experiences in many of his stories, such as **One Small Boy** (Longman).

Break in the Sun by BERNARD ASHLEY (O.U.P.; Puffin)
Patsy Bligh tries to escape her London flat and her unpleasant step-father, and return down-river to Margate, with a group of actors. Like **All My Men**, **Terry on the Fence** and **Trouble with Donovan Croft** (all Puffins), this is a realistic, exciting story of life in the London area for teenagers.

Silver Everything and **Many Mansions** by WINIFRED CAWLEY (O.U.P.)
Two down-to-earth stories about Tyneside in the 1920s, both centred on Jinnie, who clings firmly to her family pride even when they have to take the corner shop in Stratford Street.

Me and My Million by CLIVE KING (Kestrel; Puffin)
If Elvis will entrust a valuable picture, stolen from Kenwood House, to a kid brother who can't tell a No.14 bus from a No.41, things are bound to get complicated; and in this lively story by the author of **Stig of the Dump** (Kestrel; Puffin), set firmly in the heart of London, they certainly do.

10   Actors and Audiences

Fourteen-year-old George Treet, eldest boy in a family of eighteenth-century strolling players, has been claimed as the long-lost son of the dying Sir John Dexter. But the theatre is in his heart and in his upbringing, and it takes very little encouragement from the visiting Rumbold family for him to put on a solo performance . . .

I made my hurried excuses and flew to my room – to the chest I'd always known I'd be opening at just such a time as this. Out they came! King Charles's green coat! Othello's yellow tabby waistcoat with its rich silver lace! The stockings with "bas de soye shot through"! The white silk breeches! The red-heeled shoes worn by a Marshal of France! Even the grand Dutch wig with its two tails and great black bow . . . and last and most handsome of all, the blue Steinkirk cravat with its foot-deep border of lace!

Off went my dull clothes and on went my glory, till I shone like the rising sun! There was nothing of me – even to the tips of my fingers (scrubbed till pink) – that wasn't of the finest and most princely!

Then down the stairs I went and fairly burst upon the great hall with: "'Friends, Romans, countrymen!'"

And how they cheered and clapped! For this time, with their goodwill at the outset, I gave them a performance they'd never forget!

Comedy, tragedy, drama and passion! Not just fragments, but whole scenes! For many of the most excellent pieces are not writ for one performer, but need interjections, such as, "Truly!" "Indeed!" "'Tis strange!" to prick the course and whip it on. So I took all parts, shifted here and there, altered my voice, my stature, my whole person to give a rare richness . . . missed nothing . . . gave everything! (And, every now and then, stole a sly, satisfied look at my mother, who was deeply entranced: and then, proudly, to my

144

father, whose eyes never left me . . .)

"General Othello! General Othello!" screamed the Rumbold children as I ended each scene. For that performance had made the deepest impression. So at last, and to signify the end, I begged a fruit-knife and began upon that stupendous farewell in which the mightiest passions in the universe flare up, blaze – then flicker and die.

"'I kissed thee ere I killed thee, no other way but this,

Killing myself, to die upon a kiss.'"

I staggered, sank – half recovered, then knelt . . . seemed to crawl toward something precious . . . then groaned, twitched – and died!

Silence. The most absolute silence. I dared not move for seconds so's not to break the spell. My head being buried in my sleeve (to this day, I can still recall a rough edge of braiding pressing against my cheek), I could see nothing.

Then I heard someone begin to clap . . . loudly, slowly, evenly. I looked up. Everyone was staring at my father. He was on his feet. And clapping. But not with much joy. His face was pale – grey, almost – so's I wondered briefly if his heart was to blame.

"A farewell indeed!" he said – and tried to smile, though nothing was further from him!

Then he went on, staring everywhere but at me, as if the sight of me, half kneeling on my imaginary stage, was deeply humiliating to him. He said . . . I cannot exactly recall his words, for I felt a sudden sickness and shame and a deep desire to be forgot . . . he said – and I believe he was striving to be gentle against his anger – he said that much must be forgiven me on account of my upbringing. And that my understanding of what was seemly was to be judged by – by other standards.

"Good friends, what appears lofty in the players' booth unluckily seems coarse, vulgar and ridiculous when seen so close as this! So do not judge him harshly. He knew no better. But now he does . . . and – and it injures *me* to see him injured in your eyes. So – so we'll let his unlucky past die, as he says, upon a kiss. Come to me, boy!"

In a maze of horrible, unbelieving shame, I began to stand up … when, with a quick abrupt rustle, my mother left her place and came to my side.

"'No other way but this!'" she murmured – and, bending slightly, kissed my brow!

(from Devil-in-the-Fog by LEON GARFIELD)

For discussion

1 What do you think "I made my hurried excuses" means here?

2 Discuss the items of costume that George took out of the chest. What do you know (or what can you guess) about each? For instance, who is Othello and who wrote the play he appears in? Do you think King Charles's coat belonged to a real King? What about the red-heeled shoes; were they really once worn by a Marshal of France?

3 What play includes a famous speech beginning: "Friends, Romans, countrymen! … "? Find this speech, so that you can see who says it, to whom he or she is speaking, and what the plot is about.

4 How might George alter his voice, stature and whole person? Why did he need to do this? What does "shifted here and there" mean in this context?

5 Explain the meaning of the two statements: "(I) missed nothing" and "(I) gave everything", in this situation.

6(a) What was the family's reaction, *at first*, to George's performance?

(b) What did George at first think were the attitudes of his mother, and of his father (Sir John Dexter) to his acting?

7 Discuss what you know (or have found out in 2 above) about Othello, about the play in which he is the main character, and this scene in which he dies "upon a kiss". What do the following imply? – "I kissed thee ere I killed thee" and "(I) seemed to crawl toward something precious"?

8 Trace the stages by which George realises that his father is not proud, but ashamed of him. What do you think is the reason for Sir John's attitude to the "players' booth" and to George's acting? Is he simply being "snobbish"? Could there be any anger, embarrassment, guilt or jealousy amongst Sir John's feelings?

9(a) What is an "interjection"? Bearing in mind the use of exclamation marks here and elsewhere in this extract, what other word could be used to describe: "Truly!", "Indeed!" and "'Tis strange!"?

(b) What would you guess "to prick the course and whip it on" means here, and what might be the origin of these phrases?

10 Why has the printer put *two* sets of quotation marks (inverted commas) round "'No other way but this!'"? Where else in the extract have two sets been used, and why?

11 Contrast George's attitude to the scene from "Othello" ("that stupendous farewell in which the mightiest passions in the universe flare up … ") with Sir John's "other standards" of "what appears lofty". Do you think professional actors are held in very different regard today from the eighteenth-century attitudes represented here?

For written answers

1 How does the reader of this extract know that the Rumbold children have seen George act before?

2 Explain clearly, in your own words, why George refers to his "stage" as "imaginary".

3 Why didn't George move for a while at the end of his performance?

4 Was George surprised, or disturbed, at the end, when his father clapped him? If so, why?

5 What was George's first interpretation of Sir John's pale, almost grey, face?

6 What does the word "maze" imply about George's feelings of "horrible, unbelieving shame"?

148

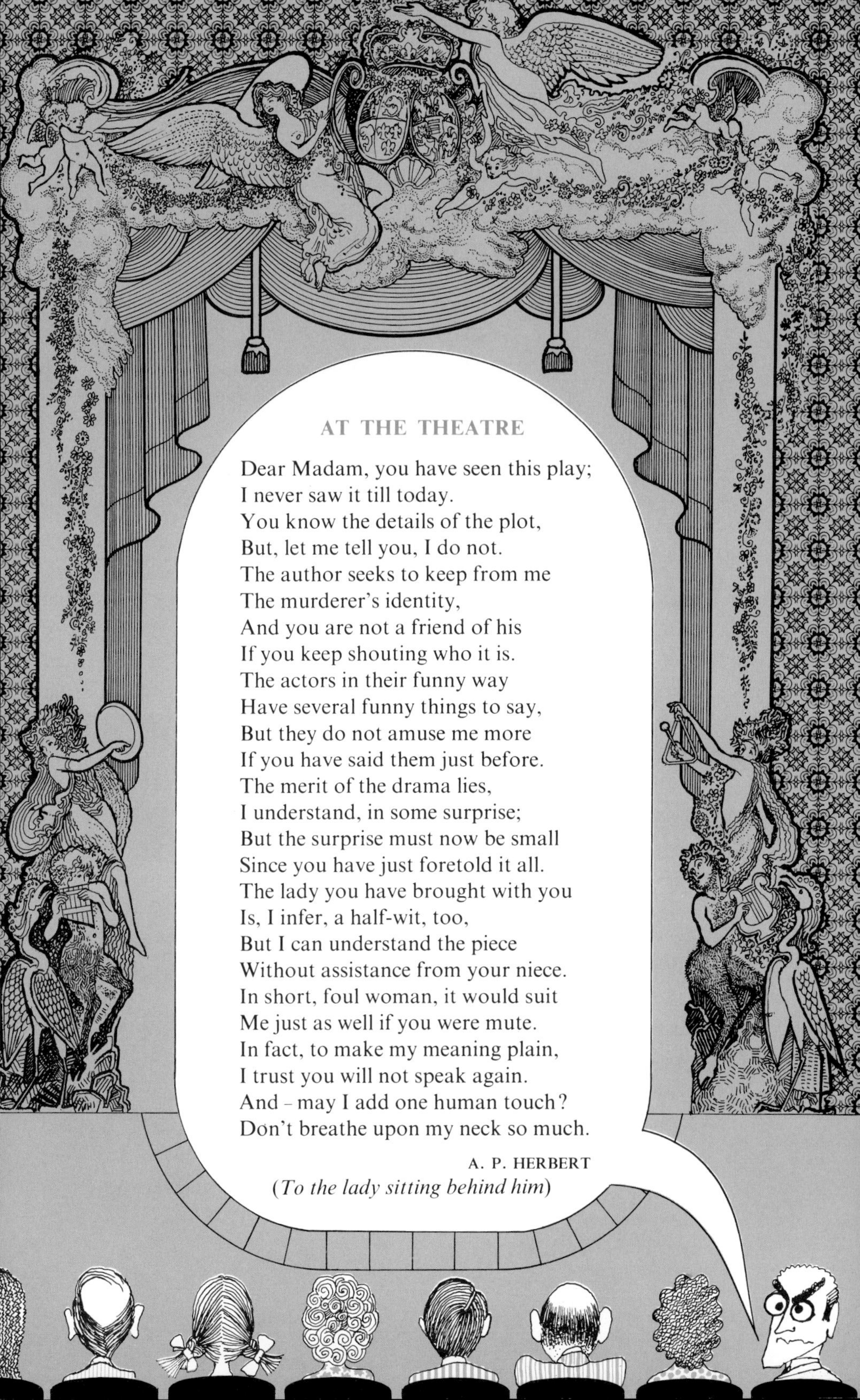

AT THE THEATRE

Dear Madam, you have seen this play;
I never saw it till today.
You know the details of the plot,
But, let me tell you, I do not.
The author seeks to keep from me
The murderer's identity,
And you are not a friend of his
If you keep shouting who it is.
The actors in their funny way
Have several funny things to say,
But they do not amuse me more
If you have said them just before.
The merit of the drama lies,
I understand, in some surprise;
But the surprise must now be small
Since you have just foretold it all.
The lady you have brought with you
Is, I infer, a half-wit, too,
But I can understand the piece
Without assistance from your niece.
In short, foul woman, it would suit
Me just as well if you were mute.
In fact, to make my meaning plain,
I trust you will not speak again.
And – may I add one human touch?
Don't breathe upon my neck so much.

A. P. HERBERT
(*To the lady sitting behind him*)

Discussing the poem

1 What kind of play is the poet watching? Is it wholly serious, do you think?

2 Can you explain the meaning of the word "foretold" in line 16; and of the word "mute" in line 22? What does "I infer" mean (and is it different from "I imply")?

3 What exactly is the lady sitting behind him doing to annoy the poet? Would it be different if he was watching this play on television? Are there particular kinds of good manners appropriate for a visit to the live theatre? If so, what are they?

For learning about language

We have learnt the difference between subject and object; it may be quite important to know whether Othello killed Desdemona or Desdemona killed Othello! Frequently, however, a sentence will continue to say more about the subject, instead of introducing an object, as in:

Othello became Governor of Cyprus.

Here Othello and the Governor are the same person.

This happens most commonly with the verb "to be" (is, are, was, were, am, have been, will be etc.) which can never be followed by an object, because the sentence will always continue to speak about the same person, thing or idea. In each of the following, we are talking about *one* person:

George Treet was an *actor*.

George Treet became *heir* to Sir John.

But this is not so in these two sentences:

George Treet respected Sir John.

Sir John disliked actors.

In the first two examples, the words "an actor" and "heir" cannot be called objects; we therefore call them **complements**, because they complete the sense by *complementing* (= adding to) the subject.

150

Exercise 1(a) Pick out the objects or complements from the following sentences. State what the verb is, in each case, and underline the object or complement word.

For example:

The last rose seemed a beautiful <u>specimen</u>.
The verb is "seemed" and its complement is "a beautiful specimen".

(1) She always grew beautiful roses.

(2) The experiment seemed a disaster.

(3) The experiment prevented a disaster.

(4) We are amateur actors.

(5) We admire professional actors.

(6) We hope to become professional actors.

(7) Sir Alexander Fleming discovered penicillin.

(8) Sir Alexander Fleming was a famous scientist.

(9) The doctor felt a fool.

(10) The doctor felt the lump on the boy's neck.

(b) Explain the following newspaper headlines, showing whether they are using complements or objects. Those marked with an asterisk * could have two meanings.

For example:

*EXPLORER RETURNS CANNIBAL CHIEF

This could mean that the explorer has returned from an expedition on which he was made a chief by some cannibals, in which case "chief" is the complement of "returns". Alternatively, it could mean that he is sending a cannibal chief back to someone, somewhere ("chief" is then the object of "returns").

(1) MECHANIC BECOMES BOSS

(2) MECHANIC CRITICISES BOSS

(3) THIEF TURNED DETECTIVE

(4) THIEF TURNED CAR OVER

(5) *ELECTRICITY SUPPLIES THE ANSWER

(6) *POST DELAYS SERIOUS MATTER

(7) *BONE REMAINS ONLY EVIDENCE

(8) MAGAZINE CONTINUES WEEKLY SUPPLEMENT

151

Exercise 2 In discussing the extract from **Devil-in-the-Fog**, you will have noted the use of single inside double inverted commas. Notice also the use of double inverted commas round words such as "Truly!" (5th paragraph) and round the words "snobbish", "interjection", and "Othello" in 8, 9(a) and 11 of the **For discussion** section.

Apart from their use round the single words, short phrases and so forth that have been quoted from sentences for comment, what further uses of inverted commas do you think are illustrated by the above instances? In what sense does the term "quotation marks" fit all these uses of inverted commas?

Inverted commas can be used:

(a) to indicate direct speech;

(b) to refer to the title of a book, play, film etc. (printers often use **bold** or *italic* type for this);

(c) to call attention to any very particular or unusual name, including special places and buildings, and curious nicknames;

(d) to indicate single words, phrases or sentences that are quoted from someone else, or from a book or other publication;

(e) to call attention to any unusual, rare, slang, foreign or made-up words used in writing.

Some printers use double inverted commas (" ") for use (a) and single (' ') for uses (b) to (e), but in handwriting it is simpler to use double for them all, and reserve single for use when you wish to use inverted commas *inside* other inverted commas.

For example:

"Have you ever read 'Romeo and Juliet'?" Jean asked.
Notice that in titles we also use capital letters for the first letters of the first word and all the other important words, but not for "the, of, in, a" etc., unless these are the first words of the titles.

(a) Justify the use of inverted commas in the following sentences, using the categories (a) to (e) above.

(1) When she says, "I know what I'm doing," she means it.

(2) Shakespeare wrote "Macbeth" and "Much Ado about Nothing" as well as "Othello".

(3) He called his house "The Dungeon" and his cat was nicknamed "Warder Pete".

(4) For "spoon" my little sister says "poon".

(5) "Weekend", "whisky" and "football" are all words the French have borrowed from the English.

(6) The only "quote" he knew was "To be or not to be".

(b) Rewrite the following sentences putting in *all* the necessary punctuation. (But do *not* enclose complete answers in inverted commas.)

(1) a tale of two cities is a novel by charles dickens set in london and paris

(2) in the play henry v henry himself speaks the famous once more unto the breach speech

(3) in cockney rhyming slang plates of meat means feet and apples and pears are stairs

(4) in gullivers travels we are told that the lilliputians called gulliver the man-mountain

(5) did you or did you not snapped the magistrate refer to the defendant as bandy-legs

Exercise 3 In Book 1, you saw how to set out the script of a play. As revision of that, study the following dramatisation of the scene described in Chapter 9, **The Customer is Always Right**. Compare this with pages 133–35. Notice how names, stage directions etc. are set out.

CHARACTERS: *Bill (a small boy of about ten), Bob (the hairdresser), Alice (his wife and assistant), the customer being shaved, three other customers waiting for a haircut.*

SCENE: *Rag Bob's Hairdressing Saloon, 1925.*
A small room with a stone floor, lit by gaslight. Several old-fashioned chairs face the fireplace where a kettle is kept hot on an open fire. Over the mantelpiece is a large mirror. Bill is in the boys' chair (a rocking-chair with the rockers sawn off) and Bob is cutting his hair with old-fashioned clippers. A customer is in the next chair, where Alice is lathering his face with a shaving-brush. The other customers sit against the opposite wall, reading magazines.

CUSTOMER (*grunting angrily*): Watch what you're doing.

ALICE: I'm watching what I'm doing.

CUSTOMER: Then what do you keep shovin' it up me nose for?

ALICE: Shovin' what up your nose?

CUSTOMER: Lather. You keep shovin' lather up me nose.

ALICE: Don't be so soft. (*Pause*) Anyway, you're not too big to have a bit of soap up your nose.

BOB (*turning to Alice; quietly*): Now, that's enough, Alice.

ALICE (*to Bob*): Do you mind keeping your big nose out of this?

CUSTOMER: My wife wouldn't have to talk to me like that.

(*Bob's hand presses firmly down on Bill's head*)

ALICE: I never knew you had a wife.

CUSTOMER: I haven't. I mean, if I 'ad one.

ALICE: You needn't worry about that; you never will have one so long as you've got an Adam's apple like that. It sticks out like Blackpool Tower.

BOB (*hissing angrily and pushing down hard on Bill's head*): Alice! Shut up!

CUSTOMER (*trying to get up*): I'm not standing for it!

(*Alice pushes the customer down, forces his head back and starts lathering his whole face, nose and eyes. The customer squirms.*)

CUSTOMER (*spluttering*): Grrrh . . . !

(*Bob lets go of Bill's head and leans over to grasp Alice, but she swings free of him. The other customers are now aware of the tension.*)

ALICE (*shouting*): You men . . .

Continue this play by making up about a page more, beginning with the unfinished last line here (do not rewrite the first part). Give Bill and the other customers (call them Customer 2, Customer 3 and Customer 4) some lines to say after Bob and Alice have left (*exit*). Where the printer has used italics, you should underline.

Exercise 4 Read the following description carefully. It is about the opening of a new production of a play by Shakespeare.

The first night at Oxford begins casually enough, an hour before curtain-up, with two stage-hands sweeping the stage. Clouds of dust are rising in the patch of light that surrounds Hamlet and Laertes, who are rehearsing the duel under the critical eye of the fight director, Ian Mackay. To one's surprise he is small and bird-like, one of the highly select company of fencing masters who arrange fights for the major companies.

However often it has been practised – and they have been practising every day for a month – the duel has to be rehearsed before every performance for safety reasons. Hamlet, after three hours on stage, is bound to be tiring. Any uncertainty can mean injury . . .

Apart from practising the fight, Derek Jacobi has been in his dressing-room since 5.30 – two hours before the show will "go up". He hasn't slept for two nights and this afternoon there was a drill going outside his hotel. "I spend the night with the show going round and round in my head – entrances, exits, cuts. I'm not able to eat yet. I'm living on Dextrosol. I feel desperately tired but when you get out there, you somehow find the energy. There must be a way of doing it without flogging yourself to death, and I've got to find it. And yet, if you don't go flat out, you're not giving 100 per cent of your performance."

To add to his worries, he has had an unspecified throat infection that has baffled the doctors all through rehearsals. Glasses of water are set out for him at strategic places in the wings. It is all that can be done.

The "half" is called over the backstage tannoy – "Half an hour, please, ladies and gentlemen" – followed, much too soon it seems, by the "quarter". Wigs, newly dressed, are fitted by the wigmaster, Robert Gardner. Hamlet has grown his own hair, beard and moustache. A wig would be impossibly hot and sweaty in such an active part. Invitations are issued to a wine-and-cheese cast party afterwards. The trumpeter can be heard warming up. People, as usual, are borrowing make-up from one another. (It is not all Leichner – a lot of young actors save money by going to Boots make-up counter.)

"Five minutes, please," says the sepulchral voice over the dressing-room loudspeakers and behind it can now be heard the subdued, bubbling sound of an assembling audience, like the breaking of a distant sea. Each actor feels at this moment nakedly exposed and vulnerable. They have their own ways of exorcising their fears. Superstition runs deep, as it does in any risky profession – motor racing, bullfighting, gambling. Actors put charms on their dressing-tables . . .

By such rituals actors try to contain their fear of the many-headed beast waiting out there for them in the dark. They are as superstitious of bad luck omens as sailors. Hence the taboos against whistling in the dressing-room, or naming that unluckiest of plays, *Macbeth* – often referred to, for safety, as "the Scottish play".

"Beginners, please," murmur the loudspeakers. Most of the beginners (it means those on first, not those who are inexperienced) are already pacing the wings in a state either of friendliness or withdrawal. Distantly one can hear the front-of-house announcement: "Ladies and gentlemen, will you kindly take your seats? The curtain will rise in one minute." The phrase lingers although there is no curtain down, as is increasingly the custom with Shakespeare productions.

There is much throat clearing in the passages and the occasional "Good luck" and "Merde". Why the French word? It is like spitting for luck – but why in French no one is sure. "Stand by, please," murmurs Marje in a super-cool voice into her microphone in the prompt corner, with a finger poised to take down the house lights.

As they fade to darkness, a spotlight hits the front of the stage; the first eerie chord is struck by the musicians and the heads of the audience come into view, like rows of cobblestones lit by moonlight. Smoke billows from a smoke canister; the waiting guards grasp their pikes and thrust forward into the smoky space to turn it into the battlements of Elsinore, and suddenly the play is *on*.

(from Facts about a Theatre Company by PETER LEWIS)

Each of the following questions, which are intended to test your understanding (or **comprehension**) of the extract above, has three possible answers; select the correct one(s). The other one or two answers, though in some cases possible, are not accurate. Answering questions of this kind is partly a process of elimination – cutting out the wrong answers.

For example:

Who was playing the part of Hamlet in this production?

(i) Ian Mackay
(ii) Robert Gardner
(iii) Derek Jacobi

You would write down "(iii)" as the correct answer, not only because it is clear from the second and third paragraphs that Derek Jacobi is the most important actor, but also because you can read that Ian Mackay and Robert Gardner, though working with this company, are not actors at all. (Do not mark the correct answer in this book; write out the numbers on a separate sheet.)

(a) 1 Which of these statements is or are true, according to the first paragraph of this extract?

(i) Ian Mackay is one of a small number of teachers of fencing who trains actors.

(ii) Ian Mackay trains small birds to sit on fences.

(iii) Ian Mackay is a theatre critic who also runs a business specialising in erecting fences.

2 Which of the following does the duel scene in this play include?

(i) a boxing match between Laertes and Ian Mackay

(ii) a fencing match between Hamlet and Laertes

(iii) a wrestling match between Derek Jacobi and Dextrosol

3 Which of the statements below means the same as the second sentence in the second paragraph ("Hamlet ... is bound to be tiring.")?

(i) The play, "Hamlet", always tires the audience.

(ii) The actor playing Hamlet has to pretend he is becoming more tired.

(iii) The actor playing Hamlet is bound to feel tired at the end of this play.

4 Which of these statements is (or are) true, according to the third paragraph of this extract?

(i) Derek Jacobi got up at 5.30 a.m. and went from his hotel to the theatre.

(ii) Derek Jacobi could not sleep for the previous two nights because soldiers were drilling outside his hotel until 5.30 a.m.

(iii) Derek Jacobi, although tired from lack of sleep, arrived at his dressing-room at 5.30 p.m.

5 Which of these statements is true of what Derek Jacobi says about performing on stage (3rd and 4th paragraphs)?

(i) He has to have a drink, or he might fall unconscious.

(ii) He has to give everything to every performance.

(iii) He has no hope of learning how to cope with the strain.

6 In the third paragraph "the show will 'go up'" means:
  (i) it will start
  (ii) it will be a success and transfer to London
  (iii) it will be a failure.

7 "The 'half' is called" (in the 5th paragraph) means:
  (i) the play is half over, and there is an interval
  (ii) the actors in the first half of the play are being called to their places
  (iii) there is half an hour to go to the beginning of the performance.

8 In this production of the play in Oxford, at what time would the "quarter" have been announced?
  (i) 5.45 p.m.
  (ii) 6.15 p.m.
  (iii) 7.15 p.m.

9 Derek Jacobi has grown his hair, beard and moustache:
  (i) because nobody in this performance is wearing a wig
  (ii) because he refuses ever to wear a wig
  (iii) because he could not wear a wig comfortably throughout this long play.

10 "Leichner" (5th paragraph) is the trade name for:
  (i) a photographic camera
  (ii) a special kind of stage make-up
  (iii) the kind of make-up you can buy in any chemist's.

(b) The following five short sentences give, briefly, the main point in each of the last five paragraphs of the extract above. They are all "correct", but in the wrong order.
  (i) This play begins with music and artificial mist as the guards keep watch on the ramparts.
  (ii) Actors feel nervous just before a performance, and most are in some way superstitious.
  (iii) At the last moment, the actors wish one another luck.
  (iv) As the audience are called to their seats, the actors required in the first scene become tense.
  (v) There are various things actors will not do before a performance, for fear of having a poor reception from the audience.

Rewrite all these sentences (in their *correct order* but making suitable changes – such as changing "the actors" to the pronoun "them") to form a continuous single paragraph which is a **summary** of the last five paragraphs of the extract on pages 156–57.

For your own writing

1 Have you any experience of acting, speaking or performing in public? If you have, did you feel at all like any of the actors in the extract in Exercise 4, or like George Treet in the main extract at the beginning of this chapter? Perhaps you have even more vivid memories of some other occasion which made you nervous such as a serious interview with someone, or an occasion when you were in trouble or " on your best behaviour " or in the public eye. Recall the occasion, making notes on how you felt: begin with a simple list of all the symptoms of nervousness as you felt them (such as shivering, blushing, perspiring, looking pale, a tight or sick feeling in the stomach, and so on). Then plan your account of the occasion, with an introductory paragraph to explain what it was, a second paragraph to show how you came to be involved, and at least one paragraph to describe your own feelings of nervousness, or how you coped with your nerves. Think of an interesting way to round off the composition in the concluding paragraph.

2 Write a short composition in play form. The simplest would be a conversation or an argument between two or three people. If you decide to tell a particular story, work out the details carefully, remembering that the story and the characters of the people involved have to be unfolded almost entirely by what they say (and do) on stage. Also avoid too many changes of scene, for these are distracting and boring for an audience.

A good single-scene plot would be that used in Jerome K. Jerome's amusing book **Three Men in a Boat**, when he tells the fishing story of the prize trout in the glass case in a riverside public

160

house. He and George enter the bar and ask an old man about the fish. The old man proudly tells them how he caught it. Enter the local carrier, who, when they tell him how they have been admiring the fish, tells them how he caught it! Enter another two local gentlemen, and they again claim to have caught the fish, as does the landlord. Finally, George climbs up for a better view, slips, clutches madly, and the case and fish are knocked to the floor and the fish broken into a thousand *plaster* fragments. It was not a stuffed trout at all!

For talk and action

1 Find out (with the help of books in the library) what the following theatrical terms mean.

box-office success	backcloth
good box-office	in the limelight
flies	a dais
wings	orchestra pit
floats or foots	stage manager
floods	producer or director
spots	green-room
tabs	repertory
drapes	a review
front-of-house	a revue
down- and up-stage	critics
stage left and stage right	a lead
playing to the gallery	to "ham"
the gods	a cue
revolving stage	an understudy
proscenium (arch)	dress rehearsal
stalls or pit	prompt(er)
theatre-in-the-round	properties

Classified at 792 with other books on the theatre, **The Theatre** by W. A. Lord and H. Webster (E.S.A.) is a good, informative book with an index, and a glossary of theatrical terms.

2 The class as a whole, or groups of the class, might try to produce a play over the next few weeks. Decide first whether it is to be "improvised" or acted from a complete script. Groups should then work on several possible plots, and the most suitable for acting can then be chosen. Casting must be done with care; it is often useful to have two people learning the main part or parts, and to decide later who is to take them, and who to "understudy". Scenery (though very little should be necessary), simple properties and costume have all to be planned well in advance. Make sure that everyone in the group or class has some part to play, on stage or off, and learns it thoroughly. The success of a play depends on *everyone*.

3 With your teacher's help, organise a group visit to the theatre. Choose a suitable play for which you can get reasonably cheap seats, and telephone the theatre to see if you can book for any of the convenient afternoons or evenings, and whether they can offer any reductions for school parties. You will then have to write a business letter confirming the booking and enclosing a cheque or Postal Order and a stamped, addressed envelope. You may also be able to get reduced rates on the trains or buses to the theatre, if the party is large enough.

For further reading

Devil-in-the-Fog by LEON GARFIELD (Longman; Kestrel; Puffin)
George's happiness as a talented member of the Treet family was utterly upset when Mr Treet suddenly revealed the secret of his birth and sent him to the dark mansion, luxurious but sinister, where death seemed to lurk outside in the fog. This is a story steeped in mystery, with exciting twists and turns.

Many of Leon Garfield's other popular books take the reader back in time (like this one and **The Strange Affair of Adelaide Harris**, recommended in Book 1), and recreate eighteenth-century scenes which are exciting, mysterious, and often comic. **Smith** is about a boy living as a pickpocket in London who steals a document that plunges him into adventure and makes him want to learn to read.

ck Holborn stows away on board ship and falls in with murderous
ates. **Black Jack**, having narrowly escaped the gallows, forces
lly (the hero) to help him. (All are published as Puffins.)

e Swish of the Curtain by PAMELA BROWN (Brockhampton)
though now a "period piece", this story still captures all the fun
d tensions of amateur acting. It tells how seven boys and girls of
e to fifteen converted a disused hall into the Blue Door Theatre
d put on their own shows.

geants of Despair by DENNIS HAMLEY (Deutsch; Puffin)
is time-travel story is based on the medieval play-cycle called the
akefield (or Townley) Mysteries, and offers an exciting struggle in
ich evil seems to be overcoming good and threatening to alter
story.

e Facts about a Theatre Company by PETER LEWIS (Deutsch)
is book, lavishly illustrated and full of information, graphically
scribes the many activities and skills that are required to mount
uccessful professional production. (Classified as 792.)

hite Boots by NOEL STREATFEILD (Collins; Puffin)
is book is about two very different girls who share the same
bition to be skating champions. The author really involves you
what happens to all the characters, boys, girls and adults, in this
citing story.

INENT·GREE
eau de sport—vincent price

11 A Place of Your Own

The four Melendy children live in New York with their father and " Cuffy", the housekeeper. At the top of the house the children have a room all to themselves . . .

The room in which they were sitting might have been called a playroom, schoolroom or nursery by most people. But to the Melendys it was known as the Office. It was at the very top of the house so that they could make almost all the noise they wanted to and it had everything such a room should have: a skylight, and four windows facing east and north, and a fireplace with a basket-shaped grate. The floor was covered with scarred red linoleum that didn't matter, and the yellow walls were encrusted with hundreds of indispensable objects: bookcases bursting with books, pictures both by the Melendy children and less important grown-up artists, dusty Indian war bonnets, a string of Mexican devil masks, a shelf of dolls in varying degrees of decay, coats and hats hanging on pegs, the leftover decorations from Mona's birthday party, and other articles too numerous to mention. In one corner of the room stood an old upright piano that always looked offended, for some reason, and whose rack was littered with sheets of music all patched and held together with Scotch tape.

In addition to various chairs, tables and toy cupboards, there was a big dingy sofa with busted springs, a blackboard, a trapeze and a pair of rings. That was all but I think you will agree that it was enough. The Melendys seemed to go on and on collecting precious articles that they could never bear to throw away. The Office was their pride and joy, and what it lacked in tidiness it more than made up for in color and comfort and broken-down luxuries such as the couch and the piano. Also it was full of landmarks. Any Melendy child could have told you that the long scars on the linoleum had been made by Rush trying out a pair of new skates

165

one Christmas afternoon; or that the spider-shaped hole in the east window had been accomplished by Oliver throwing the Milk of Magnesia bottle, or that the spark holes in the hearthrug had occurred when Mona tossed a bunch of Chinese firecrackers into the fire just for fun. Melendy history was written everywhere.

"There's that leak again," said Rush in a tone of lugubrious satisfaction. "It's getting bigger than it was last time even. Boy, will Cuffy be burned up!" He lay staring at the ceiling. "It's a funny shape," he remarked. "Like some kind of a big fat fish. And there's lots of other old dried-out leaks that have funny shapes. I can see a thing like a heart, and a thing like a baseball mitt, and a kind of lopsided Greyhound bus."

"You've missed Adolf Hitler, though," said Randy, thumping down off the trapeze and lying on the rug beside him. "See up there? That long fady line is his nose, and those two little chips are his eyes, and that dark place where you threw the plasticine is his moustache."

"I'm going to throw some more plasticine and make it into George Bernard Shaw," said Rush.

"Who's he?" inquired Randy.

"Oh, a man with a beard," said Rush. "I'd rather look at him than Hitler."

Mona put down her book.

"George Bernard Shaw is a playwright," she said. "My heavens, don't you even know *that*? He wrote a play called *Saint Joan*, all about Joan of Arc, that I'm going to act in someday."

"I bet that's why you were walking round your room, holding the curtain rod out in front of you yesterday. You had kind of a moony expression and you kept talking to yourself. I thought to myself, she's gone goofy at last."

Rush shook his head and laughed appreciatively.

(from **The Saturdays** by ELIZABETH ENRIGHT)

For discussion

1 Give examples of the "color" and "comfort" in the room.
2 Do you think the piano and the music were much used?
3 Why might the piano have looked offended?
4 Were the skates roller-skates or ice-skates?
5 Explain: "Melendy history was written everywhere."
6 What does "lugubrious" mean? How does it apply to Rush's satisfied tone?
7 Why do you think Rush preferred George Bernard Shaw to Hitler?
8 What evidence can you find in the extract that it is about American children and by an American author?
9 What effects are obtained by using the following?
(a) the yellow walls were *encrusted* (instead of "covered")
(b) hundreds of *indispensable* objects (instead of "hundreds of objects")
(c) whose rack was *littered* with sheets of music (instead of "covered")
(d) had been *accomplished* by Oliver (instead of "made")
(e) and laughed *appreciatively* (instead of "and laughed")
10 What are the advantages and disadvantages of having a children's room at the *top* of the house?
11 If at all possible do you think there should be one room set aside for the child (or children) in a house? Why? What kind of room is ideal?

For written answers

1 Where were Rush and Randy at the opening of this extract?
2 Why would Cuffy be "burned up"?
3 What was Mona doing when Rush saw her on the previous day?
4 How much can you piece together from the extract about each of the four children? Write at least a sentence describing each.
5 Without looking again at the extract, describe the Melendys' "Office" in your own words, from memory.

NELSON STREET

There is hardly a mouthful of air
In the room where the breakfast is set,
For the curtains are redolent yet
Of tobacco smoke, stale from last night.
There's a little bronze teapot, and there
The rashers and eggs on a plate,
And the sleepy canary, a hen,
Starts faintly her chirruping tweet,
And I know could she speak she would say:
"Hullo there – what's wrong with the light?
Draw the blind up, let's look at the day."

I see that it's Monday again,
For the man with the organ is there;
Every Monday he comes to the street
(Lest I, or the bird there, should miss
Our count of monotonous days)
With his reed-organ, wheezy and sweet,
And stands by the window and plays
"There's a Land that is Fairer than This."

SEUMAS O'SULLIVAN

Discussing the poem

1 What details in this poem contribute to the idea that this is a depressing scene which is the same nearly every morning? Are there any pleasant or optimistic touches?

2 Why is the last line in inverted commas?

3 What do the following mean?

"redolent"   "rashers"   "monotonous"   "reed-organ"

168

For learning about language

In Book 1 we mentioned the use of **commas** to separate anything "aside" from the main sentence. Without looking at the extract or the poem, try to decide where commas were used in the following six short pieces from them.

1 an old upright piano that always looked offended for some reason and whose rack was littered . . .
2 a play called Saint Joan all about Joan of Arc that I'm going to act in . . .
3 redolent yet of tobacco smoke stale from last night.
4 the sleepy canary a hen starts faintly her chirruping tweet . . .
5 lest I or the bird there should miss our count of monotonous days.
6 he comes . . . with his reed-organ wheezy and sweet and stands by the window . . .

Commas were used here for three purposes:

(a) To divide off an adjective phrase which follows the noun it describes (except when introduced by "of"), as in:

He took her a cup of cocoa, thick and sweet with sugar, before she went to sleep.

(b) To divide off a word or phrase **in apposition***, that is, an alternative name or an explanation of the noun, as in:

Jean, Bill's elder sister, brought home a new umbrella, a red one with a black handle.

(c) To divide off a phrase **in parenthesis**, that is, an aside that might be in brackets.

She was hoping, not without reason, that she might break the long-jump record.

Which of the short pieces 1–6 above illustrate use (a)? Which illustrate use (b), and which use (c)?

*"in apposition" means "lying alongside"

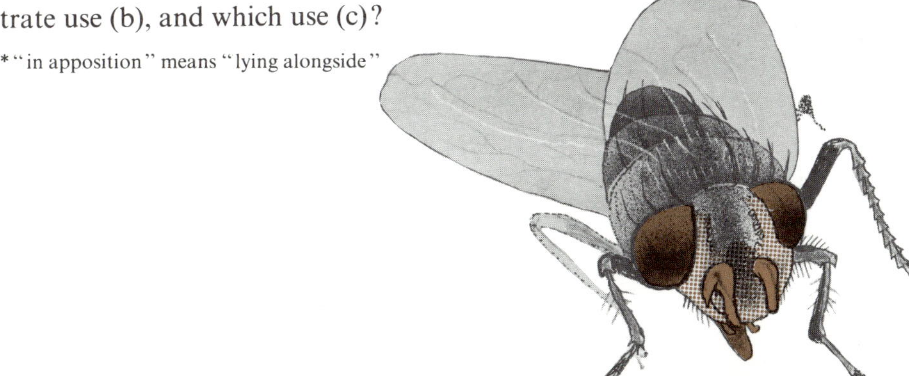

Exercise 1(a) The following five sentences sound absurd – rewrite them inserting the commas necessary to give them their proper meanings.

(1) "Would you mind washing up Oliver?" asked Mr Melendy.

(2) The children had bread jelly fruit and ice cream for their tea.

(3) The piano concert is to be held in the Parish Hall Railway Alley.

(4) The noise of the screaming teenagers thumping guitars and unmusical singers gave Cuffy a headache.

(5) This record young man will cost you ten pounds said the sales assistant.

(b) Rewrite the following, inserting the commas that are necessary.

(1) Pat Peter's younger sister looked much older in a long satin dress trimmed with grey fur.

(2) Now just fourteen she sat nervously on the edge of her chair wondering what to say if one of Peter's noisy cheerful confident friends came over to talk to her.

(3) The children's room of course was full of precious souvenirs; there were battered books on the shelves an old guitar on the wall picture postcards stuck above the beds a model aeroplane once the winner of a local competition suspended from the ceiling and a pair of rusty skates over the fire-guard.

(4) In 1603 Queen Elizabeth the last of the Tudors died and James I already King of Scotland succeeded her.

Exercise 2 In the extract, when Rush wants to describe the discoloured patch on the ceiling, he is naturally bound to compare it with something else. What does he compare it with? As we saw in Chapter 5, comparisons between different things are called **similes**. There is, of course, no point in comparing things that are identical, and if we compare truly similar things (e.g. if we say that a girl is like her mother) these are called **literal comparisons**. To be effective, similes have to be fresh and original.

Discuss the possible similes made by using each of the words or phrases in brackets in turn to complete the following sentences. Are any of them literal comparisons? Which are the most original, interesting and effective similes? Try to suggest even more striking comparisons for these people or things.

(a) She sang like (a famous singer, a bird, the soothing voice of the sea).

(b) The full moon moved across the hazy sky like (an eerie ghost, a little bent old man, a white saucer).

(c) The excavator crawled forward like (some prehistoric creature, a whale, an enormous tractor).

(d) Seen from the hilltop, the silvery river wound its way through the valley like (an eel, the coils of a rope, a shimmering necklace of pearls).

(e) The feathers were as soft and pure as (silk, down, new-fallen snow).

(f) He was as slow as (his brother, he could be, a patient slug).

(g) The dark water sparkled in the sun like (neon signs, a glass of champagne, the Milky Way).

(h) His loud voice echoed angrily round the class-room like (a clap of thunder, solemn church bells, a howling dog).

Exercise 3(a) Instead of verbs with **complements** and verbs with **objects**, many sentences have verbs that require neither complement nor object. Rewrite the sentences in this exercise, underlining the verb (remember that it may be more than one word), and state whether it has an object or complement or neither. (Adverbs and adverb phrases, of course, can be added to *any* kind of verb.) Set out answers as in these three examples.

   1 James <u>was</u> a king. (subject – verb – complement)

   2 James <u>used to write</u> books. (subject – verb – object)

   3 James <u>ruled</u> for several years. (subject – verb – adverb phrase)

(1) Baden-Powell founded the Boy Scouts.

(2) Baden-Powell himself became Chief Scout.

(3) Baden-Powell died in 1941.

(4) You ought to join a scout troop.

(5) You ought to be a scout.
(6) On Thursday the weather changed.
(7) The heat melted the tar on the roads.
(8) The butter melted in the cupboard.
(9) Smith will continue captain of the team.
(10) Smith will continue the same goal-scoring tactics.
(b) Complete the following with a suitable complement, object or adverb phrase, as indicated:
Example: He returned ... (adverb phrase – how?)
Answer: He returned on the train.
(1) He returned ... (adverb phrase – when?)
(2) He returned ... (object – what?)
(3) The jewels were ... (complement – what?)
(4) The jewels were ... (adverb phrase – where?)
(5) The only occupant of the car appeared to be ... (complement – what?)
(6) How can you remain ... (complement – what?)
(7) She certainly seemed ... (complement – what?)
(8) She appeared ... (adverb phrase – how?)
(9) Yesterday the bull broke ... (object – what?)
(10) Yesterday the bull broke out ... (adverb phrase – where?)

Exercise 4 What are **synonyms**? Words of *opposite* meaning are called **antonyms**. Often we can find an exact antonym, as with "black" and "white", but sometimes we cannot be so definite: the opposite of "lost" might be "found" or "saved", and the opposite of "rough" might be "smooth", "gentle" or "calm".
(a) Discuss possible antonyms for each of the following:

| love | angry | perfect | supple | barren |
| diligent | solemn | clear | steep | wisdom. |

(b) Check all the meanings of the words in the following groups, and pick out from the synonyms the antonym in each group.

For example: request, ask, demand, beg, crave, <u>deny</u>.
(1) emperor, majesty, dictator, protector, president, subject.
(2) witty, sullen, humorous, smart, waggish, facetious.

172

(3) satirical, sarcastic, complimentary, critical, cynical, sardonic.
(4) surcharge, rebate, reduction, discount, allowance, concession.
(5) savoury, dainty, palatable, appetising, nauseous, delicious.
(6) precede, succeed, antedate, forerun, presage, anticipate.
(7) entirely, completely, partially, altogether, wholly, fully.
(8) inception, conclusion, commencement, inauguration, beginning, opening.
(9) alight, disembark, depart, arrive, reach.
(10) concern, grief, sorrow, distress, affliction, felicity.

Exercise 5(a) All the following words are names of kinds of rooms. Rearrange them in alphabetical order.

studio	cell	dressing-room	dormitory
mezzanine	galley	box-room	gallery
refectory	boudoir	salon	pantry
saloon	lounge	box	
garret	cloakroom	scullery	
nursery	ante-room	mess-room	

(b) Below there is one definition for each of the nouns in the above list. Pair each definition with its appropriate noun.

For example: studio – where a painter, sculptor or photographer works.

(1) for young children to sleep and play in
(2) in which visitors wait to see someone important
(3) built into the roof of a house
(4) where guests can sit in a hotel
(5) for changing clothes, especially in the theatre
(6) where outer garments can be left
(7) where a lady can find privacy
(8) for a small private party at a theatre
(9) for storing cases, trunks etc
(10) for cooking, on a ship
(11) where a monk, nun, or prisoner lives
(12) where a Parisian lady of fashion entertained her guests
(13) for drinking in, in a public house

(14) for washing dishes etc.
(15) in which provisions are kept
(16) for eating in, especially in a college
(17) where a company (of soldiers or sailors) eat together
(18) between two storeys, often low in height
(19) containing a number of beds, especially in a boarding-school
(20) for exhibiting works of art

For your own writing

1 Study this very exact description of a room:

The room measures four metres by three. It is on the first floor and there is one window, facing south and overlooking a garden. The door is in the centre of the opposite wall. In the corner on your right as you enter is a single bed with a small reading-light over it, controlled by a pull-cord switch hanging from the ceiling above it. A small bedside table stands between the bed and the door. On your left as you enter, and facing the window, stands a large wardrobe, about one and a half metres across and two metres high, with a full-length mirror on the outside of its single door. Under the window is a writing-desk and a chair, with a table-lamp on the desk, and on the left-hand wall is a chest of drawers for clothes.

The walls are papered with a pattern of thin, vertical grey stripes on a white background. The ceiling is grey, with a central light in a white glass globe. On the left-hand wall is a painting of a landscape with a lake and a steamer in it; and over the bed, on the right-hand wall, is a large notice-board, painted yellow, decorated mainly with pictures of sportsmen cut from magazines. There is a transistor radio on the chest of drawers and a cricket bat and pads stand in the corner to the right of the desk. The curtains are yellow with a delicate red pattern of stars, and the carpet, which covers nearly all the floor, is charcoal grey.

Notice that it gives the facts: first the location and size of the room, then the position of the main items of furniture, finally some details of decoration and smaller fixtures. It does not give opinions about how attractive the room is, nor is it a personal account of a visit to it and what happened there. It is the sort of exact description a police report might require.

174

Write a similarly factual and full description of your own room or the class-room or some other room you know well. Use the same impersonal style.

2 In describing the room you were writing as clearly and exactly as possible. For this composition you should be more personal and imaginative. Use original and striking similes and choose words with care. Plan the composition by thinking carefully about any place you like to retreat to – whether real or imaginary – and your reasons for liking it. This is important: ask yourself *why* you like those surroundings and that particular furniture, equipment or colour scheme. Your ideas and reasons will keep the composition lively and personal.

Here are some suggested titles:

A PLACE OF MY OWN.

MY IDEAL ROOM.

HOW I WOULD FURNISH AND DECORATE A ROOM OF MY OWN.

WHY EVERY TEENAGER SHOULD HAVE HIS OR HER OWN ROOM.

OUR DEN *or* TREEHOUSE *or* " CASTLE ".

This composition could also be in the form of a poem, similar to the one by Seumas O'Sullivan on page 168, perhaps about your favourite place to retire to, at some particular time of day or season of the year.

For talk and action

1 Prepare for a class discussion on housing and town-planning, making up arguments for and against the following:

Garages should be provided for all houses and flats.

More people should be prepared to live in flats rather than houses.

More thought should be given to the needs of young children and old people (especially in designing flats).

All houses and flats should be built and owned by the government or local authorities, and not by private landlords who let them for profit.

Towns should be re-planned so that large areas are free of cars.

Parking charges in city centres should be made so expensive that motorists have to use public transport.

All houses and flats should be centrally heated and air-conditioned.

2 Draw an exact plan of the room you described in 1 of **For your own writing**. The room shown in the plan below has many features in common with the one described on page 174. If you can, also draw a picture of the ideal room or favourite place you described in 2 of the same section. Alternatively, you could draw a plan of this ideal room.

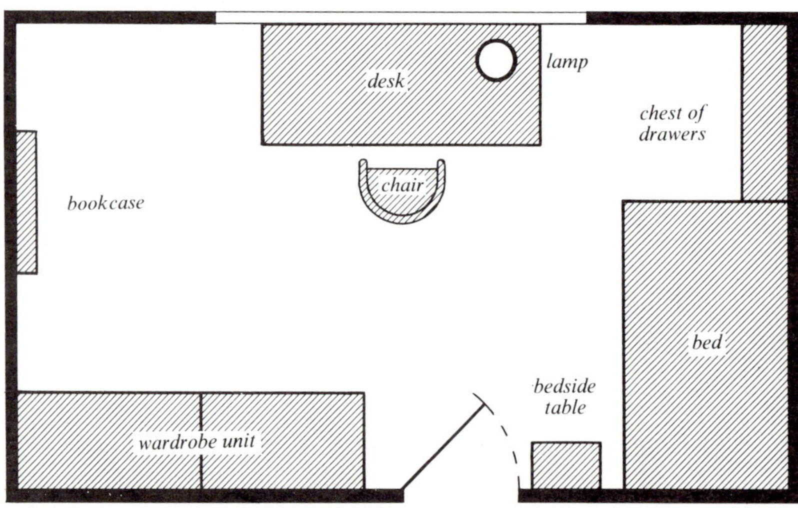

For further reading

The Saturdays by ELIZABETH ENRIGHT (Heinemann; Puffin)
The Melendy children decide one wet Saturday to pool their pocket money so that each of them can go out in turn on successive Saturdays with a considerable sum to spend. Not all these expeditions are successful, but their later Saturdays, spent together, include some even greater disasters!

Other books by Elizabeth Enright about the Melendys include **The Four-Storey Mistake** (Heinemann) in which they are baffled by the secret room in their new house when they go to live in the country.

Una and Grubstreet by PRUDENCE ANDREW (Heinemann)
The baby's room in an empty house is just the refuge Una needs to save Christopher (or Ronnie) Heaven when she believes he has been battered by his mother. Una is eleven, motherly, worried about her father's new girl-friend, and she doesn't stop to consider the consequences of kidnapping someone's baby.

My Side of the Mountain by JEAN GEORGE (Bodley Head; Macmillan; Puffin)
Sam lives with his large family in New York, but decides to go and live alone in the Catskill Mountains. Taking only a penknife, an axe, a ball of string and flint and steel, he manages to look after himself living in a hollow tree for over a year.

Hal by JEAN MACGIBBON (Heinemann; Puffin)
The bit of waste ground that Barry could see from his window is a very special place to the West Indian girl, Hal, and her cosmopolitan band of friends. This is the story of how Barry comes to join in the job of creating an adventure playground there, and how that helps him become a success at a school he thought he'd never dare to attend.

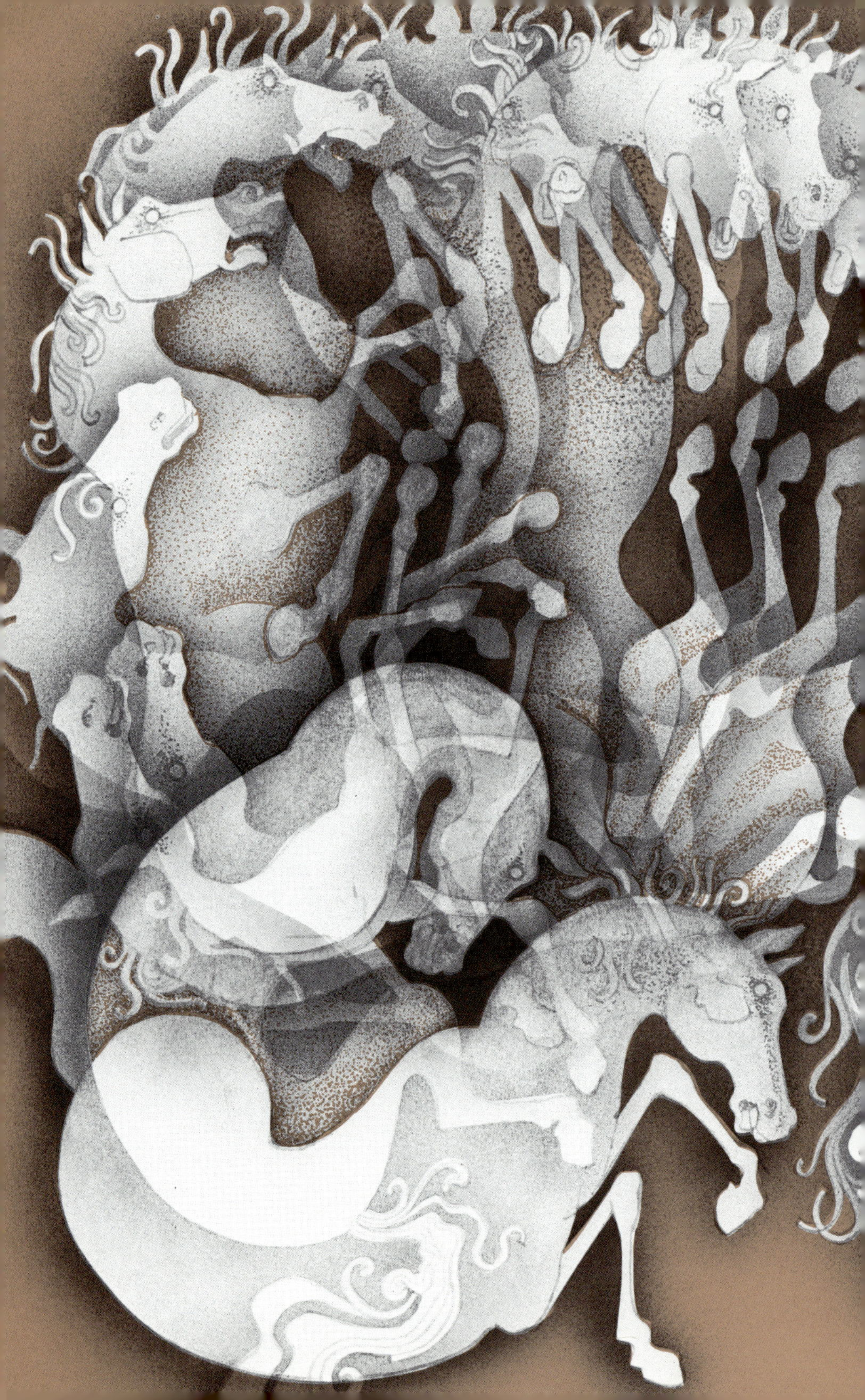

12 If You Take My Advice ...

For a long time Ken McLaughlin has wanted a foal of his own and at last his father gives him permission to choose one from those on their ranch. A week later, Ken announces his choice to his father, mother and his brother, Howard ...

"I'll take that sorrel filly of Rocket's; the one with the cream tail and mane."

Ken made his announcement at the breakfast table.

After he spoke there was a moment's astonished silence. Nell groped for recollection, and said, "A sorrel filly? I can't seem to remember that one at all – what's her name?"

But Rob remembered. The smile faded from his face as he looked at Ken. "*Rocket's filly*, Ken?"

"Yes, sir." Ken's face changed too. There was no mistaking his father's displeasure.

"I was hoping you'd make a wise choice. You know what I think of Rocket – that whole line of horses – "

Ken looked down; the colour ebbed from his cheeks. "She's fast, Dad, and Rocket's fast – "

"It's the worst line of horses I've got. There's never one amongst them with real sense. The mares are hellions and the stallions out-laws; they're untamable."

"I'll tame her."

Rob guffawed. "Not I, nor anyone, has ever been able to really tame any one of them."

Kennie's chest heaved.

"Better change your mind, Ken. You want a horse that'll be a real friend to you, don't you?"

"Yes – " Kennie's voice was unsteady.

"Well, you'll never make a friend of that filly. Last fall, after all the colts had been weaned and separated from their dams, she and

179

Rocket got back together – no fence'll hold 'em – she's all cut and scarred up already from tearing through barbed wire after that bitch of a mother of hers."

Kennie looked stubbornly at his plate . . .

"Well," McLaughlin barked. "It's your funeral – or hers. Remember one thing. I'm not going to be out of pocket on account of this – every time you turn around you cost me money – " . . .

The foals are herded together in the corral. Then all except Ken's filly, Flicka, are driven out again.

But Flicka did not intend to be left. She hurled herself against the poles which walled the corral. She tried to jump them. They were seven feet high. She caught her front feet over the top rung, clung, scrambled, while Kennie held his breath for fear the slender legs would be caught between the bars and snapped. Her hold broke, she fell over backwards, rolled, screamed, tore around the corral.

One of the bars broke. She hurled herself again. Another went. She saw the opening, and as neatly as a dog crawls through a fence, inserted her head and forefeet, scrambled through and fled away, bleeding in a dozen places . . .

Walking down from the corrals, Rob McLaughlin gave Kennie one more chance to change his mind. "Better pick a horse that you have some hope of riding one day. I'd have got rid of this whole line of stock if they weren't so damned fast that I've had the fool idea that someday there might turn out one gentle one in the lot, and I'd have a racehorse. But there's never been one so far, and it's not going to be Flicka."

"It's not going to be Flicka," chanted Howard.

"Maybe she *might* be gentled," said Ken; and although his lips trembled, there was fanatical determination in his eye.

"Ken," said McLaughlin, "it's up to you. If you say you want her, we'll get her. But she wouldn't be the first of that line to die rather than give in. They're beautiful and they're fast, but let me tell you this, young man, they're *loco*!"

180

Ken flinched under his father's direct glance.

"If I go after her again, I'll not give up *whatever comes,* understand what I mean by that?"

"Yes."

"What do you say?"

"I want her."

"That's settled then," and suddenly Rob seemed calm and indifferent. "We'll bring her in again tomorrow or next day – I've got other work for this afternoon."

(from My Friend Flicka by MARY O'HARA)

For discussion

1 Why did Ken want Flicka? What did he admire about her?

2 How did Ken's father, Rob McLaughlin, know already that Flicka was a difficult filly?

3 This incident shows that Flicka was almost untameable: does it show any worthwhile qualities in the filly?

4 Why did Ken's lips tremble as he returned home? Why was he so determined?

5 What *did* Rob mean by "I'll not give up whatever comes"?

6 Explain the following:
"sorrel"   "colour ebbed from his cheeks"   "hellions"
"guffawed"   "last fall"   "weaned and separated from their
dams"   "scarred up"   "a corral"   "fanatical determination"
"indifferent".

7 Why has the printer put the first line (of the extract, not the introduction), and some other words and short phrases, in italics? What would be the equivalent of these italics in handwriting?

8 Do you admire Ken's determination? Was he foolish or sensible in his attitude?

9 Would *you* have given in to Ken if you were in Rob's place?

10 Should children be allowed to have the things they really want? What kind of treatment makes children spoilt and selfish?

For written answers

1 What was the name of Ken's mother?
2 What do you think is meant by a horse being "loco"?

THE RUNAWAY

Once when the snow of the year was beginning to fall,
We stopped by a mountain pasture to say, "Whose colt?"
A little Morgan had one forefoot on the wall,
The other curled at his breast. He dipped his head
And snorted at us. And then he had to bolt.
We heard the miniature thunder where he fled,
And we saw him, or thought we saw him, dim and grey
Like a shadow against the curtain of falling flakes.
"I think the little fellow's afraid of the snow,
He isn't winter-broken. It isn't play
With the little fellow at all. He's running away.

Discussing the poem

1 What do you think the following mean?
   "a little Morgan"   "Sakes"
   "winter-broken"   "gone to stall and bin"
2 Why do you think the colt behaved like this, first almost climbing
the wall, then snorting, then running away and galloping back?
3 Is Robert Frost sympathetic to the colt? Give examples of his
close observation of the details of the colt and its behaviour.

3 Explain in your own words what was wrong with this whole line of horses.
4 Why did Ken's father keep Rocket and her offspring at all?
5 Retell in your own words how Flicka broke out of the corral.

I doubt if even his mother could tell him, 'Sakes,
It's only weather.' He'd think she didn't know!
Where is his mother? He can't be out alone."
And now he comes again with clatter of stone,
And mounts the wall again with whited eyes
And all his tail that isn't hair up straight.
He shudders his coat as if to throw off flies.
"Whoever it is that leaves him out so late,
When other creatures have gone to stall and bin,
Ought to be told to come and take him in."

ROBERT FROST

For learning about language

We have seen that many verbs need either an object or a subject complement to complete the sense. Are the words in italics in the following examples objects or complements?

Ken wanted a *foal*.
He chose *Flicka*.
Flicka was a sorrel *filly*.
She seemed a fast young *horse*.

Verbs that need a complement, however, may have a simple adjective as complement, instead of a noun:

Flicka is a fast horse.   Flicka is *fast*.
Ken's father seemed a fierce man.   His father seemed *fierce*.
The grass became a wet marsh.   The grass became *wet*.

Exercise 1(a) Decide whether the following have noun (or pronoun) or adjective complements; and **(b)** rewrite each so that it becomes the other type, keeping the meaning approximately the same.

Example: His father was not a rich man. (noun complement)
Answer: His father was not rich. (changed to adjective complement)

(1) The result of the match seemed a certainty.
(2) She seemed very capable.
(3) The house became a zoo full of animals.
(4) The castle was ruined.
(5) The boy felt a fool.
(6) The tree appeared to be rotten.
(7) The play is a great success.
(8) Some criminals turn honest men.
(9) The explorer returned a disillusioned man.
(10) During the rescue, the night remained a calm one.

Exercise 2 What is an **antonym**? What is the antonym of "possible"? When searching for an antonym for "perfect", in the last chapter, did you choose "imperfect"? In both these cases the antonym can be formed by adding the letters im- before the word.

In Book 1 we learnt that a group of letters (a syllable or syllables) added at the end of a word is called a **suffix**. A syllable added at the beginning is called a **prefix**. The following are common **antonym prefixes**:

in-, im-, un-, il-, ir-, dis-.

Perhaps the most common is un- (as in: real – unreal). Each of the

above prefixes will fit two or more of the following twenty words. Rewrite the words with their antonym prefixes.

For example:

religious – irreligious;   legal – illegal;   honest – dishonest

happy	formed	curable	regular
logical	agree	patient	musical
appropriate	resolute	literate	order
qualify	gratitude	definite	mortal
readable	legible	appear	resistible

Exercise 3 In Chapter 2, we considered **verb phrases** where one verb is made up of several words, usually to indicate the *tense* of the *head-word*.

For example:

We will bring her.

Here the word "will" indicates the future tense of "bring". But other words also may form part of a verb phrase.

For example:

We will bring her in.

This can be regarded as the future tense of the verb "to bring in"; the verb here is: "will bring . . . in"; the head-words are: "bring in".

Study the following examples from the extract. Which of the words in italics are head-words or other verbs, and which are other words incorporated into the verb phrases?

to be able – Not I, nor anyone, *has* ever *been able* to really tame any one of them.

to get back – She and Rocket *got back* together.

to turn around – Every time you *turn around* you cost me money.

to get rid of – I*'d have got rid of* this whole line of stock.

to turn out – There *might turn out* one gentle one.

to give in – She wouldn't be the first to die rather than *give in*.

to go after – I*'ll go after* her again.

to give up – I*'ll* not *give up*.

(a) Write out in full the verb phrases in the following examples, underlining the head-words. To help you, the first five verb phrases have been printed in italics.

(1) The enemy soon *gave in*.

(2) Mother *could* not *get* the stain *out*.

(3) You *have been running up* a considerable debt.

(4) The van *picked up* all our luggage at the station.

(5) I *shall be putting* my holiday *off* indefinitely.

(6) She may well get on in her new job.

(7) The dog was definitely going for the postman at the time.

(8) They ran the plan down so much that few people believed in it.

(9) Two friends like them would never fall out over such a trifle.

(10) The landlady cannot put up any more lodgers.

(b) Replace the head-words in each case with another single head-word, taken from the list in brackets below, and keeping the tense the same. Rewrite the sentence, as in this example:

The car *was* already *taking up* all the garage space.

    1 Verb: to take up. Head-words: taking up.
    2 The car was already occupying all the garage space.

(occupy; accommodate; succeed; surrender; accumulate; postpone; attack; criticise; quarrel; collect; remove)

Exercise 4 Changing the position of an adverb in a sentence often alters the meaning of that sentence. Discuss the differences in the following:

    Only last night she said she liked horses.
    Last night she only said she liked horses.
    Last night she said only she liked horses.
    Last night she said she only liked horses.
    Last night she said she liked only horses.

Changing the position of an adverb phrase in a sentence may also alter the meaning. Discuss these sentences:

    In your best books now copy out the notes again.
    Now copy out the notes in your best books again.
    Now copy out the notes again in your best books.

Rewrite the following sentences, altering (or improving) their meanings by moving an adverb or adverb phrase (or altering the punctuation). In the first five sentences the adverb or adverb phrase has been printed in italics.

(a) The rebellion was crushed before any lives had been lost *by the army*.

(b) The candidate who had finished *quickly* left the room.

(c) He forgot to do the job *completely*.

(d) Fill up the scuttle which you will find in the cellar *with coke and anthracite*.

(e) *At least* the girls in the party knew how to cook.

(f) A criminal who steals often gets caught.

(g) Dogs only are admitted with their owners.

(h) Quick! Follow that man in a taxi.

(i) Lost: one small black kitten by an old age pensioner last seen with a red ribbon round her neck.

(j) This stone was erected in memory of Admiral James Jameson tragically killed in action by his fellow officers.

PROTOCOL is BIOLOGICAL

Exercise 5 Advertisers are very fond of giving their products scientific-sounding names, and of using long impressive words to describe them. Can you suggest some examples of this?

In the following example the trade name is in fact most inappropriate, although it *sounds* suitable:

> FOR SMALL CUTS AND BRUISES, APPLY A LITTLE **POLLUTION**: THE CREAM THAT SOOTHES AND CLEANSES.

POLLUTION, the dictionary tells us, means "uncleanness, impurity".

Explain why in each of the following advertisements the trade name is equally inappropriate.

(a) TIRED? LISTLESS? LACKING IN ENERGY? TRY **INERTIA** TABLETS TODAY.

(b) **BLUNDERBUS**, THE WONDERBUS – FOR SILENT, CAREFREE TRAVEL.

(c) MASSAGE NO GOOD? FRICTION INADEQUATE? **ELECTROCUTION** IS THE *SCIENTIFIC* ANSWER TO YOUR PROBLEMS.

(d) FOR A LONGER, HEALTHIER LIFE, TAKE **RADIOACTIVE MALT** DAILY.

(e) THE NEW **VISOR-VISTA** IS THE ONLY CAR WITH UNINTERRUPTED ALL-ROUND VISION.

(f) ALL THE ATHLETES SAY: "**SOPORIFIC** IS TERRIFIC – FOR THAT EXTRA EFFORT THAT WINS!"

(g) *OUR* SWEETS ARE NUTTY, NOURISHING AND TRULY **NOXIOUS**.

(h) RECORDS ON THE **CACOPHONOUS** LABEL GIVE YOU THE BEST IN SMOOTH SOUNDS.

(i) HOW TO WIN FRIENDS AND INFLUENCE PEOPLE – USE A **BLUDGEON**, THE KEY TO PERSONAL SUCCESS.

(j) ARE YOU AMBITIOUS? THERE IS ROOM AT THE TOP OF *YOUR* PROFESSION FOR THE PERSON WHO HAS TAKEN A COURSE IN **PROCRASTINATION** – THE PSYCHOLOGIST'S ANSWER TO LACK OF SELF-CONFIDENCE.

When you have explained all these, make up some of your own on similar lines.

188

For your own writing

1 Have you ever wanted something as much as Ken did? Did your parents advise you against it and did you have to get round them? How did you find the money?

Decide what is your most precious possession and write some notes about it: how you obtained it, any difficulties you had to overcome or sacrifices you had to make, and why you value it so highly. Then write a composition on one of these four topics:

How you obtained your most precious possession.

Why you value the possession so highly.

The loss of your possession (whether you found it again, or not).

The one thing you would most like to have.

Whichever you choose, try to bring out your own feelings, and the tensions these may cause at home or inside yourself.

2 Each member of the class should choose one topic from the list below for a short factual article, based on library research, within the general theme of: THE HORSE AND MAN.

The early domestication of the horse.

Horse breeds and breeding.

Horses in farming.

Horses in myth and legend.

The development of harness.

Armour for horses.

Cavalry regiments.

The use of the horse in battle.

Pit ponies.

Racehorses of the past.

Horse trials and gymkhanas.

Horse-drawn vehicles.

Pack-horses.

Stables and coaching inns.

The art of the blacksmith.

Famous horsemen and horsewomen.

Famous horse-races.

Pony-trekking.

Polo.

Horses in ceremony and pageantry.

In the library, use reference books and books under reference numbers: 636.1 (domestic animals), 599.7 (zoology), 798 (horsemanship), 357 (cavalry, military science), 380 (transport).

For talk and action

1 Horses (like dogs) have been such an important part of man's work and sport for thousands of years that many sayings and proverbs are connected with them. Here are a few examples:

Never look a gift-horse in the mouth.

Do not change horses in mid-stream.

You can take a horse to water, but you can't make it drink.

To put (someone) through his or her paces.

To spur (someone) on.

At the end of one's tether.

Horse-play.

A slowcoach.

To put the cart before the horse.

Neck and neck.

Explain the meaning and use of each of these, and see how many more you can collect (and explain).

2 Groups or individuals could contribute articles on the theme of The Horse for a class display, a folder or an issue of the class magazine. With illustrations and additional material, the work completed in 2 of **For your own writing** should form a basis for this.

3 Many people are eager to learn how to ride and to look after their own horses or ponies. Plan either a riding school, or the best accommodation in which to keep a privately owned pony. In either case draw diagrams and prepare a manual of advice on the care of the animal(s) or the art of riding.

For further reading

My Friend Flicka by MARY O'HARA (Methuen; Mayflower)
Flicka is finally captured, but, as if to prove Rob McLaughlin's statement that she would die rather than give in, she very nearly kills herself in attempting to escape yet again.

Thunderhead and **The Green Grass of Wyoming** (both Methuen; Mayflower) are the sequels to this classic story by Mary O'Hara. There are many stories about horses and ponies, but these must be three of the best ever written; and in many ways they are much more than stories about horses.

The Spuddy by LILLIAN BECKWITH (Hutchinson; Arrow)
This is the story of an independent mongrel dog, The Spuddy, befriended by Andy and then by Jake, skipper of the fishing boat "Silver Crest". In the final tragedy, The Spuddy shows his heroic quality and Andy, till then dumb, finds he can speak.

The Yearling by MARJORIE KINNAN RAWLINGS (Heinemann; Pan)
The yearling in this famous story is a fawn which young Jody Baxter saves and rears on his father's homestead in Florida. But the life is hard and dangerous, and in the end he has to face the terrible decision to shoot the yearling that he has loved and cared for.

13   **On the River**

Three Polish children, Ruth, Edek and Bronia, accompanied by their friend Jan, are journeying to Switzerland to find their father, who had fled there after escaping from a Nazi prison camp. They travel part of the way in two canoes; but then the girls lose their only paddle and their canoe becomes grounded . . .

And they sat there shivering and clinging to each other till the shadows brightened and they could see the whole sweep of the river, white and broken in the middle, rock-strewn and shallow at either side, with the wood-muffled hills hemming it in, and not a soul in sight. No sign of Edek and Jan. They could not have felt lonelier.

Then Bronia saw something which gave them hope. Down in the water, near the point of the V-shaped rock, was a stick that looked as if it might serve as a paddle. She climbed down to get it and found it was the very paddle they had lost. This was luck indeed.

They turned the canoe over and poured the water out. Then, with new confidence, they launched it again. Stepping aboard, they headed for midstream. And the current caught them and carried them on towards the rapids.

The river grew faster, and the bank flashed past. Soon they were in a kind of gorge, where the river squeezed past great boulders, some of them as high as houses. Some of the swells were over a foot high, and the spray dashed over the bow and stung their faces. The water roared here so that even the loudest shout could not be heard. Out to the left there were huge oily surges that looked as if they would pound you down into the depths if you got caught in them.

Bronia closed her eyes and clung to her sister's waist. Ruth was not as scared as she had expected to be. With a triumphant sense of exhilaration she flashed in with her paddle, heading always for the open stream, away from the white broken water where the rocks lay hidden. Now and then a boulder loomed up and she knew that if they struck it they would be dashed to pieces. But a quick dip of the paddle at the right moment was enough to shoot them safely past.

In no time the river broadened, the boulders eased, and the banks were wooded again. The terrors of the rapids were over. Ruth hoped that Edek and Jan, whose two-seater was much less easy to manœuvre, had been as successful as they had.

There seemed no need for the paddle now, for the water was clear of rocks and the current smooth and swift. They could lie back and let the canoe take care of itself.

Bronia closed her eyes and fell asleep. Ruth lay back and watched the blue sky overhead and the climbing sun. It was to be another scorching day, and she too became sleepy and dozed.

A grating, tearing sound brought her to her senses, and she woke to find herself thigh-deep in water. The canoe had grounded on a shoal and a sharp stone had ripped the canvas underneath. She looked about her. The river was very broad here, and they were near the right bank, where it was shallow and easy to wade ashore. So they stepped out and scraped the waterlogged craft over the pebbles to the bank and hauled it ashore.

(from **The Silver Sword** by IAN SERRAILLIER)

For discussion

1 Why were the girls "shivering and clinging to each other"?

2 Which of the girls was the elder?

3 Is there any evidence in this extract to suggest that they had been canoeing at night?

4 Was it summer or winter? How do you know?

5 Do you imagine that the girls' canoe was larger or smaller than the boys'?

6 Why was Ruth "not as scared as she expected to be"?

7 Was it really true that they could "let the canoe take care of itself" once they were past the rapids?

8 What do the following mean here?
"hemming in" "the swells" "exhilaration" "to manœuvre" "a shoal" "waterlogged".

9 What effects are created by using the following?
   (a) the *wood-muffled* hills (instead of "woods and hills")
   (b) the river *squeezed* past great boulders (instead of "flowed")
   (c) huge *oily surges* (instead of "waves")
   (d) would *pound* you down (instead of "pull")
   (e) she *flashed in with* her paddle (instead of "dipped")
   (f) a boulder *loomed up* (instead of "appeared")
   (g) *scraped* the waterlogged craft (instead of "pulled" it)

10 Is canoeing a dangerous pastime? What precautions and training are necessary? What are the attractions of canoeing?

For written answers

1 Were the girls travelling upstream or downstream? Give a reason for your conclusion.

2 How did Ruth pick out where the rocks in the rapids "lay hidden"?

3 What was Ruth using the paddle for in the rapids?

4 Why did the girls feel tired?

5 How did Ruth come to find herself thigh-deep in water?

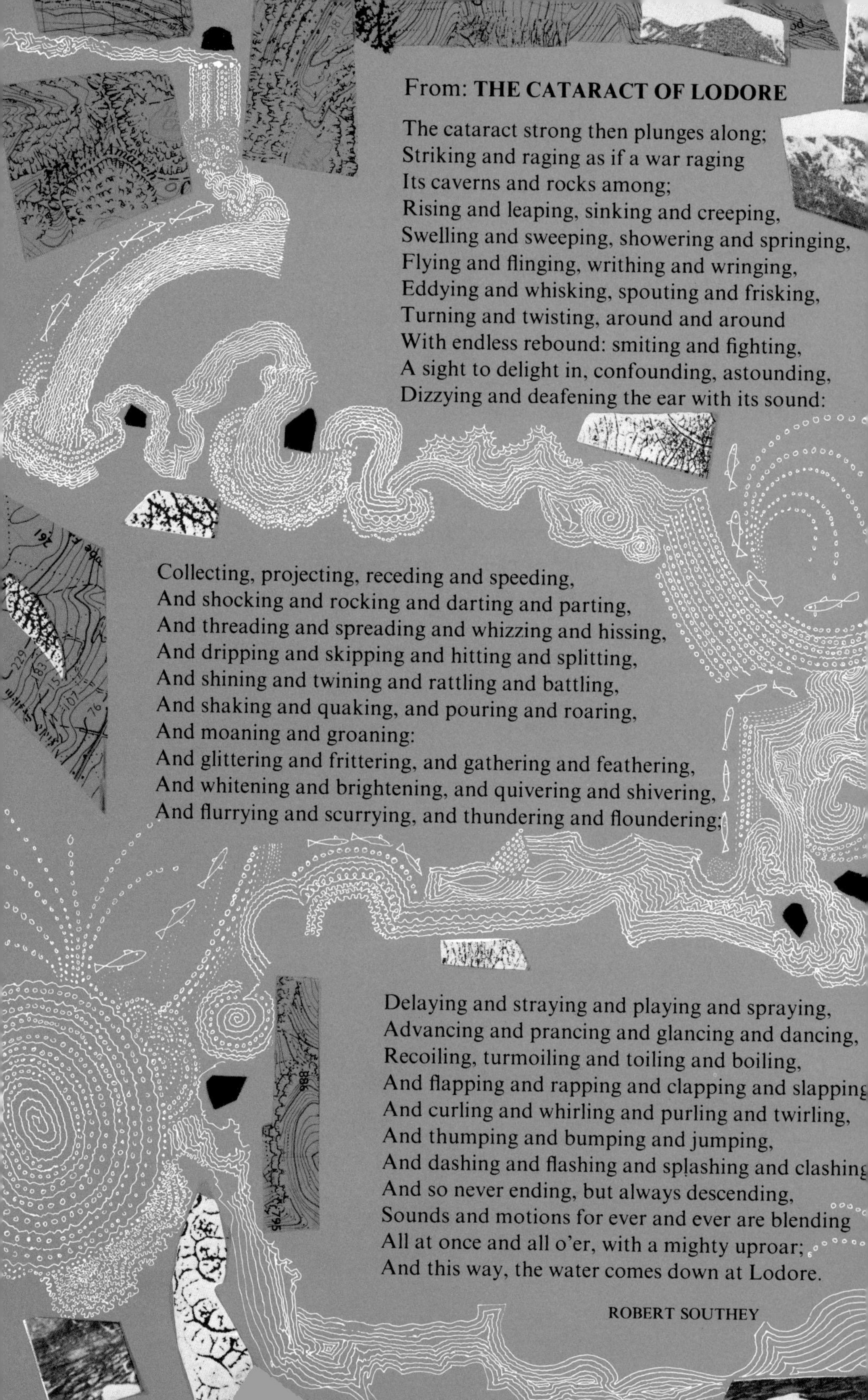

From: THE CATARACT OF LODORE

The cataract strong then plunges along;
Striking and raging as if a war raging
Its caverns and rocks among;
Rising and leaping, sinking and creeping,
Swelling and sweeping, showering and springing,
Flying and flinging, writhing and wringing,
Eddying and whisking, spouting and frisking,
Turning and twisting, around and around
With endless rebound: smiting and fighting,
A sight to delight in, confounding, astounding,
Dizzying and deafening the ear with its sound:

Collecting, projecting, receding and speeding,
And shocking and rocking and darting and parting,
And threading and spreading and whizzing and hissing,
And dripping and skipping and hitting and splitting,
And shining and twining and rattling and battling,
And shaking and quaking, and pouring and roaring,
And moaning and groaning:
And glittering and frittering, and gathering and feathering,
And whitening and brightening, and quivering and shivering,
And flurrying and scurrying, and thundering and floundering;

Delaying and straying and playing and spraying,
Advancing and prancing and glancing and dancing,
Recoiling, turmoiling and toiling and boiling,
And flapping and rapping and clapping and slapping
And curling and whirling and purling and twirling,
And thumping and bumping and jumping,
And dashing and flashing and splashing and clashing
And so never ending, but always descending,
Sounds and motions for ever and ever are blending
All at once and all o'er, with a mighty uproar;
And this way, the water comes down at Lodore.

ROBERT SOUTHEY

Discussing the poem

1 Examine the rhymes used in this poem: notice where one line rhymes with the following one or with one several lines below, and where one half of a line rhymes with the other half, and so on. What is the purpose of the variation in rhyme pattern? Why are some lines longer than others?
2 What is the effect of using so many words ending in -ing? Is this appropriate in the description of a waterfall?
3 Pick out words in the poem where the sound represents the meaning, as with "hissing" and "splashing".

For learning about language

Examine the content of the poem. Would you say that these lines are describing *how* the water falls down, or do they describe the whole waterfall?

Now examine the following examples:
(a) I watched the leaves *quivering in the breeze*.
(b) The *quivering* leaves were very beautiful.
(c) John stood there *quivering with excitement*.
(d) He *was quivering* all over.

In (a), the phrase in italics is definitely an adjective phrase: "quivering" describes the leaves, not how I watched them. Similarly in (b) "quivering" is an adjective. In (c), the phrase could be adjectival (describing John) or adverbial (how John stood). In (d) it is possible to maintain that "quivering" is an adjective complement (as you might say: "John was *brown* all over"), but it is simpler to call it part of the verb "to quiver" (John quivers, John quivered, John was quivering, etc.).

Thus, words formed from verbs and ending in -ing can be:
1 part of adjective phrases
2 single adjectives
3 part of adverb phrases (or adverbs)
4 part of some tenses of the verb.
These -ing words are called **present participles** of verbs.

Exercise 1 Which of the four uses given on page 197 does each of the present participles, printed in italics below, represent?

Example: The tourist was *talking* to the bishop.

Answer: talking = part of the past tense of "to talk".

(a) They sat there, *shivering* and *clinging* to each other.

(b) They were *clinging* to each other.

(c) *Stepping* aboard, they headed for midstream.

(d) The captain is *stepping* aboard now.

(e) Ruth flashed in with her paddle, *heading* always for the open stream.

(f) Ruth watched the *climbing* sun.

(g) Ruth watched the sun *climbing*.

(h) It was to be another *scorching* day.

(i) A *grating*, *tearing* sound brought her to her senses.

(j) We are *discussing* the poem.

(k) My friend had been *thinking* of buying a canoe.

(l) I am *hoping* for some help with this exercise.

Exercise 2 Present participles are the source of two very common kinds of confused expression in English. Firstly, it is easy to confuse a present participle with a complete verb. Remember that it is only part of a verb, and requires words such as "am", "is", "are", "was", "were", "have been" etc. (part of the verb "to be") to make it complete. A present participle is therefore *not* sufficient to complete a statement sentence. Thus:

> People rushing, pushing and stumbling down the steps, all in an
> unreasonable hurry to get home.

still needs a verb to complete it, and ought to read:

> People *were* rushing ...   People *are* rushing ...

Secondly, present participles, and phrases introduced by present participles, are usually assumed to describe the nearest noun (or pronoun), especially if this is the subject of the sentence. Thus:

> Riding her cycle down the road, a dog dashed under Jane's
> wheel.

really means that the dog was riding Jane's bicycle! How should this be rewritten to make the intended meaning clear?

198

Some of the examples in Exercise 1 show how the present participle can be used as one method of combining short statements into longer sentences:

I watched the leaves; they quivered in the breeze.

becomes:

I watched the leaves quivering in the breeze.

What two statements are combined in the following sentence?

John stood there quivering with excitement.

(which could equally well be "Quivering with excitement, John stood there.")

Rewrite the following sentences, where two statements have been combined with "and", so that the two are combined with the use of a present participle, as in the example above.

(a) He left the others at the entrance and he found an underground loading wharf.

(b) She signalled madly and swept down the slope.

(c) There were several bowls of roses and they were filling the room with a soft perfume.

(d) We found him and he was mowing the grass for his father.

(e) The caretaker reminded himself that there were no such things as ghosts, and slowly opened the door of the darkened class-room.

(f) She left a brief note explaining where she had gone and hurried out of the house.

(g) "Come out of there at once!" he cried, and beat loudly on the door with his fists.

(h) They had no hope of success and returned dispiritedly.

(i) She returned across the moor alone and felt very lonely and frightened.

(j) The ferryman shipped his oars and pulled the unfortunate passenger out of the water.

Exercise 3 Rewrite the following, making sufficient alterations or additions to say quite clearly what the author meant to say.

> Example: Whilst reading a book in the garden, a fly got into Paul's eye.
>
> Answer: Whilst Paul was reading a book in the garden, a fly got into his eye.

(a) Weeping sadly they found the poor little child alone.

(b) Entering the cave, the smell was quite overpowering.

(c) Three little children playing hopscotch in the street.

(d) We flew over the Statue of Liberty flying from London to New York.

(e) The old man, having three sons and no daughters, and wanting to provide for his own old age.

(f) Crossing the English Channel the sea was very rough.

(g) On all sides men laughing, children playing, women gossiping and on the stand the band playing lively military music.

(h) After reading his latest book, Ian Serraillier is certainly one of my favourite authors.

(i) The queue of people waiting for their turn.

(j) Returning home late last night, the stars were very beautiful.

Exercise 4 Much of the effect of the extract from the poem by Robert Southey is due to the **rhyme**. The rhyming of words at the ends of lines has been common in English verse for centuries: in couplets, for instance, one line is rhymed with the next:

> This books can do – nor this alone: they give   a
> New views to life, and teach us how to live;   a

In quatrains, alternate lines rhyme:

> Beneath this stone, a lump of clay,   a
> Lies Uncle Peter Dan'els,   b
> Who, early in the month of May,   a
> Took off his winter flannels.   b

Notice how "code letters" can be used to indicate a rhyme scheme.

Each of the following questions refers to the extract from the poem printed on page 196.

(a) Find and write out, with the "code letters", the seven lines which rhyme:

a, b, a, c, d, d, e.

(b) Write out any three examples of "internal rhyme" (where two or more words rhyme with each other within one verse line).

(c) Find and write out, with the "code letters", four verse lines which rhyme a, a, b, b.

Would you describe the rhyme-scheme of this poem as a "regular" one?

Exercise 5 Rhymes are similar sounds repeated at the *end* of the word. In English we also have a very strong and ancient tradition of **alliteration**, the repetition of consonant sounds, especially at the *beginning* of words.

For example:

Flying and flinging, writhing and wringing,

is an example in the poem, where fl- and wr- are repeated.

(a) Find six other examples of alliteration from the extract from the poem and in each case identify the letters and sounds that are alliterated.

(b) Think of at least six examples of alliteration in popular and traditional phrases, such as

"Curiosity killed the cat"

or "Better safe than sorry".

Write them out and identify the alliteration.

(c) Find at least six examples of alliteration used in current advertising slogans.

For example:

"Guinness is good for you"

is one that has been publicised for many years, with the alliteration of the g- sound. Why do you think alliteration is used in advertising slogans?

(d) When words are formed directly from the sounds of things or actions, this is called **onomatopoeia**.

For example:　　　splash　　　snap　　　click　　　tinkle
are words representing sounds and actually *sounding like* what they represent.

The same term, onomatopoeia, is applied to using the sounds of *any* words or phrases to imitate particular noises. Can you find an example in the extract from the poem by Robert Southey? Here is one from Dylan Thomas's poem "Fern Hill":

. . . the foxes on the hills barked clear and cold.

(1) What creatures might make each of these noises?

neigh	snarl	coo	chirp	buzz
bray	moo	purr	twitter	hum
gobble	bleat	cluck	bellow	hoot
growl	caw	cheep	howl	squeal

(2) Make up the most lively and interesting sentences you can, using the following onomatopoeic words.

For example:　　　wheeze
The vintage pump engine coughed, wheezed and thumped as water gushed from the pipe.

clatter	clash	patter	rustle	sizzle
blast	plump	whirr	clack	wail

(3) Make a list of as many more onomatopoeic words as you can think of.

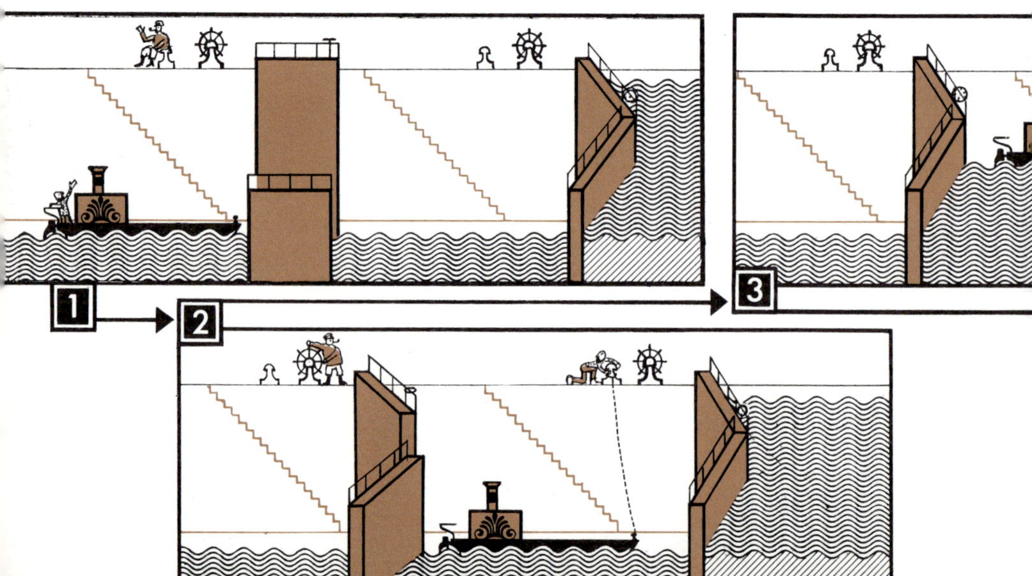

For your own writing

1 In Chapter 11 we worked out an exact description of a room. After studying the diagrams below, write an exact description of how boats are raised and lowered on a canal by means of locks. Do *not* make this a personal story. Your aim is to give a clear and ordered account of how *any* lock would work. Begin by saying what a lock is for, and describe a typical one. Then explain the process, making it clear how the gates are held closed by water pressure, how the water level can be raised and lowered in the lock, and how the gates themselves are opened and closed.

2 Most people find water fascinating. Discuss briefly what is particularly attractive (or alarming) about (a) still, calm water, (b) strongly flowing, deep water, (c) rapid, turbulent water, (d) falling water.

Do you like watching ripples, foam, spray, eddies, whirlpools, fountains or the wake of a ship? Watch a drop of water forming on and then falling from a slowly dripping tap, or the current as it drags water weeds in a stream or river. Make a list of comparisons that seem effective, and a list of words that describe the sight, sound or feel of water.

Write an imaginative description of any riverside or waterside scene. Choose *any* river, stream or lake scene that you know, and decide on the weather, the time of day and year, the number of

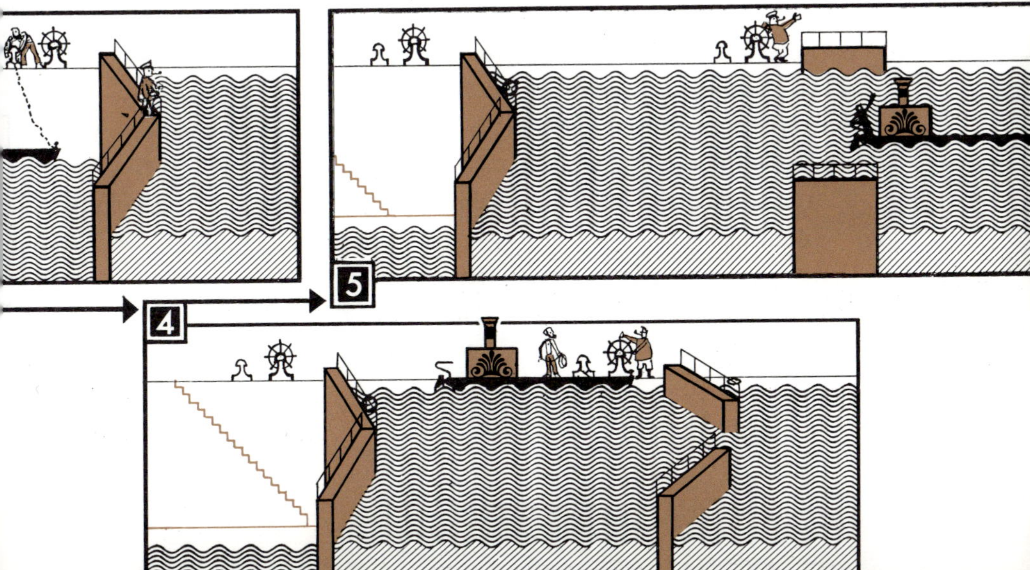

people about, and so on. Write as clear and as vivid an account of the water as you can, mentioning the river traffic if you wish, but pay special attention to the beauty and fascination of the water itself, to the trees and water weeds, birds and fish, by, on or in the water. Remember to write in paragraphs.

For talk and action

1 Which are the three longest rivers in the British Isles? Find out what you can about them, perhaps using this information to draw a map showing their courses and the most important or interesting riverside towns, together with notes about historical events or existing places of interest associated with the rivers.

2 Alternatively, if you live near a fairly large river, you should be able to collect much interesting information about it. For instance, what industries are found on its banks, and how have these changed over the centuries? Who built the bridges, and when? What authority is responsible for keeping the river clean and the banks in good condition? What is the fishing like? How much traffic is there on the river? Does the water feed reservoirs? Are there locks, fords, weirs, waterfalls or rapids? What historic scenes have been associated with the river? What wildlife and plant-life are to be found?

All this might well be enough to occupy the whole class in visits and research and in map-making, illustrations and writing up factual information. One issue of the class magazine could be devoted entirely to this theme. Some of you could even devise cartoons to illustrate various aspects of river safety.

3 Prepare an illustrated talk to the class on one of the following subjects. (The library section 797 includes nearly all the water-sports; some other library reference numbers are given in brackets.)

Yachting	Fishers and waders (598.2)
Rowing	River fishing (799)
The Boat Race	**Three Men in a Boat**
Henley Regatta	Swans and "swan-upping" (598.2)

Enjoying canoeing

Building a canoe

Canoeing holidays

Sailing a dinghy

Holidays afloat

Thames barges (623)

Water skiing

Speedboats (623)

Hovercraft (623)

Hydrofoils (623)

Punting

Water fowl (598.2)

Paddle-boats and other pleasure-boats

Water buses and ferries

Trees of the river bank (582)

Mammals on the river bank (599)

Water supplies of cities (628.1)

Locks, dams and weirs (626)

The world's finest bridges (624)

Tunnelling beneath rivers (624)

Soft and hard water (551)

The Silver Sword by IAN SERRAILLIER (Cape; Heinemann; Puffin) This exciting story of how four children trekked across war-devastated Europe, from Poland to Switzerland, is based on fact. Ian Serraillier also wrote **There's No Escape** (Cape; Heinemann; Puffin) about enemy-occupied Europe – in which a young meteorologist is parachuted into France to bring out a radar scientist.

The Boy and the River by HENRI BOSCO (translated by Gerard Hopkins) (O.U.P.) Pascalet lives near a river in southern France, where his parents have forbidden him to play. But he hears about the river's attractions from a poacher, finds a boat and meets another boy, Gatzo, on an island. They row off to explore a network of remote waterways.

The Dolphin Crossing by JILL PATON WALSH (Macmillan; Penguin) Of this exciting story based on the evacuation of British troops from Dunkirk in 1940, the author wrote: "There really were schoolboys who joined the many civilians in ferrying the British army back across the Channel. I hope this is also a truthful book in another sense; when real people take real risks, they really get killed."

Jack and Richard Church were brought up in Battersea before the First World War. Their parents could afford few luxuries, but music came to play a vital part in Jack's life, as literature did in Richard's . . .

I cannot explain what attracted my twelve-year-old brother to this sonata of Beethoven, the only piece of worthwhile music in our home. His only instruction at that time had been given by Mother, to the limited extent already described. She had neither time, opportunity nor energy to further her own interest in music, and I am not certain that she possessed more of that interest than she exhibited on Sunday evenings, with her husband or a few friends who showed even less musical sophistication.

Then one day a gaunt young man with long hair and a nervous cough came to tune the piano. I noticed his thin, dirty hands, with

finger-nails like claws, that rattled on the keys and scratched the face-board behind them. He smoked cigarettes the whole time he was at work: and that was an unusual habit in 1900.

Jack and I were vastly interested. We stood side by side watching him that Saturday morning. He took out the front of the piano, exposing the strings and the rusty pegs. That was wonderful enough. But he talked to us while he worked, breaking off the conversation at intervals while he struck a note and called forth a clank from the three strings whose neighbours had been muted by a metal tool stuck through them. He talked to Jack, over my head, and my attention wandered.

Jack, however, was doubly interested, for two sides of his nature were engaged by this long-haired professional. He saw the mechanism of the piano at work, and learned, by demonstration, how the pressure on the soft pedal brought up a long damper of felt and applied it to the strings, to cause that faraway effect which made the

listener urgent to run upstairs, or into the kitchen, seeking the music so ventriloquially removed.

I could feel, by the tone of the conversation between Jack and the tuner, that this method of inducing a pianissimo was not approved. Jack's face wore the bleak inscrutability habitual when he was bored or disgusted. His nose became bigger and bonier, and his eyes retreated into their sockets.

In spite of his disapproval of the structure of our Broadwood White, Jack was able to give particular attention to the other part of the tuner's flood of soliloquy. It was about music, and it poured advice over the bullet-head of my brother, who stood gravely beneath it, like a religious enthusiast receiving baptism by total immersion.

During a pause, after the tuning was done, he produced the Beethoven sonata, and asked the tuner to give him an inkling how it should be attacked.

The result was like that of opening a weir. The thin, bow-backed figure of the piano-tuner shook with latent energy. He tossed his hair back, cracked his bony knuckles, and began to play the sonata in G major, Opus 31, No. 1 (published in 1803), which, as music-lovers will recollect, opens with a startling statement, a running gesture, and then the assertion of a theme whose dogma is beyond all doubt.

The tuner emphasised that dogma with the vehemence of a Savonarola castigating the pleasure-loving Florentines. Jack and I swayed like water-weeds in the flood, making the same mesmeric movements under the invisible punches of the music. Then, after the violent assertion and running to and fro, the second part of the sonata, heard by us both for the first time in our lives, came out with a long, rapid melody that tore us up by the roots and flung us downstream; the main stream of the art of music.

The musician was equally touched by his own magic, for as he played this melody, he leaned over it, watering it with his flowing hair, which almost touched the ivories. I was deeply impressed, as much by the spectacle as by the music. All was new to me: the performer, his odd manners and appearance, the nature of the music and the fluidity of the performance. That is why I have never forgotten that half-hour, as long as one of the half-hours spent by Adam and Eve in the Garden, before their Disobedience set the clocks ticking.

When the performance ended, the pianist sat, nervously working the muscles of his cadaverous face, and wiping his dirty hands on a dirtier handkerchief. He was sweating freely and emitting an odour as of mice, or bats. Then he turned to Jack, and looked at him. But Jack was lost. He stood before the keyboard, staring at the notes, settled into a shy obstinacy. I could read that index. He was struggling with something: an emotion against which his cautious and sardonic mind was warning him. He ignored the unhealthy figure at the piano, and he ignored me.

Thus, for several moments, we made a statuary group, the musician and I waiting for my brother to show some sign. But we were to be disappointed, for suddenly he looked up, quietly thanked the tuner, and left the room. He must, however, have gone to Mother and spoken to her, for when she appeared, without Jack, to pay the tuner, she asked him if he would give the boy some lessons, a request to which he agreed.

From that time, Jack put in some practice daily, and went regularly for a weekly lesson.

(from **Over the Bridge** by RICHARD CHURCH)

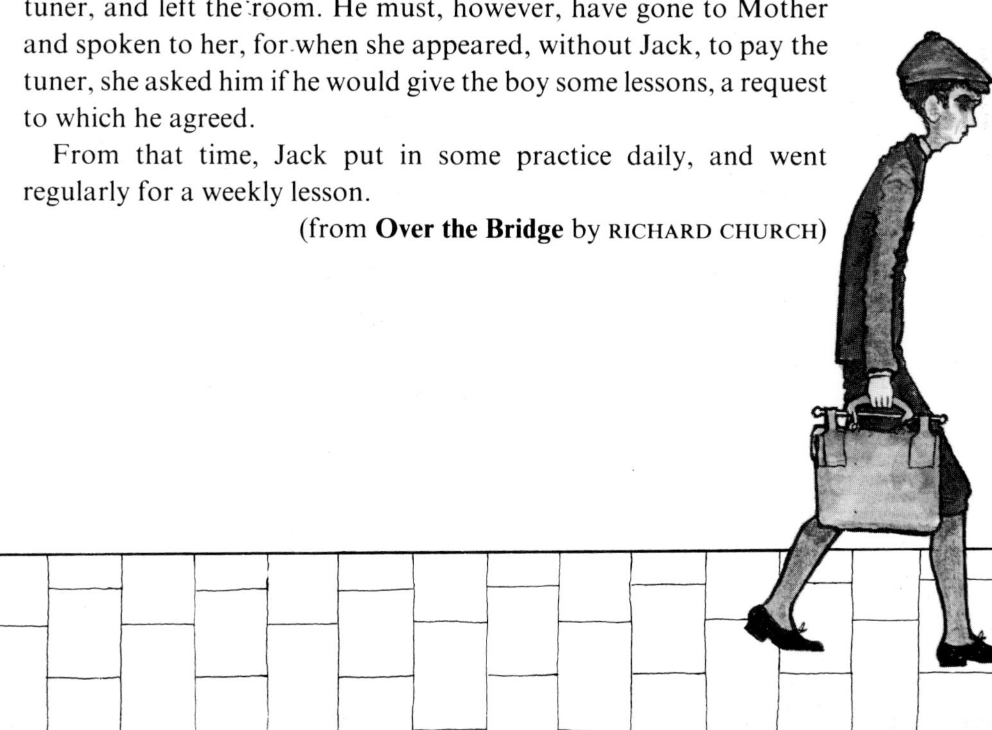

For discussion

1 Discuss any words and phrases in the extract whose meaning is not immediately clear including:

"sophistication"   "latent energy"
"gaunt"   "vehemence"
"muted"   "castigating"
"so ventriloquially removed"   "mesmeric movements"
(what is a ventriloquist?) "his cadaverous face"
"pianissimo"   "I could read that index"
"bleak inscrutability"   "his ... sardonic mind"
"flood of soliloquy"   "a statuary group".

2 Near the end of the extract, the piano tuner is described as "the unhealthy figure at the piano". What indications are we given earlier about his poor health?

3 What indications are there that the tuner had a lot of nervous energy?

4 "Broadwood White" was the trade name of the piano. What indication is there that it was not a very good piano? Is there reason to think it was poorly designed, rather than neglected?

5 Jack was four years older than Richard (the writer). What details reflect the fact that Richard was only eight?

6 What, apparently, were the "two sides of Jack's nature" referred to in the fourth paragraph of this extract? What state of mind did Richard judge Jack to be in after the recital?

7 There are a number of rich or detailed comparisons used in this extract. Discuss in detail what is compared to what in the following examples:

(a) "(Jack) stood gravely beneath it, like a religious enthusiast receiving baptism by total immersion." (sixth paragraph)

(b) "The result was like that of opening a weir." (eighth paragraph)

(c) "The tuner emphasised that dogma with the vehemence of a Savonarola castigating the pleasure-loving Florentines." (Savonarola was a late fifteenth-century religious reformer in the city of Florence who preached against wickedness in the Church, and was

210

so effective that he persuaded the citizens to burn everything they were ashamed of.) (ninth paragraph)

(d) "Jack and I swayed like water-weeds in the flood … Then … the second part of the sonata … came out with a long, rapid melody that tore us up by the roots and flung us downstream; the main stream of the art of music." (ninth paragraph)

(e) "… watering it (the piano?) with his flowing hair" (tenth paragraph)

(f) "that half-hour, as long as one of the half-hours spent by Adam and Eve in the Garden, before their Disobedience set the clocks ticking." (tenth paragraph)

8 In your experience, does the "spectacle" of seeing musicians performing add something to the effect of the music? If so, does this apply equally to *all* kinds of music – light, serious, pop, jazz, rock – and to all kinds of instruments? What other visual effects are used with music (at discos, or in films or on television)?

9 If possible, listen to a recording of the Sonata in G major that the piano tuner played (Beethoven's Sonata No. 16, Opus 31, No. 1). What is the difference between the first and second parts (or movements)? How far does Richard Church describe the music effectively in words?

For written answers

Basing your answers as closely as you can on the evidence in this extract, write two full paragraphs, in your own words.

1 Describe Jack's appearance as you imagine it, and his personality, and how he reacts to this experience.

2 Describe the "odd manners and appearance" of the piano tuner as he impressed Richard that day.

MUSIC COMES

Music comes
Sweetly from the trembling string
When wizard fingers sweep
Dreamily, half asleep;
When through remembering reeds
Ancient airs and murmurs creep,
Oboe oboe following,
Flute answering clear high flute,
Voices, voices – falling mute,
And the jarring drums.

At night I heard
First a waking bird
Out of the quiet darkness sing . . .
Music comes
Strangely to the brain asleep!
And I heard
Soft, wizard fingers sweep
Music from the trembling string,
And through remembering reeds
Ancient airs and murmurs creep;

Discussing the poem

1 Look carefully in this poem for (a) whole lines repeated, and (b) single words repeated (often within the same line). Discuss the reasons for their repetition, and also the reasons for any slight variations. What effect does the poet wish to achieve?

2 What different kinds of instrument are represented here? Can you think of any reason why some instruments do *not* seem to be represented?

3 Discuss the words the poet uses, particularly the adjectives. Why are strings "trembling", or reeds "remembering", or drums "jarring"? Would you call these examples of onomatopoeia?

For learning about language

Jack learnt all the pieces.
This is a simple statement sentence. What are the subject, verb and

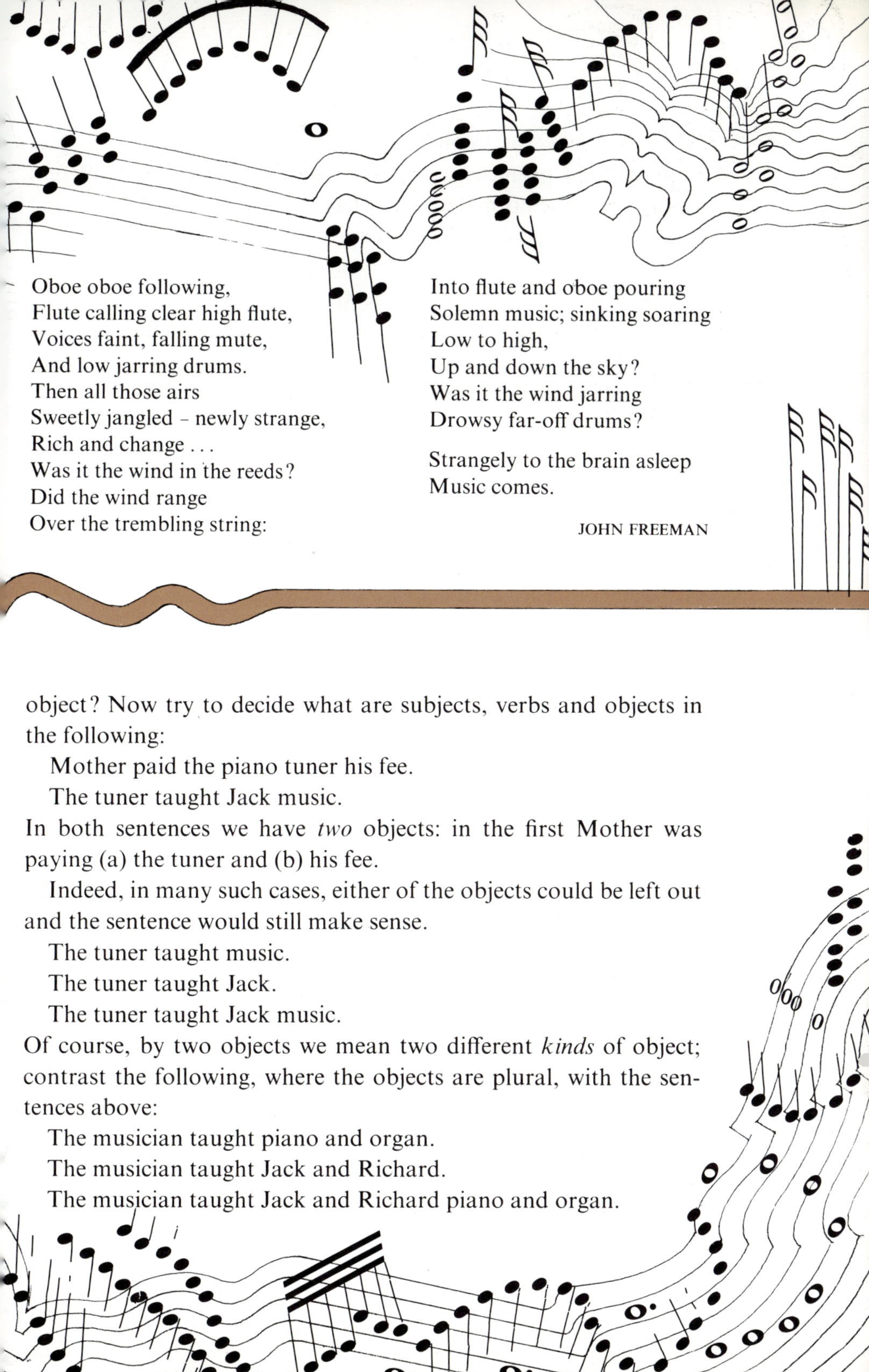

object? Now try to decide what are subjects, verbs and objects in the following:

Mother paid the piano tuner his fee.

The tuner taught Jack music.

In both sentences we have *two* objects: in the first Mother was paying (a) the tuner and (b) his fee.

Indeed, in many such cases, either of the objects could be left out and the sentence would still make sense.

The tuner taught music.

The tuner taught Jack.

The tuner taught Jack music.

Of course, by two objects we mean two different *kinds* of object; contrast the following, where the objects are plural, with the sentences above:

The musician taught piano and organ.

The musician taught Jack and Richard.

The musician taught Jack and Richard piano and organ.

A number of verbs frequently take two objects: give, lend, find, bring, ask, tell, promise, are all examples. The objects are of different kinds: one is the normal object, what is given, lent, found etc., and is called the **direct object**. The other is usually the person (or people) to whom or for whom it is given, lent, found etc., and is called the **indirect object**. But note that, if the words "to" or "for" are actually used before the person, it is no longer called an object of the verb:

The musician taught the piano to Jack.

"Jack" is *not* here called the indirect object of "taught".

Exercise 1 Write out (in four columns) the subject, verb, indirect object and direct object of the following sentences:

	SUBJECT	VERB	INDIRECT OBJECT	DIRECT OBJECT
Example:	Jack	played	his mother	a tune

(a) Tracy's mother gave her a beautiful necklace.

(b) I can lend you fifty pence.

(c) The musician found Mrs Church a piano.

(d) The class will send the Children's Home a cheque.

(e) My uncle brought me a souvenir.

(f) Will you ask the speaker another question?

(g) The Headmaster promised the school a half-holiday.

(h) May we offer your friend a drink?

(i) That experience taught the boys a lesson.

(j) New members have to pay the treasurer an entrance fee.

Exercise 2 Word order alone tells us whether a noun is subject, direct object or indirect object. Identify the subjects and objects in these sentences:

The home help insulted the supervisor.

We gave the home help a new supervisor.

We also gave the supervisor a new home help.

When pronouns are used instead of nouns, standard English changes many of them according to whether they are subject or object. (There is no difference between the direct and indirect object

forms.) Write down the object forms of these pronouns.

I, you, he, she, it, we, you, they.

Turn to page 110 to check that you are correct.

In addition, the pronoun "who" (which is used to ask questions and to introduce adjective phrases and clauses) has an object form "whom".

For example: Who wants to come? (subj.)
                 Whom do you want? (obj.)

– though in spoken English "Who do you want?" sounds quite natural, and is certainly accepted in everyday speech.

The subject and object forms of pronouns are often confused, or varied in local dialects of English. Each of the following sentences includes one such pronoun. Rewrite them as standard written English.

Example: Shall us all help him do it?

Answer: Shall *we* all help him do it?

(a) Jim and me want to start a new youth club.
(b) All us boys are very keen on it.
(c) Him and his friends will not support us in our venture.
(d) Who will help us and who can we help?
(e) The people who we want to help really do need us.
(f) Please give Jim and I all the support you can.
(g) It was me who first thought of the scheme.
(h) As we all took part, whom should take the credit?
(i) He and his friends will never be as successful as us.
(j) It was they who we very much wanted to beat.

Exercise 3 Look again at the **comparisons** in the extract. Most of them are **similes**, and state clearly that some person or thing is like another in one or more particular ways:

The result was like that of opening a weir.

Jack and I swayed like water-weeds in the flood.

But others *imply* (hint at) a comparison, treating one thing as if it really were another. What is the comparison being made in these quotations from the extract?

... the invisible punches of the music.

a long, rapid melody that tore us up by the roots and flung us downstream.

An implied comparison, when one thing or person is treated as if it is something else, is called a **metaphor**. It is really a "compressed simile". This has already been mentioned briefly in Chapter 6 on page 95.

What is compared to what in these metaphors and similes? Which are metaphors and which similes?

(a) *Like a bee gathering honey* she turned over the leaves of the music.

(b) In the darkness the pianist's hands had *to creep and crawl, finding their way* to the right notes by themselves.

(c) The river *squeezed past* great boulders.

(d) Some of the boulders were *as high as houses.*

(e) We *heard the miniature thunder* where the colt fled.

(f) He shakes his coat *as if to throw off flies.*

(g) The waterfall *arched gracefully* over the brink of the cliff.

(h) He saw the stone columns in the light *sliced from the dark by his torch.*

(i) Years of dripping water were *held in stone* before him.

(j) He wanted to move off into *the limestone forests.*

Exercise 4 Make up sentences with interesting and original comparisons (similes *or* metaphors) to describe the following:
(a) the sea in winter
(b) a tiny stream in a quiet valley
(c) a large crane at work on a building site
(d) a combine harvester at work
(e) a ballet dancer
(f) a train emerging from a tunnel
(g) a still, warm evening
(h) silence returning after a burst of noise
(i) tall trees moving in the wind
(j) great, white cumulus clouds.

Exercise 5 Rewrite the following paragraph, inserting capital letters (some have been put in for you), one set of inverted commas, commas, full stops and apostrophes.

Schuberts Eighth Symphony known as the unfinished wasnt in fact left unfinished for any obvious reasons such as the composers death two of the composers friends Joseph and Anselm Hüttenbrenner had had him elected an honorary member of a famous musical society and in 1823 he sent anselm this uncompleted symphony in gratitude for his two friends kindness schubert did not die until 1828 after he had written his great ninth symphony forty years later Herbeck a famous conductor obtained the manuscript of the eighth symphony from anselm now an old man by promising to perform one of anselms own overtures its world premiere was in vienna in 1865 and its certain that schubert never heard it performed.

For your own writing

1 Listen to a piece of music, and let your imagination roam freely as you listen. If possible, hear it twice, and at least one of the times with your eyes closed in complete concentration. Immediately afterwards make written notes about your thoughts: the pictures, ideas, story or words that came to your mind as you listened.

Try then to develop this into a short poem or a piece of very vivid prose writing. Here is an example by a pupil. This one (like the poem on pages 212–13) is closely concerned with describing the music itself. You might prefer to describe the day-dreams prompted by it.

2 What kinds of music do you like, and why? Try to analyse your feelings. Is rhythm or melody more important to you? As you listen, do you like to dance or to beat out a rhythm with (say) your fingers, or do you allow your imagination to suggest a whole world of ideas and mental pictures? If vocal music is one of your favourites, how important are the words to you, and does it make much difference if they are in a foreign language? What are your favourite instruments? Think of adjectives or comparisons that would best describe them when played really well. Who are your favourite performers? What does their interpretation have that others lack? Write notes on all these points.

Now try to rearrange your rough notes into a complete composition on the subject of:

MY FAVOURITE MUSIC.

Arrange the material into paragraphs, so that the reader is led from some general ideas about music, and its appeal, to your own particular tastes. Include paragraphs on composers and performers, but illustrate throughout from your own experiences: refer to records, concerts, musical programmes on television or radio, any instruments you play, and try all the time to show *what* you like about music.

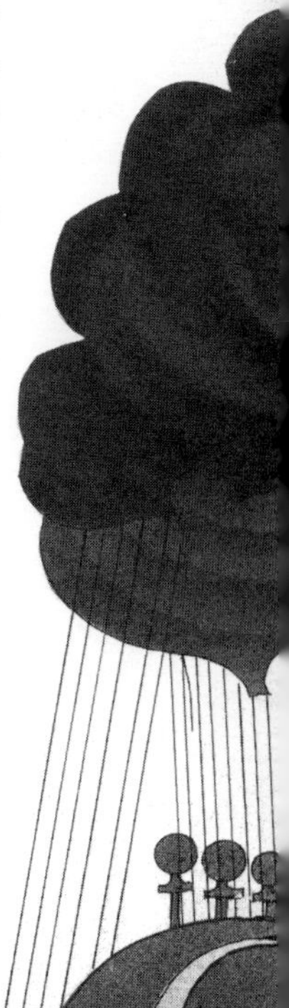

For talk and action

1 Prepare a short talk on *one* musical instrument – anything from a penny whistle to a church organ. You should include an exact description of the instrument (with diagrams that can be pinned up or drawn on the board), and how it produces its range of sounds. If possible, have one with you, and be prepared to play it to illustrate your points. In any case, have some information about the history of the instrument, how it is made, and about musicians who have used them or been famous for playing them.

Alternatively, make this an illustrated article for the class magazine.

2 A group of the class could make a survey of musical tastes in the class, or the class as a whole could undertake a survey of music throughout the school. First, decide on the questions you want to answer: are you simply concerned with a "Top Ten" of artists and kinds of music, or would you like to investigate how many records people have, or how long they spend listening to music, or whether they play an instrument, or whether they would like more music to be taught at school, and so on? Next, decide on methods: a questionnaire or personal interviews? Finally, make sure that the information will come back in a form that can be assessed and used in a written account; decide whether results should be shown as percentages, etc.

An interesting variation of this would be to interview a number of members of staff about their attitudes to music and music teaching in school.

For further reading

Over the Bridge by RICHARD CHURCH (Heinemann)
In this vivid, first-hand account of life in Battersea (and later Dulwich) at the beginning of this century, the family's ordinary home, Jack's love of music, and Mr Church's passion for cycling, are all recorded with accuracy and affection. (Classified as 920 CHU.)

Richard Church also wrote the adventure stories **The Cave** and **Down River** (see Chapter 4, page 69).

She Shall Have Music by KITTY BARNE (Dent)
Karen Forest's family are not particularly musical, and it is only after some disappointing setbacks that Karen finds a really good teacher and works her way up to win a scholarship to a London college of music.

The Great Composers series (published by Faber) includes **Bach**, **Britten**, **Byrd** and **Holst** (by IMOGEN HOLST), **Beethoven** and **Handel** (by STANLEY SADIE) and **Elgar**, **Mendelssohn** and **Vaughan Williams** (by MICHAEL HURD). These are fascinating biographies, full of information and commentary on the works of these masters. (Classified as 780.92.)

Instruments of Popular Music, **Processional Music**, etc. by LILLA M. FOX (Lutterworth)
This series of clear, lively, well-illustrated books forms a comprehensive survey of past and present musical instruments, interesting even to non-musicians. (Classified as 786.)

A Swarm in May by WILLIAM MAYNE (O.U.P.)
John Owen, youngest chorister at the Cathedral Choir School, refuses to carry on tradition by acting as the Cathedral's bee-keeper, thinking he dislikes bees. But in helping the organist with his swarm, he finds he was wrong, and also makes some remarkable discoveries among the Cathedral towers.

The Lark in the Morn by ELFRIDA VIPONT (O.U.P.)
Kit Haverard, youngest of a musical family, discovers when staying with relations after an illness, that she has real musical talent and can sing. With her friends she goes to boarding-school and through the ups and downs of musical training. Her story is continued in **The Lark on the Wing** (O.U.P.).

DOUG SCOTT:

As I belayed Dougal
up the Hillary Step it gradually
dawned upon me that we were going
to reach the summit of Big E. I took another
photograph of Dougal and wound on the film to find that
it was finished. I didn't think I had any more film in my
rucksack, for I had left film and spare gloves with the bivvy sheet
and stove at the South Summit. I took off my oxygen mask and
rucksack and put them on the ridge in front of me. I was sat astride
it, one leg in Nepal and the other in Tibet. I hoped Dougal's steps
would hold, for I could think of no other place to put his rope than
between my teeth as I rummaged around in my sack. I found a
cassette of colour film that had somehow got left behind several
days before. The cold was intense and the brittle film kept breaking
off. The wind was strong and blew the snow Dougal was sending
down the Nepalese side right back into the air and over into Tibet.
I fitted the film into the camera and followed him up. This was the
place where Ed Hillary had chimneyed his way up the crevass
between the rock and the ice. Now with all the monsoon snow on
the mountain it was well banked up, but with snow the consistency
of sugar it looked decidedly difficult.

222

15 Man and Nature

Everest was first conquered by Sir Edmund Hillary in 1953, and during the following twenty years several expeditions reached the top; but all attempts by the challenging South-west Route had failed. On 24th September 1975, two members of Chris Bonington's party finally succeeded, though this expedition was to pay a heavy price when the weather changed . . .

A
wide
whaleback
ridge ran up
the last 300 yards.
It was just a matter of
trail breaking. Sometimes the
crust would hold for a few steps
and then suddenly we would be stumbling
around as it broke through to our knees. All
the way along we were fully aware of the enormous
monsoon cornices, overhanging the 10 000-foot East

223

Face of Everest. We therefore kept well to the left.

It was whilst trail breaking on this last section that I noticed my mind seemed to be operating in two parts, one external to my head. In my head I referred to the external part somewhere over my left shoulder. I rationalised the situation with it making reference to it about not going too far right in the area of the cornice, and it would urge me to keep well to the left. Whenever I stumbled through the crust, it suggested that I slowed down and picked my way through more carefully. In general it seemed to give me confidence and seemed such a natural phenomenon that I hardly gave it a second thought at the time. Dougal took over the trail breaking and headed up the final slope to the top – and a red flag flying there. The snow improved and he slackened his pace to let me come alongside. We then walked up side by side the last few paces to the top, arriving there together.

All the world lay before us. That summit was everything and more that a summit should be. My usually reticent partner became expansive, his face broke out into a broad happy smile and we stood there hugging each other and thumping each other's backs. The implications of reaching the highest mountain in the world surely had some bearing on our feelings. I'm sure they did on mine, but I can't say that it was that strong. I can't say either that I felt any relief that the struggle was over. In fact, in some ways it seemed a shame that it was, for we had been fully programmed and now we had to switch off and go back into reverse. But not yet, for the view was so staggering, the disappearing sun so full of colour that the setting held us in awe. I was absorbed by the brown hills of Tibet. They only looked like hills from our lofty summit. They were really high mountains, some of them 24 000 feet high, but with hardly any snow to indicate their importance. I could see silver threads of rivers meandering down between them, flowing north and west to bigger rivers which might have included the Tsangpo. Towards the east Kangchenjunga caught the setting sun, although around to the south clouds boiled down in the Nepalese valleys and far down behind a vast front of black cloud was advancing towards

224

us from the plains of India. It flickered lightning ominously . . .

DOUGAL HASTON: We were sampling a unique moment in our lives. Down and over into the brown plains of Tibet a purple shadow of Everest was projected for what must have been something like 200 miles. On these north and east sides there was a sense of wildness and remoteness, almost untouchability. Miraculous events seemed to be taking place in the region of the sun. One moment it seemed to dip behind a cloud layer lying a little above the horizon. End Game – thought we. But then the cloud dropped faster than the sun and out it came again. Three times in all. I began to feel like a Saul on the road to Tarsus. More materially, right in front of me was an aluminium survey pole with a strip of red canvas attached. The Japanese ladies in the spring hadn't mentioned leaving or seeing anything. Puzzlement for a moment. Then the only answer. There had been a Chinese ascent of the North East Ridge claimed, just after the Japanese ascent. Some doubt, however, had been cast on the validity of this, due to the summit pictures lacking the detail associated with previous summit shots. It was good to have the ultimate proof in front of us. Having to play the doubt game in climbing is never a pleasant experience.

Slowly creeping into the euphoria came one very insistent thought as the sun finally won its race with the clouds and slid over the edge. The thought? Well, we were after all on the top of the world but it was still a long way back to Camp 6 and it was going to be dark very soon and then what would we do? We knew we could get back to the South Summit in the half light. On the previous nights there had been a very bright moon and it seemed reasonable to assume we could retrace our steps down the Face if this came out. If it didn't, as a last resort we could bivouac. That after all was the reason for bringing the tent sac. I'd always reckoned a bivouac possible at such altitude, but that doesn't mean to say I looked upon the project with a great degree of enthusiasm. We finally turned our back to the summit and set off down.

(from **Everest the Hard Way** edited by CHRIS BONINGTON)

For discussion

1 Discuss any technical or unfamiliar language used in the extract. What do the following mean?

"I belayed Dougal up"

"the bivvy sheet" and "a bivouac"

"had chimneyed his way up the crevass"

"I rationalised the situation"

"My usually reticent partner became expansive"

"the euphoria"

2 Discuss what a "wide whaleback ridge" with "enormous monsoon cornices" would be like. Describe the shape of the last 300 yards before the summit, as they saw it. What difficulties and dangers did the snow present?

3 Why, do you think, did Dougal Haston "slacken his pace" as they neared the summit?

4 What was their nickname for the summit? What reminders were there of Sir Edmund Hillary's first successful ascent, and what evidence did they find of other ascents, in the spring of 1975?

5 What had been unusual about the Japanese ascent, and what doubt was there about the Chinese party's ascent? Why was Dougal Haston pleased to have that doubt resolved?

6 Explain why Doug Scott felt some sense of anticlimax at the summit. What is he comparing himself with when he uses the words "fully programmed"? Does this comparison seem effective to you?

7 "End Game" (page 225) is a metaphor. What recreational activity is it taken from, and what does it mean (a) literally, (b) in this comparison?

8 Dougal Haston has misquoted the Bible story of the conversion

of "Saul of Tarsus". Look up Acts 9, check the correct details, and show why the "miraculous" sunset reminded him of that Bible story.

9 What was the striking difference between the weather to the north and east, and the weather to the south (and perhaps west)? Which way was the wind blowing?

10 Discuss what this extract tells us about the use of oxygen at this height (about 29 000 feet or 8840 metres above sea-level), comparing these experiences with those described by Wilfrid Noyce in the poem on the next page.

For written answers

1 "The snow improved" (third paragraph). What was difficult and dangerous about the state of the snow, until those last few paces to the top?

2 Explain clearly why the climbers "kept well to the left" (second paragraph). What was the danger to the right?

3 Describe fully, in your own words, the phenomenon of Doug Scott's mind "operating in two parts", comparing this with Wilfred Noyce's description of climbing at 21 000 feet, in his poem overleaf.

4 Compare the feelings expressed by the two climbers (Doug Scott and Dougal Haston) about (a) the achievement of reaching the highest summit in the world, and (b) the view from the top. Which of them seems to be more deeply moved by the experience?

5 Explain in your own words the problems the two climbers faced (or feared they might face) in descending from the summit, in view of the likely weather changes.

227

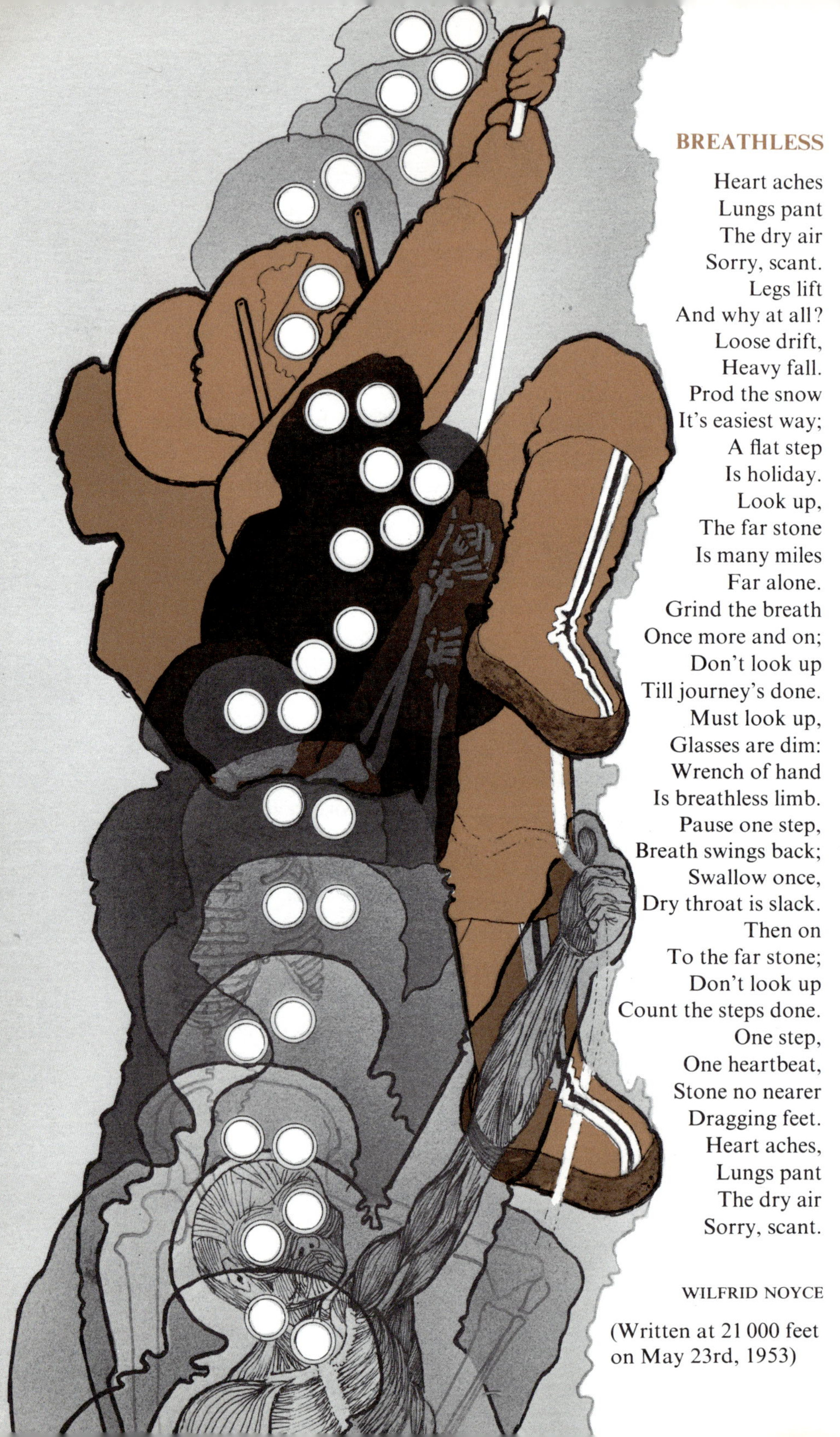

BREATHLESS

Heart aches
Lungs pant
The dry air
Sorry, scant.
Legs lift
And why at all?
Loose drift,
Heavy fall.
Prod the snow
It's easiest way;
A flat step
Is holiday.
Look up,
The far stone
Is many miles
Far alone.
Grind the breath
Once more and on;
Don't look up
Till journey's done.
Must look up,
Glasses are dim:
Wrench of hand
Is breathless limb.
Pause one step,
Breath swings back;
Swallow once,
Dry throat is slack.
Then on
To the far stone;
Don't look up
Count the steps done.
One step,
One heartbeat,
Stone no nearer
Dragging feet.
Heart aches,
Lungs pant
The dry air
Sorry, scant.

WILFRID NOYCE

(Written at 21 000 feet
on May 23rd, 1953)

Discussing the poem

1 Does the poem live up to its title? How are the length of line (and the number of "stressed" syllables), and the rhyme, used to emphasise the climber's state?
2 Why do you think the poet repeats the first four lines as the last four lines of the poem?
3 What is the importance of "the far stone" to the climber?
4 Sum up in plain prose the physical effects of great effort at great heights. Can you account for these effects on the body?

For learning about language

Read the following extract carefully. It is about what the author sees as the extravagant use mankind makes of energy resources.

Primitive man had to make do with the power of his muscles. Food was his only fuel. His energy needs were modest. The average well-fed person uses just a little more energy than a steadily glowing 100-watt bulb.

5   As time went by man began to make use of materials around him, and his use of fuel steadily grew. At first wood was gathered to make fires for heat and light. Much later, animals were domesticated so that they could carry people and pull carts and farming equipment – just like a tractor today. Windmills and water-wheels enabled our fore-
10 fathers to undertake many more tasks, while the development of wind-powered sailing ships gave them the opportunity to make long sea voyages. Civilisation grew and spread.

    Then, in the late seventeenth century, an Englishman, Thomas Savery, developed the first steam-driven engine. The industrial age was
15 dawning and civilised man began to exploit coal in large quantities. In 1870 those living in Western Europe and America were using about thirty-five times as much energy each day as the first primitive men.

    By now, however, the first commercial oilwells had been drilled. Within the space of a century humankind entered the complicated age
20 of cars, space travel, supersonic aircraft, worldwide communications, television and plastics. Modern farming methods which include machinery, fertilizers and chemical treatments help to ensure that the world's fast-rising population is fed. All of these developments have been made possible, in some way, by the use of fossil fuels.

25 We may not have recognised the fact that energy lies at the heart of this progress. One third of all the world's daily use of energy goes into industry, where machines have largely replaced muscles. Almost as much energy is used in homes for heating and lighting. Transport accounts for a further 20%, indicating how accustomed we have become
30 to using cars, buses, trains, ships and aircraft . . .

It is a sad fact that people in the United States of America, with their big cars and over-heated or over-cooled buildings, use 330 times as much energy as those living in Ethiopia. To take another example, each year a single person living in the USA uses on average the amount of
35 energy that is contained in about twelve tonnes of coal. This is six times the average for the world as a whole. He does not handle all this fuel himself, of course. Some of it is used to power machines or instruments at his place of work. Some more might have been used to make the car in which he drives around. Yet in India, where the population is far, far
40 larger than in America, each person has to get by with less than 200 kilograms worth of coal each year.

(from **Running Out of Fuel – Solving the Energy Puzzle** by RAY DAFTER)

Exercise 1 In the following statements or questions, you are given several possible answers, and (according to this extract) only one is fully true. Write down the number of the correct answer in each case; as before, do not write anything in this book.

1 On his own, a man can be regarded as a working machine, and the fuel he uses is:

    (i) food   (ii) muscle-power   (iii) electricity   (iv) horse-power.

2 The statement that "primitive man's . . . energy needs were modest" (line 2) means:

    (i) he did not like to talk about his strength
    (ii) he used his energy to make himself clothes to wear
    (iii) he required little food and fuel compared with a modern man
    (iv) he used a lot of energy working hard.

3 The first steam-engines were developed in Britain in:
    (i) the 1660s   (ii) the 1680s   (iii) the 1760s
    (iv) the 1780s   (v) the 1860s   (vi) the 1870s.

4 The statement "civilised man began to exploit coal" (line 15) means:

    (i) he began to make use of coal

230

(ii) he made a big profit out of coal-mines
(iii) he used explosives to get the coal out of the ground
(iv) he began to understand where to find coal
(v) he sold coal to other countries.

5 Which of the following statements, according to the extract, is most true of the situation in 1870?
(i) People in Western Europe were using thirty-five times as much energy a day as those in the U.S.A.
(ii) People in America were using about as much energy each day as primitive men.
(iii) The average person in America and Western Europe was using about thirty-five times the daily energy consumption of the average primitive man.
(iv) The average commercial oil consumption in America was thirty-five times that in Western Europe.

6 By which year had the first commercial oil-wells been drilled? Which of the following is most accurate, according to the writer?
(i) 1700   (ii) 1770   (iii) 1800
(iv) 1870   (v) 1900

7 Which of the following is true, according to the extract?
Heating and lighting homes accounts for:
(i) 10%   (ii) 20%   (iii) 30%   (iv) 50%   (v) 70% of the world's daily energy consumption.

8 According to the writer, transport is:
(i) the biggest   (ii) the second biggest   (iii) the third biggest   (iv) the least important consumer of energy in the world today.

9 A single person living in the U.S.A. uses, on average,
(i) twelve tonnes of energy a day throughout the year
(ii) twelve tonnes of coal a year to heat his home
(iii) the equivalent of twelve tonnes of coal for all his energy needs in a year
(iv) twelve times as much energy in a year as the average person in the rest of the world.

10 A tonne is 1000 kilograms. Does the writer mean that on average every Indian uses:
(i) one sixth   (ii) one twelfth   (iii) one sixteenth   (iv) one sixtieth
(v) one six-hundredth of the energy used by every American in the U.S.A.?

Exercise 2 Each of the following six sentences summarises one of Ray Dafter's paragraphs, but they are now in the *wrong order*. Rewrite the six sentences in the correct order to form a continuous summary of the points the writer has made in the extract on pages 229–30.

(i) In the last one hundred years men have exploited oil and gas as well as coal.

(ii) At first, men used their own physical energy.

(iii) In the eighteenth and nineteenth centuries coal, burnt to run steam-engines, greatly increased energy consumption.

(iv) But this vastly-increased energy consumption is available only to advanced industrial nations.

(v) Much energy is now used by industry and for heat, light and transport.

(vi) They then made use of energy from wood, animals, wind and water.

Exercise 3 Because the extract printed on pages 229 and 230 is from a factual book, it is written in an impersonal style. One important element of this is the use of the **passive voice**: instead of "Men at first gathered wood to make fires", the writer has put:

At first wood was gathered to make fires.
Instead of "Much later, people domesticated animals", Ray Dafter wrote:

Much later, animals were domesticated.
The first version of each of these examples is in what is called the **active voice**: the subjects ("men" and "people") were *doing* something actively. Why is the term **passive** a good term for the second versions? Look at the *subjects* of the verbs "was gathered" and "were domesticated" and notice how they relate to these verbs.

Give an active version of each of these sentences (the first six are from the extract before Exercise 1); the passive verbs are given in italics.

(a) The first commercial oilwells *had been drilled.*

(b) The world's fast-rising population *is fed.*

(c) All these developments *have been made possible*, in some way, by the use of fossil fuels.

(d) Almost as much energy *is used* in homes for heating and lighting.

(e) Some of the fuel *is used* to power machines or instruments at his place of work.

(f) Some more (fuel) *might have been used* to make the car in which he drives around.

(g) Many attempts to conquer Everest *were defeated* by the weather or the lack of oxygen.

(h) First, a good base camp *will be constructed* near the foot of the mountain.

(i) For many weeks, the mountains *were enveloped* in thick cloud.

(j) The climbers *were* at first *puzzled* by the red flag attached to the aluminium pole.

Exercise 4 When we turn active voice to passive voice we take the natural object of the verb and make it subject. Take the objects of the verbs in the following active sentences, and make them the subjects, turning the verbs into the passive voice. Notice in these examples that we can retain the original subject by putting it after the word "by".

Active: My grandfather *was designing* that bridge in 1942.

Passive: That bridge *was being designed* by my grandfather in 1942.

But often there is no point in doing so.

Active: People *find* anemones in rock pools.

Passive: Anemones *are found* in rock pools.

Be careful to keep the tenses the same, in the passive.

(a) Aunt Jane rode this bicycle.

(b) A scorer keeps the score in cricket.

(c) The voters elected him to Parliament.

(d) They sell vinegar here by the litre.

(e) A special deputation will meet the Queen.

(f) Someone will launch the new liner on Friday.

(g) A primitive man probably invented the wheel by accident.

(h) A bullet or something has wounded the general in the arm.

(i) A shower of tomatoes, bad eggs, cabbages and other rubbish met the official as he spoke.

(j) They are postponing the match until next week.

Exercise 5 All the following statements are **ambiguous**, that is to say, each has more than one possible meaning. Try to state clearly what two (or more) meanings each can have; and try to explain, using the grammatical terms you have already learned, why the statement is ambiguous.

For example: I hope I am well on the way up.
This could mean:

1 I hope I am in good health during this ascent.

2 I hope I have made good progress towards the top.

In 1, "well" would be an adjective, complement of "am"; in 2, "well" is an adverb, modifying the phrase "on the way".

(a) The ascent was for experienced climbers only in the summer season.

(b) The Climbing Committee made an alteration in the route that was intended to help beginners.

(c) Chris found Doug a reliable man to rope with.

(d) The woman climber was a mother with a very young baby who was able to equal the best of the men.

(e) She seems to like rock-climbing better than you.

(f) We could see them on the summit waving a flag from the hotel.

(g) He looked long and hard when he reached the summit.

(h) They were on the highest peak of a mountain range that had never before been conquered.

(i) Their boots were no good on the ice patches because they were so slippery.

(j) We descended to our companion on the rope.

(k) Headline:

FAMOUS ROCK CLIMBER HURT ON FACE

(l) Headline:

MOUNTAIN GUIDES COACH IN SNOW

234

For your own writing

1 Several of the world-wide problems facing mankind are closely linked to each other. Discuss the connection of the energy crisis (look again at the extract from Ray Dafter's book, on pages 229–30) with the problems of pollution (by oil, by mining and chemical industries, and by the waste products from nuclear power), and the problems of population growth and how to grow and distribute enough food for the world.

Write a short story or a discussion essay in which you imagine yourself transported ahead in time about fifty or a hundred years. Show what changes you think will have happened by then. Will people have found new sources of energy, to replace "fossil fuels"? Will the world's population still be growing? Will there be enough food for everyone, perhaps from fish-farming or protein-rich vegetables? Will people still be using vast amounts of energy travelling and moving goods about, or will effective, simple communications mean that we can work, learn and enjoy our leisure in our own homes? Will the natural world be better preserved and looked after, or will people still be cutting down vast forests and forcing rare animals, birds, fish and plants into extinction?

2 Write a shortened, impersonal version of the story of the final ascent of Everest by Doug Scott and Dougal Haston in 1975, using only about 200 words. Use mainly your own words, but base your account closely on the two given in the extract, and do not add completely imaginary details. Write in the third person (both the accounts in the extract are in the *first* person). Include details of the snow, the slopes the two men climbed, what they found at the summit, how they reacted to the achievement and to the view, and of the weather at the time.

For talk and action

1 Do some simple research into possible answers to the following questions about man and his natural environment; prepare either a written folder or an illustrated talk on at least one of these topics. They might be suitable for some group research.

(a) The energy crisis: what do people need energy and fuel for, and in what ways can we either manage with less or find new, cheap and safe sources of energy to replace fossil fuels and nuclear power?

(b) World food supplies: how can starvation and malnutrition be reduced or eliminated? Will we need to use new methods of food production (e.g. fish-farming or growing protein-rich vegetables)?

(c) Pollution: how can we prevent the damage done by oil-slicks, chemical leaks, the large-scale use of artificial fertilisers or pesticides, and the waste products from nuclear power-stations?

(d) Endangered animals and plants: what various land, sea or air animals, or insects or plants, have been exterminated over the past one hundred years? What should we do to conserve and preserve our natural environment? What effects might it have if we clear the world of jungles and plough the grasslands? Should fishing and hunting be more strictly controlled?

(e) Our use of space: in what ways may we either improve or threaten the world we live in by exploring the solar system, visiting the moon or other planets, or putting up more satellites and space stations to orbit the earth?

2 Find out about the life and discoveries of famous explorers:

John Cabot	Sir Martin Frobisher	Ferdinand Magellan
H. M. Stanley	Christopher Columbus	Francisco Pizarro
James Cook	David Livingstone	Vasco Da Gama
Henry Hudson	Sir Ernest Shackleton	Roald Amundsen
Mungo Park	Sir Walter Raleigh	Abel Tasman.
Marco Polo	Auguste and Jean Piccard	

Each member of the class should then make up two questions based on their lives, suitable for a class quiz later.

3 Find out what opportunities there are today for young people to find challenge and adventure. What are: The Duke of Edinburgh's Award Scheme, Outward Bound courses, Voluntary Service Overseas, International Voluntary Service, the British Schools Exploring Society (or the Royal Geographical Society)? How would you set about (a) learning rock-climbing, pot-holing or canoeing, (b) going

236

fell-walking or pony-trekking with organised parties, and (c) planning a tour using Youth Hostels?

4 Prepare a talk or an illustrated folder on rock-climbing and mountaineering. Include equipment, techniques and some outstanding achievements in this field.

For further reading

Everest the Hard Way edited by CHRIS BONINGTON (Hodder & Stoughton; Arrow)
A distinguished climber himself, the author draws on these first-hand accounts of the other members of his memorable 1975 expedition on a previously unconquered route up the highest and most challenging mountain on earth. This is a tense and emotional story of triumph and tragedy under enormous pressure.
It is quoted at length in **My Favourite Mountaineering Stories** by SIR JOHN HUNT (Lutterworth) which is an excellent collection.

Running Out of Fuel – Solving the Energy Puzzle by RAY DAFTER (Wayland)
We now understand something of the cost of an energy-hungry civilisation. This book surveys the startling facts in a clear, direct way and attempts to answer the question of how long we can continue to squander our resources. (Classified as 662.6.)

The Kon-Tiki Expedition by THOR HEYERDAHL (Allen & Unwin; Longman; Penguin)
In this extraordinary, real-life adventure, the author and five companions proved that a primitive balsa-log raft would drift safely 6900 kilometres across the Pacific to Polynesia, a journey they believed peoples from South America had done centuries before. (Classified as 910.4.)

How to Survive by BRIAN HILDRETH (Puffin)
What would you do if you were lost on the mountains or in the forest, or stranded after an air crash? Could you make fire, find food, avoid exposure? This book is packed with good advice for any such emergency. (Classified as 614.)

16 Visiting

Sandra meets Mike when they both take part in an archaeological "dig" on the Maythorn Hills. She invites him back to tea and finds that her grandmother, Mrs Leigh, does not altogether approve of her choice of a friend. Before tea Mike and Sandra have been upstairs to wash their hands . . .

She led the way down. She stopped short on the threshold of one room, and backed out again as though surprised. He had just time to see, over her shoulder, a pale blue room with a big dining-table and nothing on it except a bowl of roses. "Where are we having tea, Gran?" she called.

"Where do you expect, darling?" came Mrs Leigh's voice from nearby. "Isn't it usual to have tea in the drawing-room?"

They went into the next room. Mrs Leigh was sitting at a trolley-table with the cups and saucers in front of her.

"I just thought we'd be sitting up," Sandra apologised. "I mean, we do sometimes use the dining-room when it isn't grown-ups, and – "

"But, darling, I thought you were so insistent that you *are* grown up – or nearly?" Mrs Leigh's expression was mild and innocent, as if her one object in life was to please her granddaughter. But Mike had his doubts. "Do sit down, Michael," she told him.

"Thanks, Mrs Leigh."

He subsided into the nearest armchair and wished he had chosen a smaller one. Subside was the word. It was so deep and soft it engulfed him like a swamp. He wondered desperately how he would ever get out of it again. Meanwhile, how was he going to manage his cup and saucer, the little plate and the finicky little tea-knife and the various good things which were being offered him? . . .

It wasn't only the eating and drinking that were awkward. It was the talk.

Mrs Leigh kept asking questions. She was ever so polite – you couldn't say she was rude – but the general effect was snooty. It was as though she had just turned over a stone, and found Mike underneath it, and wasn't too pleased with what she saw.

She made him feel that even the way he talked was wrong. Not just his accent, but the words he used.

"Your teacher?" she would echo him. "Oh, I see – a *schoolmaster*."

"No, Mrs Leigh, it's a lady."

"Oh, really? And tell me, do you like being taught by a woman?"

"She's not bad."

"I'm very glad to hear *that*."

I suppose (Mike said to himself) that's what people mean when they talk about "gentle" sarcasm. He didn't like sarcasm of any kind.

He ought never to have come, he thought miserably. The idea of tea at Sandra's place had sounded all right, but he wasn't really having tea with Sandra, he was having tea with Sandra's grandmother. Sandra wasn't saying much, though she was looking pretty mad when Mike glanced in her direction. *She* must have spotted what her gran was up to.

"So you don't learn Latin at your school? Dear me, I don't think I have ever met a schoolboy who didn't have to learn Latin. Won't you find it a great handicap if you ever want to go to the University? But no, I suppose you won't be going ... Though one never knows these days. With all these grants and scholarships I suppose there is no reason why anyone shouldn't go to the University." ...

Mike was heartily thankful when the clock struck five and (though he knew it was only a few minutes' walk to the station) he could start saying it was time to go.

"Must you really? I expect you'd like to wash your hands again – honey is such terrible stuff, isn't it?" She smiled. She couldn't have looked nicer or more friendly. "Well, you know your way up, Michael."

240

"Thanks very much, Mrs Leigh. Won't be a sec.," he muttered to Sandra.

He got himself out of the room and upstairs. His hands *were* faintly sticky and the mirror showed a smear which the cream sandwich had left on his lip. Mam might have said the same sort of thing to Rex – made a joke of it, and pushed him out to the scullery to "wipe his whiskers" – but Mam would have done it somehow differently. She wouldn't have made Rex feel small . . .

(from The Maythorn Story by GEOFFREY TREASE)

For discussion

1 Why did Mrs Leigh choose to have tea in the drawing-room?

2 Why was the word "subside" so appropriate?

3 What was sarcastic about Mrs Leigh's "I'm very glad to hear *that*"?

4 Do you agree with Mike in disliking *all* kinds of sarcasm? What is unpleasant about sarcasm? How does it differ from irony?

5 " . . . as if her one object in life was to please her granddaughter." What was Mrs Leigh's object in conducting the tea-party and the conversation in this way? What did Sandra feel about this?

6 Sandra's surname was Clifford and her grandmother had been careful to see that Mike knew he should call her Mrs Leigh. How often does he do so? Does this seem deliberate or unnatural, do you think?

7 How did Mrs Leigh make Mike feel that he talked badly?

8 What were Mrs Leigh's ideas about who should go to university? Would you agree with her?

9 What is the contrast between the way Mrs Leigh dealt with a guest's sticky fingers and face and the way Mike's Mam would have handled the same situation? Does it tell us anything about the two women?

10 "She made him feel that even the way he talked was wrong." Discuss the circumstances in which each of the words in these five sets of four *synonyms* might seem most appropriate:
    (a) drawing-room – sitting-room – lounge – parlour;
    (b) teacher – schoolmaster/mistress – lecturer – tutor;
    (c) grown-ups – adults – elders – seniors;
    (d) women – ladies – females – girls;
    (e) wash your hands – use the bathroom – wipe your whiskers – clean up.

11 Why are the words "dig", "gentle" and "wipe his whiskers" in inverted commas? Explain the use of italics for various words and phrases in this extract.

12 Discuss what you think are the important things to remember when entertaining guests who feel rather strange and bewildered in your house.

13 Are there *any* occasions when it would be right for someone to make a guest "feel small"?

For written answers

1 Which room did they have tea in, and why did this surprise Sandra?

2 What kind of schoolboy do you think Mrs Leigh had met, up to her meeting with Mike?

3 Did Mike need to go at five o'clock? If not, why did he start saying it was time to go?

4 Was Mrs Leigh really using her "tactics" against Mike, or against Sandra? Give an explanation for your answer.

5 Without referring to the rest of this book, make some deductions about the kind of home Mike came from and the kind of boy he was.

For learning about language

Using a present participle, as in Chapter 13 (page 199), is not, of course, the only way of joining sentences more interestingly than with "and", "but", "or", "then", etc. Consider this example:

Sandra had met Mike on a "dig" and she took him home to a tea-party but this was not a great success.

This could be written:

Sandra, who had met Mike on a "dig", took him home to a tea-party, which was not a great success.

The pronouns *who, whom, which, that,* and the adjective *whose* can all be used in this way, but there are certain common mistakes to be avoided in standard written English. As we saw in Chapter 14, "who" is the subject of the verb that follows it, "whom" is the object, and these two are often confused. A good way to remember this is to think of "who" as equivalent to "he" and "whom" as equivalent to "him", as in these sentences:

Sandra met a young man *and he* was very friendly.

Sandra met a young man *who* was very friendly.

Sandra met a young man *and* her grandmother did not like *him*.

Sandra met a young man *whom* her grandmother did not like.

Secondly, *who, whom* refer to people, *which* refers to things:

A person who . . .   A bicycle which . . .

Thirdly, *that* can refer to persons *or* things, and be subject or object, but it must not be confused with *what*:

He is the kind of person *that* you can respect.

(Not "what you can respect"!)

Fourthly, *whose* (= of whom, of which) is easily confused with *who's* (= who is, who has):

Who's there?

Whose book is it?

Exercise 1 Join the two parts of each of the following, replacing the words in italics by "who", "whom", "that", "which" or "whose" and making any other changes necessary in standard written English.

243

(a) Mike bought a lot of cakes *and they* were by no means all sticky.
(b) The assistant has gone off duty *and he* served you.
(c) Pegasus was a horse *and it* was supposed to have wings.
(d) The old lady has moved *and* you used to run errands for *her*.
(e) *Sandra's* parents were abroad *and so* Sandra lived with her grandmother.
(f) Is this the bicycle? Was *this bicycle* stolen?
(g) The thieves stole several items from the store *and they* were never caught.
(h) The thieves stole several items from the store *and they* were never recovered.
(i) The thieves stole several items from the store *and it* was closed for the day.
(j) This is the manager *and his* store was robbed.

Exercise 2 Rewrite the following sentences as standard English, correcting the spelling and grammar.
(a) Those tickets what you gave me were forgeries.
(b) The youth who we saw outside the house was later arrested.
(c) Who is that? The man whose won the competition.
(d) George is the candidate whom, we hope, will be elected chairman of the club.
(e) The candidate which gets two thirds of the votes is elected.
(f) Can you think of anyone in the class who's work is more impressive?
(g) I heard what you said and I found the papers what you asked for.
(h) A man whose lost everything and whose house has been destroyed obviously needs help.
(i) Who's hat is this? Does it belong to anyone that we know?
(j) We asked her what she had done with the money what she had earned.

Exercise 3(a) Write the noun or pronoun of feminine gender that corresponds to each of the following masculine nouns or pronouns.

For example: prince – princess

244

wizard	bull	colt	son-in-law
marquis	peacock	buck	nephew
duke	fox	stag	stallion
heir	him	bachelor	dog
ram	drake	bridegroom	himself

(b) Write the plural forms of the following nouns or pronouns.
For example: tomato – tomatoes

brother-in-law	mine (noun)	handkerchief	jockey
man-of-war	pretence	handful	fly
its	apprentice	fantasy	lass
himself	transparency	octopus	reindeer
mine (pronoun)	radio	memento	mongoose

(c) Give the second person pronouns corresponding to these first person pronouns.

For example: we – you

I	us	ours	myself	ourselves

Exercise 4 In all the following sentences *except one*, there is a lack of "agreement" between subject and verb, or elsewhere in the sentence; for instance, in some there is a change from plural to singular:

They was quite sure they was right.

which should be either:

"They were . . ." or "He/She was . . ."

Rewrite in standard English the following sentences, making corrections wherever necessary (but do *not* alter the tenses).

(a) There was plenty of opportunities for promotion.

(b) I was going to give ourselves a treat.

(c) Half a kilo of tomatoes were being sold for seventy pence.

(d) Each of the children at the party had their own pads and pencils.

(e) Give John and I a chance, and we shall succeed.

(f) She were a real beauty, that boat was!

(g) Let each of us return to his own house for the night.

(h) He and she then find herself in a very clean and richly furnished room.

(i) There are not one man in thousands who knows that secret.

(j) Of the two milk bottles, neither were empty and one was full to the top.

Exercise 5 Sandra invited Mike to tea quite informally, without a written invitation. If she had been arranging a larger party (perhaps for a birthday) she would probably have used a written invitation card and expected a written reply, so that she would know how many guests to prepare for. Invitation cards can be bought to suit all occasions, but it is often more friendly and personal (and cheaper!) to make your own.

Very formal invitations are traditionally in the third person (as if both host and guest were acting through a secretary):

> *Lady Amelia Jones*
> *requests the pleasure of the company of*
> *John Fortescue*
> *at a soirée at her home*
> *on Friday, 10th August, 19—*
> *at 8 o'clock.*
>
> *R.S.V.P. to*
> *The Glade,*
> *Botsworth,*
> *Hants.,*
> *SO12 8PL.*   *Dress optional*

The answer should also be in the third person:

> *John Fortescue*
> *thanks Lady Amelia Jones*
> *for her kind invitation*
> *to a soirée at her home*
> *on Friday, 10th August 19—,*
> *at 8 o'clock.*
> *He is pleased to accept.*

(a) What is a soirée?

(b) At what time of day would you expect to go to a cocktail party, or to a sherry party, or to a wedding breakfast?

(c) What kind of food would you expect to be offered to eat at each of these: a dinner party, a cheese and wine party, a barbecue, a buffet lunch?

(d) What does R.S.V.P. stand for, and what does this mean in English?

For your own writing

1 For most of us, most of the time, less formal (and more friendly) invitations are more appropriate. Here is the kind of letter Sandra might have written to Mike to invite him to a birthday party, if Mrs Leigh had not disapproved of him so much. Notice that she includes the time the party will end – perhaps her grandmother made her do this because she had visions of a noisy teenage party going on all night. Anyway, it will help Mike when it comes to looking up trains home.

> *Apple Garth,*
> *Beacon Lane,*
> *Little Maythorn,*
> *Somerset,*
> *LM6 5ST.*
> *1st July, 19——.*

Dear Mike,

I am having a small party here on Saturday, July 16th, from 6 o'clock until about 10.00 p.m., to celebrate my birthday, and I very much hope you will be able to come.

Most of the crowd you met up on the Beacon when you were last here will be coming, and we are looking forward to seeing you again.

> *Yours sincerely,*
> *Sandra.*

P.S. Let me know if you can come. I do hope you can.

Write Mike's reply, either accepting or refusing this invitation. Pay careful attention to the correct setting out and punctuation of his address (17 Alma Road, Ninefields, Harborough, HB7 2ST) and the date.

2 When Mike returned home, he found it very difficult to tell his family about having tea at "Apple Garth". He realised that he could not even hint at Mrs Leigh's superior manner without making his parents angry and himself embarrassed. Yet most people have had experiences like Mike's: times when they felt ashamed, embarrassed or inadequate. Try to describe one such experience, whether real or imaginary. Be careful to build up the atmosphere and background with detailed description, and pay particular attention to the *people* involved. Let their appearances and personalities come out as clearly as Mrs Leigh's do in the extract. The incident does not have to be connected with visiting or entertaining, of course, so long as it is (or was) embarrassing.

For talk and action

1 Prepare an article for the class magazine or some talks to the class on giving a party to entertain friends of your own age. Groups might divide the subject between them, including:

Inviting the guests – advice on numbers, invitations, balancing the sexes, etc.

Breaking the ice – introductions, games and other devices to help people mix and get to know each other.

Music and dancing – with ideas on novelty dances.

Team games, noisy games; pencil and paper games.

Party magic, acting or charades.

Food and costs.

Unusual ways of serving the food and drink.

Recommended books for party-givers.

2 Find out more about archaeology. What is a "dig"? What kinds of places do archaeologists dig in? What are they looking for? Find some illustrations of important archaeological discoveries, and some examples of "finds" in your own area. How do archaeologists

date their finds? If you find something of interest, where should you take it, or report it?

Books on archaeology are classified under 913 and 571.

3 An awkward tea-party might be a useful situation for an impromptu play. It should offer scope for very definite characters: proud, nervous, talkative, shy, angry, sarcastic, rude, polite. Decide on a basic situation and set of characters (perhaps using the story of Mike at Sandra's as a starting-point), and then see how the play can be developed spontaneously.

For further reading

The Maythorn Story by GEOFFREY TREASE (Heinemann)
Mike's town world of Harborough and Ninefields, with the difficult girl Shirley next door, and the derelict "island site" where he had played for years, later becomes curiously mixed up with the world of Sandra and archaeological finds on the Maythorn Hills.

Geoffrey Trease is also well known for his exciting historical novels.

Cue for Treason (Puffin) concerns a young actor involved with Robert Cecil's secret service and a plot to kill Queen Elizabeth I.

The Seas of Morning (Puffin) takes a London schoolboy to Rhodes with the Knights of St John.

Introducing Archaeology by MAGNUS MAGNUSSON (Bodley Head)
Here is an interesting outline of the history of archaeology from the time of the Babylonian archaeologist, King Nabonidus, to the modern technique of radio-carbon dating. (Classified as 913.031.)

The Changeling by ZILPHA KEATLEY SNYDER (Lutterworth)
This is a shrewd, entertaining story of two girls growing up in California: Martha, easily frightened, but from a respectable, stable home; and her close friend, Ivy, from the notorious Carson family. Ivy insists that she really is a changeling from another world.

Digging Up the Past by SIR LEONARD WOOLLEY (Greenwood)
This is a personal, expert account of work, by one of the most famous British archaeologists. (Classified as 913.031.)

17 Run for Your Life

The Wizard Ged has finally brought together the two lost halves of the ring of Erreth-Akbe that has the power to bring peace to Earthsea; but he is now held prisoner in the deepest of dungeons by Tenar, priestess of the Tombs of Atuan and servant of the Dark Ones. Ged has convinced Tenar that she must trust him, so that they can both escape from the power of the Dark Ones . . .

As she fumbled at the door, unlocking it, he said, "I wish I had my staff," and she replied, still whispering. "It's just outside the door. I brought it."

"Why did you bring it?" he asked curiously.

"I thought of . . . taking you to the door. Letting you go."

"That was a choice you didn't have. You could keep me a slave, and be a slave; or set me free, and come free with me. Come, little one, take courage, turn the key."

She turned the dragon-hafted key and opened the door on the low, black corridor. She went out of the Treasury of the Tombs with the ring of Erreth-Akbe on her arm, and the man followed her.

There was a low vibration, not quite a noise, in the rock of the walls and floor and vaulting. It was like distant thunder, like something huge falling a great way off.

The hair on her head rose up, and without stopping to reason she blew out the candle in the tin lantern . . .

But he did not move. She realised that she must lead him. Only she knew the way out of the Labyrinth, and he waited to follow her. She set out, stooping because the tunnel here was so low, but keeping a pretty good pace. From unseen cross-passages came a cold breath and a sharp, dank odour, the lifeless smell of the huge hollowness beneath them. When the passage grew a little higher and she could stand upright, she went slower, counting her steps as they approached the pit. Lightfooted, aware of all her movements, he

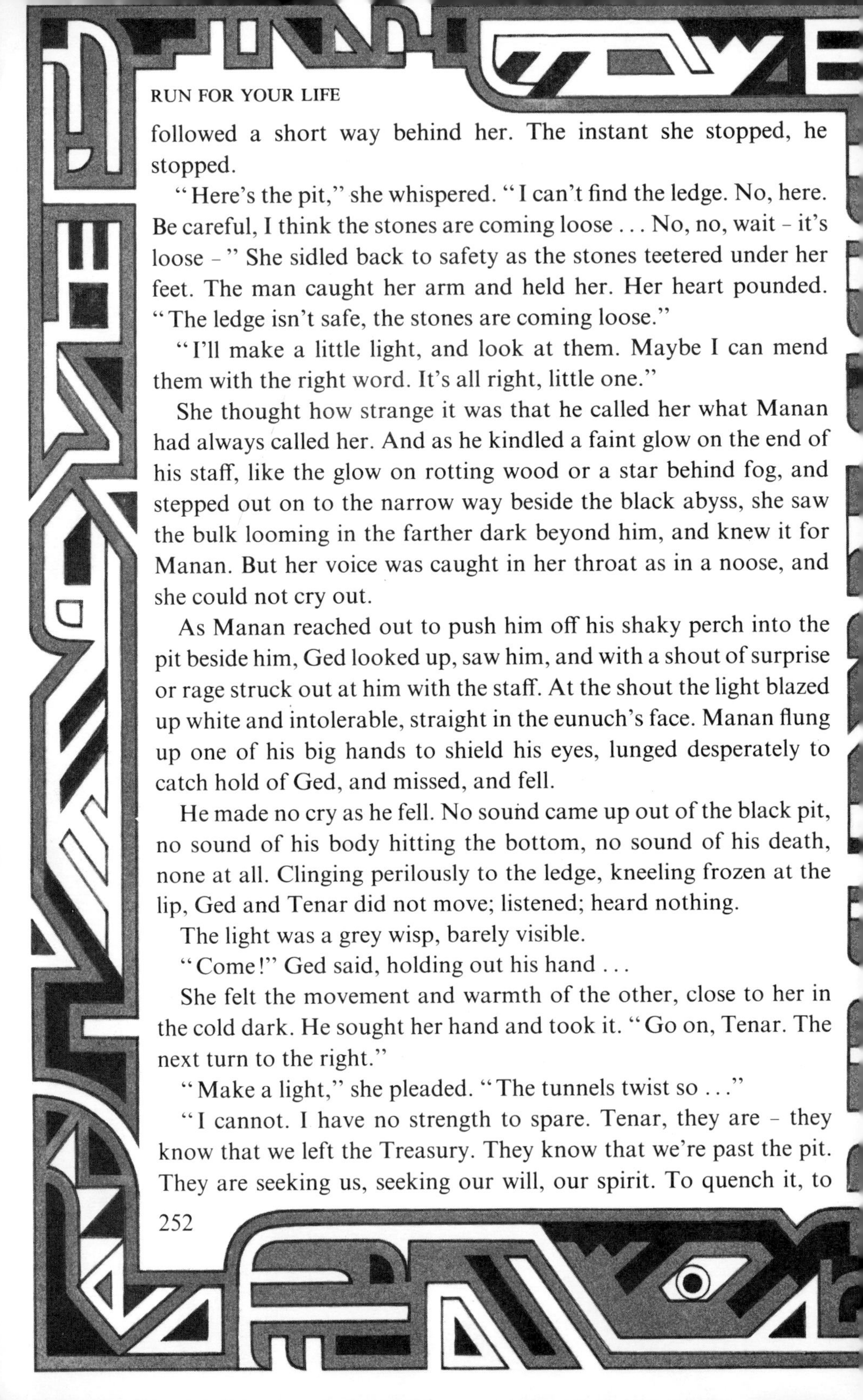

followed a short way behind her. The instant she stopped, he stopped.

"Here's the pit," she whispered. "I can't find the ledge. No, here. Be careful, I think the stones are coming loose . . . No, no, wait – it's loose – " She sidled back to safety as the stones teetered under her feet. The man caught her arm and held her. Her heart pounded. "The ledge isn't safe, the stones are coming loose."

"I'll make a little light, and look at them. Maybe I can mend them with the right word. It's all right, little one."

She thought how strange it was that he called her what Manan had always called her. And as he kindled a faint glow on the end of his staff, like the glow on rotting wood or a star behind fog, and stepped out on to the narrow way beside the black abyss, she saw the bulk looming in the farther dark beyond him, and knew it for Manan. But her voice was caught in her throat as in a noose, and she could not cry out.

As Manan reached out to push him off his shaky perch into the pit beside him, Ged looked up, saw him, and with a shout of surprise or rage struck out at him with the staff. At the shout the light blazed up white and intolerable, straight in the eunuch's face. Manan flung up one of his big hands to shield his eyes, lunged desperately to catch hold of Ged, and missed, and fell.

He made no cry as he fell. No sound came up out of the black pit, no sound of his body hitting the bottom, no sound of his death, none at all. Clinging perilously to the ledge, kneeling frozen at the lip, Ged and Tenar did not move; listened; heard nothing.

The light was a grey wisp, barely visible.

"Come!" Ged said, holding out his hand . . .

She felt the movement and warmth of the other, close to her in the cold dark. He sought her hand and took it. "Go on, Tenar. The next turn to the right."

"Make a light," she pleaded. "The tunnels twist so . . ."

"I cannot. I have no strength to spare. Tenar, they are – they know that we left the Treasury. They know that we're past the pit. They are seeking us, seeking our will, our spirit. To quench it, to devour it. I must keep that alight. All my strength is going into that. I must withstand them; with you. With your help. We must go on.''

''There is no way out,'' she said, but she took one step forward. Then she took another, hesitant as if beneath each step the black hollow void gaped open, the emptiness under the earth. The warm, hard grip of his hand was on her hand. They went forward . . .

''We are coming to . . .'' Her voice failed her.

''To the centre of the darkness. I know. Yet we're out of the Labyrinth. What ways out of the Undertomb are there?''

''Only one. The door you entered doesn't open from within. The way goes through the cavern and up passages to a trapdoor in a room behind the Throne. In the Hall of the Throne.''

''Then we must go that way . . .''

''I cannot go there.''

''Tenar, I hold the roof up over our heads, this moment. I keep the walls from closing in upon us. I keep the ground from opening beneath our feet. I have done this since we passed the pit where their servant waited. If I can hold off the earthquake, do you fear to meet one human soul with me? Trust me, as I have trusted you! Come with me now.''

They went forward.

The endless tunnel opened out. The sense of a greater air met them, an enlarging of the dark. They had entered the great cave beneath the Tombstones . . .

At the entrance so great a weight of blind and dire hatred came pressing down upon her, like the weight of the earth itself, that she cowered and without knowing it cried out aloud, ''They are here! They are here!''

''Then let them know that we are here,'' the man said, and from his staff and hands leapt forth a white radiance that broke as a sea-wave breaks in sunlight, against the thousand diamonds of the roof and walls: a glory of light, through which the two fled, straight across the great cavern, their shadows racing from them into the white traceries and the glittering crevices and the empty, open grave. To a low doorway they ran, down the tunnel, stooping over, she

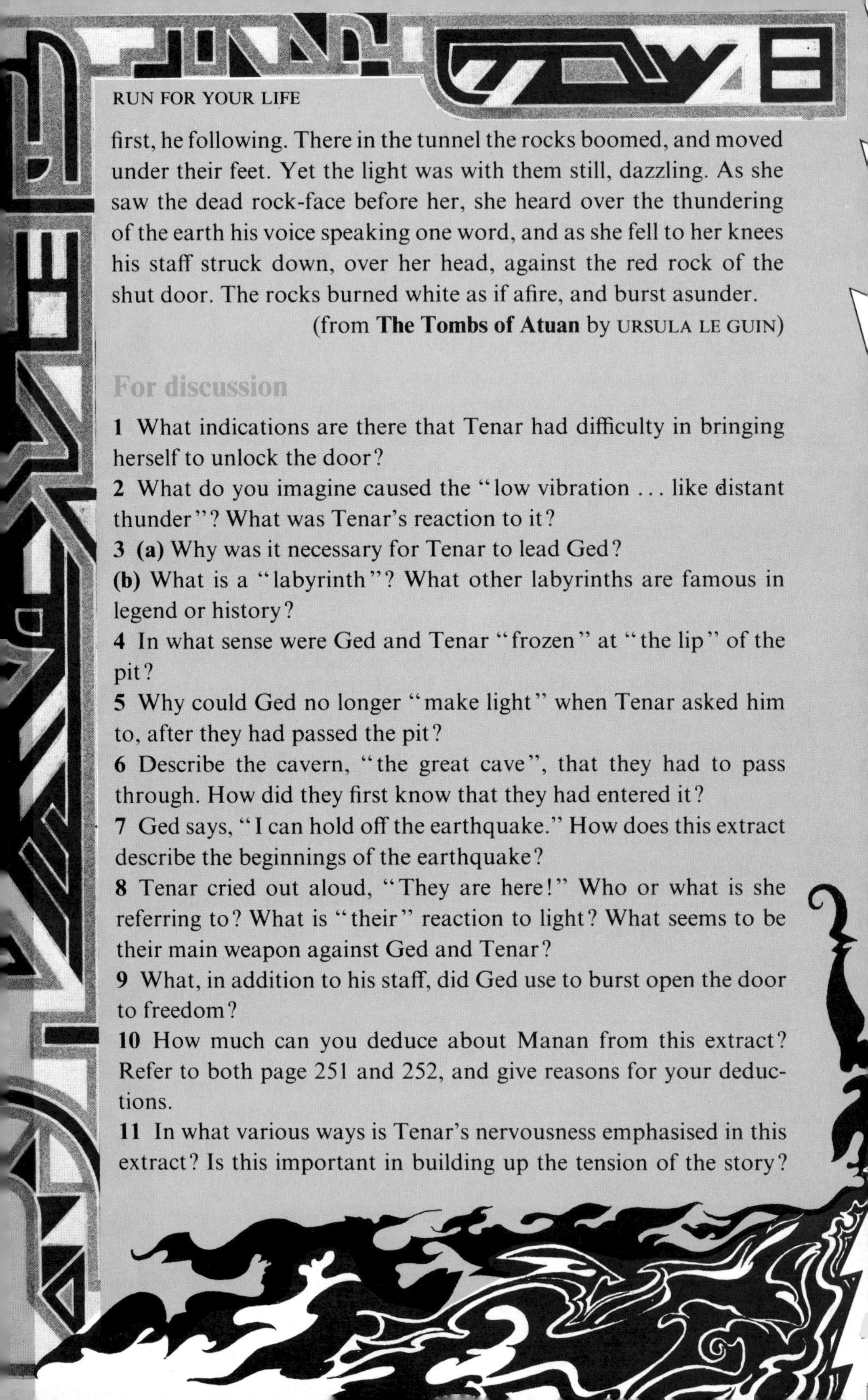

first, he following. There in the tunnel the rocks boomed, and moved under their feet. Yet the light was with them still, dazzling. As she saw the dead rock-face before her, she heard over the thundering of the earth his voice speaking one word, and as she fell to her knees his staff struck down, over her head, against the red rock of the shut door. The rocks burned white as if afire, and burst asunder.

(from **The Tombs of Atuan** by URSULA LE GUIN)

For discussion

1 What indications are there that Tenar had difficulty in bringing herself to unlock the door?

2 What do you imagine caused the "low vibration … like distant thunder"? What was Tenar's reaction to it?

3 (a) Why was it necessary for Tenar to lead Ged?

(b) What is a "labyrinth"? What other labyrinths are famous in legend or history?

4 In what sense were Ged and Tenar "frozen" at "the lip" of the pit?

5 Why could Ged no longer "make light" when Tenar asked him to, after they had passed the pit?

6 Describe the cavern, "the great cave", that they had to pass through. How did they first know that they had entered it?

7 Ged says, "I can hold off the earthquake." How does this extract describe the beginnings of the earthquake?

8 Tenar cried out aloud, "They are here!" Who or what is she referring to? What is "their" reaction to light? What seems to be their main weapon against Ged and Tenar?

9 What, in addition to his staff, did Ged use to burst open the door to freedom?

10 How much can you deduce about Manan from this extract? Refer to both page 251 and 252, and give reasons for your deductions.

11 In what various ways is Tenar's nervousness emphasised in this extract? Is this important in building up the tension of the story?

12 How does this extract emphasise the humanity of Ged, in contrast to the cruel and impersonal forces of evil against which he struggles?

13 Discuss the meanings of the following:

"dragon-hafted"   "to quench it"
"a sharp dank odour"   "she cowered"
"she sidled back"   "white traceries"
"the stones teetered"   "glittering crevices"
"the black abyss"   "burst asunder".

For written answers

Questions 1 to 5 can be answered from the first half of the extract, down to: " 'Come!' Ged said, holding out his hand . . ." on page 252.

1 "That was a choice you didn't have." What choices *were* open to Tenar at this point in the story?

2 What made Tenar go slower, "counting her steps"?

3 What form of address had Manan always used when talking to Tenar?

4 Ged, beside the pit, is described as being on a "shaky perch". Where exactly was he standing at that moment?

5 Explain in your own words how Manan died.

The next question should be answered from the whole extract.

6 List (a) at least three ways in which Ged's humanity is emphasised, and (b) at least three ways in which his supernatural powers, as a Wizard, are illustrated. Write your answer as a continuous short paragraph, mainly in your own words.

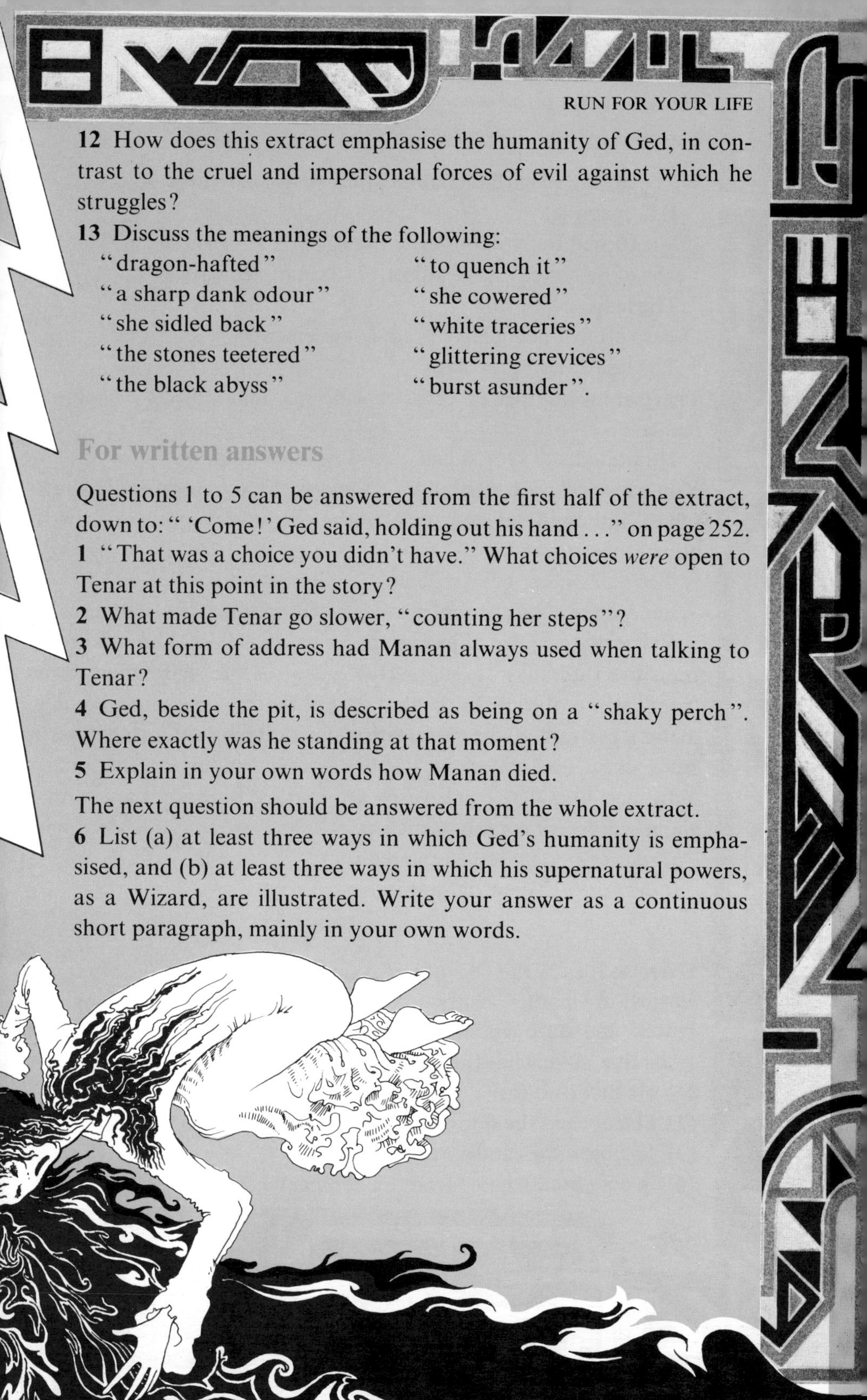

For learning about language

We have seen in earlier chapters that some verbs take objects.

For example:

She turned the dragon-hafted *key*.

Verbs of being may have adjectives as complements:

The ledge is not *safe*.

Other verbs of being have noun complements:

The light was a grey *wisp*.

There are a number of verbs that do not take objects or complements:

He waited.   She sidled.   We are coming.

You cannot "wait anything" – these verbs are complete in themselves, although, of course, adverbs (or adverb phrases) can be added to such verbs:

The hair on her head rose up.   She set out.

What are the subjects, verbs and adverbs in those two sentences?

Verbs that require objects to make complete sense are said to be **transitive** (literally: "going across", that is, the sense goes across from verb to object). Verbs that do not require objects (or complements) are said to be **intransitive**. Dictionaries often label verbs *trans.* or *v.t.* and *intrans.* or *v.i.*; find some examples in a dictionary. You may find that some verbs are marked as both, each with a slightly different meaning, such as:

Transitive: Ged moved the red rock.

Intransitive: Tenar did not move.

Exercise 1(a) Write out the verbs (in full, bearing in mind what you learned in Chapter 12 about verb phrases) from the following sentences, and state whether each is transitive or intransitive. If it is transitive, state what the object word is.

(1) He made no cry.

(2) She opened the door on the low, black corridor.

(3) She blew the candle out.

(4) A cold breath came from unseen passages.

(5) He followed behind her.

(6) He followed her.

(7) Manan lunged desperately at Ged.

(8) The light blazed up, straight in Manan's face.

(9) She could not cry out.

(10) I can mend them with the right word.

(b) Make up short sentences using each of the following verbs (1) transitively, with an object, and (2) intransitively, without an object.

For example:

ride   (1) He rode his bicycle home.

                (2) He rode very well.

fight	return	turn	run
cover	leave	play	slide
sweep	cook		

Exercise 2 Many verbs can be transitive or intransitive, but in a few cases standard written English has two similar verbs, one transitive, the other intransitive.

For example:

To lie (intransitive) = to be in a horizontal position.

To lay (transitive) = to put (something) down.

Other examples are to fall (intrans.), to fell (trans.) and to rise (intrans.), to raise (trans.).

"Lie" is particularly confusing, because its past tense is "lay", and because there is a third verb, "to lie" (intrans.) = to tell an untruth. Here are the various forms of these three verbs: which is which?

He lies, he lied, he is lying, he has lied.

He lies, he lay, he is lying, he has lain.

He lays, he laid, he is laying, he has laid.

Rewrite the following sentences, choosing the correct standard English form of lie, lay etc. to fill each of the gaps (only *one* word is required for each gap).

(a) I ____ awake most of last night.

(b) Dad asked me to ____ the table.

(c) He cackled as if he had just ____ an egg.

(d) He ____ to us then when he said he was ____ in the bushes listening to the smugglers.

(e) The grass where the oak beam had ____ was flattened and discoloured.

(f) Mother was ____ down, trying to rest.

(g) The professor ____ the specimen down carefully on the sheet of glass.

(h) ____ that parcel down for a minute, John.

(i) Our horse was then ____ fourth in the race.

Exercise 3 Read, and discuss any difficult words in, the following description of a natural disaster, a hurricane on the United States coast of the Gulf of Mexico.

Hurricane Frederic was far from its peak of fury as I drove through the deserted streets of Mobile, Alabama, for a last look. But already roaring winds loaded with rain funneled between buildings. Traffic lights danced crazily on their wire strings, then crashed into the streets. Signs, tree limbs, garbage cans, and sheet metal hurtled through the air. Windows popped; glass sprayed like shrapnel.

I retreated to my hotel about 8:30 p.m., as the center, or eye, of Frederic neared western Mobile. Eventually the city was enveloped in the most violent sector of the storm: the "eyewall", a maelstrom of wind and rain raging around the hurricane's calm core. Wind spiraled in bands towards the eye, signaled by a banshee wail that rent the night. Lightning flashed down the wall of the sky; thunder shook the hotel, and once a dread hurricane-spawned tornado rumbled past in the darkness. More than a few who have heard these horrendous noises of a hurricane have died of heart attacks.

The wind strengthened steadily until, in the fiercest assault of the century on Mobile Bay, Frederic lashed the coast with sustained winds of 133 miles per hour. The maximum gusts of history's great hurricanes have rarely been clocked, because most measuring instruments cannot stand before them. At the mouth of Mobile Bay, wind gauges on Dauphin Island recorded gusts of 145 miles per hour before Frederic swept them away. Peak gusts rocked the hotel with battering-ram blows. The floor of my room swayed like the deck of a ship ...

The thudding strikes of wind came harder and more often as the night wore on. Gusts slammed through gaping windows and knocked the inner walls of some rooms out into the hallways. Sometime near midnight Frederic jolted the entire hotel, cutting off electric power and plunging the building into darkness.

With other guests I groped down emergency stairs to the lobby. Water streamed from the cracked ceiling. Broken glass crunched under our feet. Hours later I went out into a gray, gusty dawn to walk the streets of a brutally beaten city.

Mobile was a shambles. Roofs were torn off, glass and even brick walls caved in, church steeples toppled, debris piled high. At Bellingrath Gardens, a luxuriantly landscaped estate, tornadoes like artillery fire had topped and uprooted oaks, pines, and other trees. Throughout Mobile, giant live oaks that had stood for two centuries now lay blocking avenues and flattening houses.

In only a few hours Hurricane Frederic had swept Mobile back to an earlier era. Gone were air conditioning, ice, television, telephones, and, in many areas, drinking water. Gasoline could not be pumped, newspaper presses were silent, and only candles and lanterns dispelled night-time darkness.

(from an article by BEN FUNK in the **National Geographic Magazine**)

Ben Funk refers to himself as a "veteran Florida reporter". In what ways is this style of writing what you would expect from a journalist who has to make such horrors seem real? Notice for instance his use of repetition, alliteration and comparisons. Now, answer the following questions about the extract, in writing.

1 Ben Funk talks of a "last look". What does he mean?

2 Describe in your own words the "center" of a hurricane, making clear what the "eyewall" is.

3 What do you think is the relationship between a "hurricane" and a "tornado", according to the extract? How do they differ?

4 (a) What was the maximum wind speed recorded on this occasion?

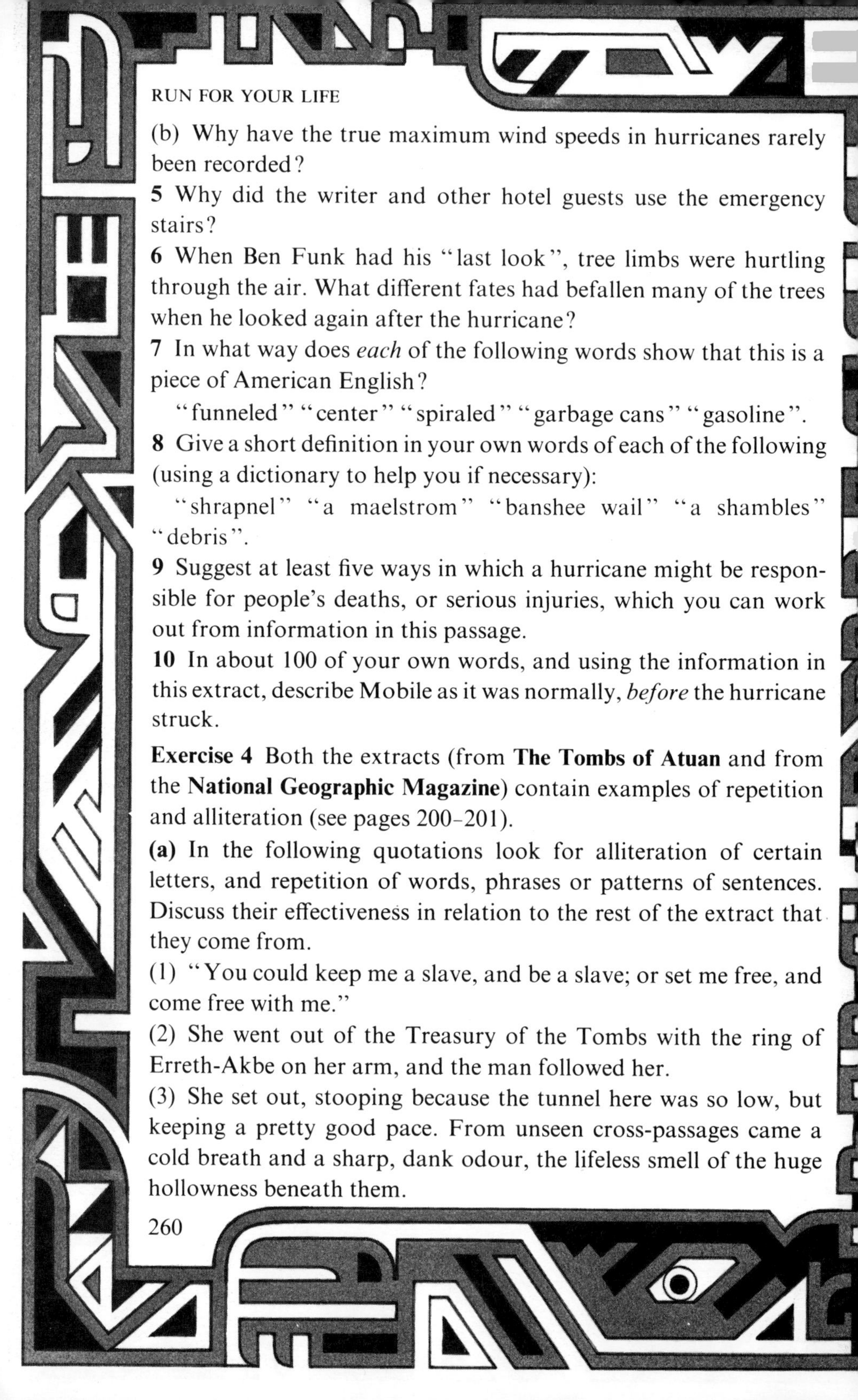

(b) Why have the true maximum wind speeds in hurricanes rarely been recorded?

5 Why did the writer and other hotel guests use the emergency stairs?

6 When Ben Funk had his "last look", tree limbs were hurtling through the air. What different fates had befallen many of the trees when he looked again after the hurricane?

7 In what way does *each* of the following words show that this is a piece of American English?

"funneled" "center" "spiraled" "garbage cans" "gasoline".

8 Give a short definition in your own words of each of the following (using a dictionary to help you if necessary):

"shrapnel" "a maelstrom" "banshee wail" "a shambles" "debris".

9 Suggest at least five ways in which a hurricane might be responsible for people's deaths, or serious injuries, which you can work out from information in this passage.

10 In about 100 of your own words, and using the information in this extract, describe Mobile as it was normally, *before* the hurricane struck.

Exercise 4 Both the extracts (from **The Tombs of Atuan** and from the **National Geographic Magazine**) contain examples of repetition and alliteration (see pages 200–201).

(a) In the following quotations look for alliteration of certain letters, and repetition of words, phrases or patterns of sentences. Discuss their effectiveness in relation to the rest of the extract that they come from.

(1) "You could keep me a slave, and be a slave; or set me free, and come free with me."

(2) She went out of the Treasury of the Tombs with the ring of Erreth-Akbe on her arm, and the man followed her.

(3) She set out, stooping because the tunnel here was so low, but keeping a pretty good pace. From unseen cross-passages came a cold breath and a sharp, dank odour, the lifeless smell of the huge hollowness beneath them.

(4) "Tenar, they are – they know that we left the Treasury. They know that we're past the pit. They are seeking us, seeking our will, our spirit. To quench it, to devour it."

(5) More than a few who have heard these horrendous noises of a hurricane have died of heart attacks.

(6) Roofs were torn off, glass and even brick walls caved in, church steeples toppled, debris piled high.

(b) Find and write out at least five more similar short quotations which are examples of alliteration, repetition, or both. Write your own comments on each to explain what sounds or words or phrases are repeated. If possible, add your own comments on their effectiveness in making the writing more exciting, powerful, or vivid.

For your own writing

1 The extract from **The Tombs of Atuan** contains a supernatural earthquake, whereas the one from the **National Geographic Magazine** (in Exercise 3) describes a natural disaster caused by Hurricane Frederic. Both include vivid, frightening description. In the second one a journalist is trying to help magazine readers to grasp the scale of the destruction and the power of the wind. If there have been other natural disasters in the news recently – caused by floods, volcanic eruptions, gales, even blizzards – it would be interesting to collect different accounts of them, and compare them. Do the journalists seem sympathetic to the victims of the disasters?

Write your own newspaper report of the effects of any major disaster or accident, real or imaginary. Remember that a newspaper expects brief, action-packed reports, with much "human interest" based on eyewitness accounts and interviews, and personal detail about or from survivors or rescuers. Notice how Ben Funk has made his account both personal and factual, vividly exciting yet clear in its explanations.

2 Write a short story involving an escape of some kind (though not repeating anything you wrote in Chapter 4 in connection with a disaster underground). Your escape could be from any kind of imprisonment, pursuit or natural disaster. Notice how Ursula Le Guin has built up the tension in the extract at the beginning of this chapter, and how her language, the comparisons and the descriptions generally, all make us share the intense feelings of the two main characters as they run for their lives in the dark through the Labyrinth.

For talk and action

1 Collect information on any recent international relief effort, following some natural disaster such as an earthquake or a violent storm. Famine and homelessness caused by natural agencies such as drought and flood and also by man-made political tensions and revolutions are common in the world. Put together newspaper cuttings and pictures from magazines, and find out the geographical and historical or scientific background, with suitable maps and diagrams. All this could be combined into a folder or wall display, and might then lead on to some kind of fund-raising effort to aid the relief operations.

2 Write business letters seeking information from the main international relief organisations, such as:

> Oxfam, 274 Banbury Road, Oxford, OX2 7DZ.
> Christian Aid, 240 Ferndale Road, London, SW9 8BH.
> Save the Children Fund, Mary Datchelor House, 17 Grove Lane, Camberwell, London, SE5 8RD.
> The British Red Cross Society, 9 Grosvenor Crescent, London, SW1X 7EJ.

Send only one letter on behalf of the class in each case! The posters and pamphlets could then be used to make a display explaining the scope of each organisation's work: both their long-term aims and how they act in emergencies.

3 Prepare talks on topics suggested in 1 and 2 above, and hold a more general discussion on the importance of international relief work. What preparations should be made for possible future disasters? What safeguards are needed to make sure that relief really reaches the people it is intended to help?

For further reading

The Tombs of Atuan by URSULA LE GUIN (Gollancz; Heinemann; Penguin)
Although a self-contained story, this is the middle of three related tales in which Ursula Le Guin has created a whole world where reality and fantasy meet. In the first book **A Wizard of Earthsea**, the young Ged grows in his knowledge, till pride tempts him to let loose evil that he alone must in the end defeat. This second story concerns the quest for the Ring of Erreth-Akbe in defiance of the dark forces of the underworld. The third, **The Farthest Shore**, takes the hero, older and wiser now, on the longest and most dangerous journey of all, to a final battle that tries to the utmost his strength and magic power.

A Valley Full of Thieves by CHRIS HAWES (Macmillan; Topliners)
Brother and sister seek safety in a war-torn land, when both King's side and People's side are against them.

Beyond the Dark River by MONICA HUGHES (Hamish Hamilton)
In this exciting story, set in Canada after a future disaster, an Indian boy and girl from a remote community escape, to learn more of the world and themselves.

The Wind Eye by ROBERT WESTALL (Macmillan; Peacock; Penguin)
Could a saint a thousand years dead work miracles? The Studdard family, each faced with challenging and dangerous forces, have to decide about St Cuthbert.

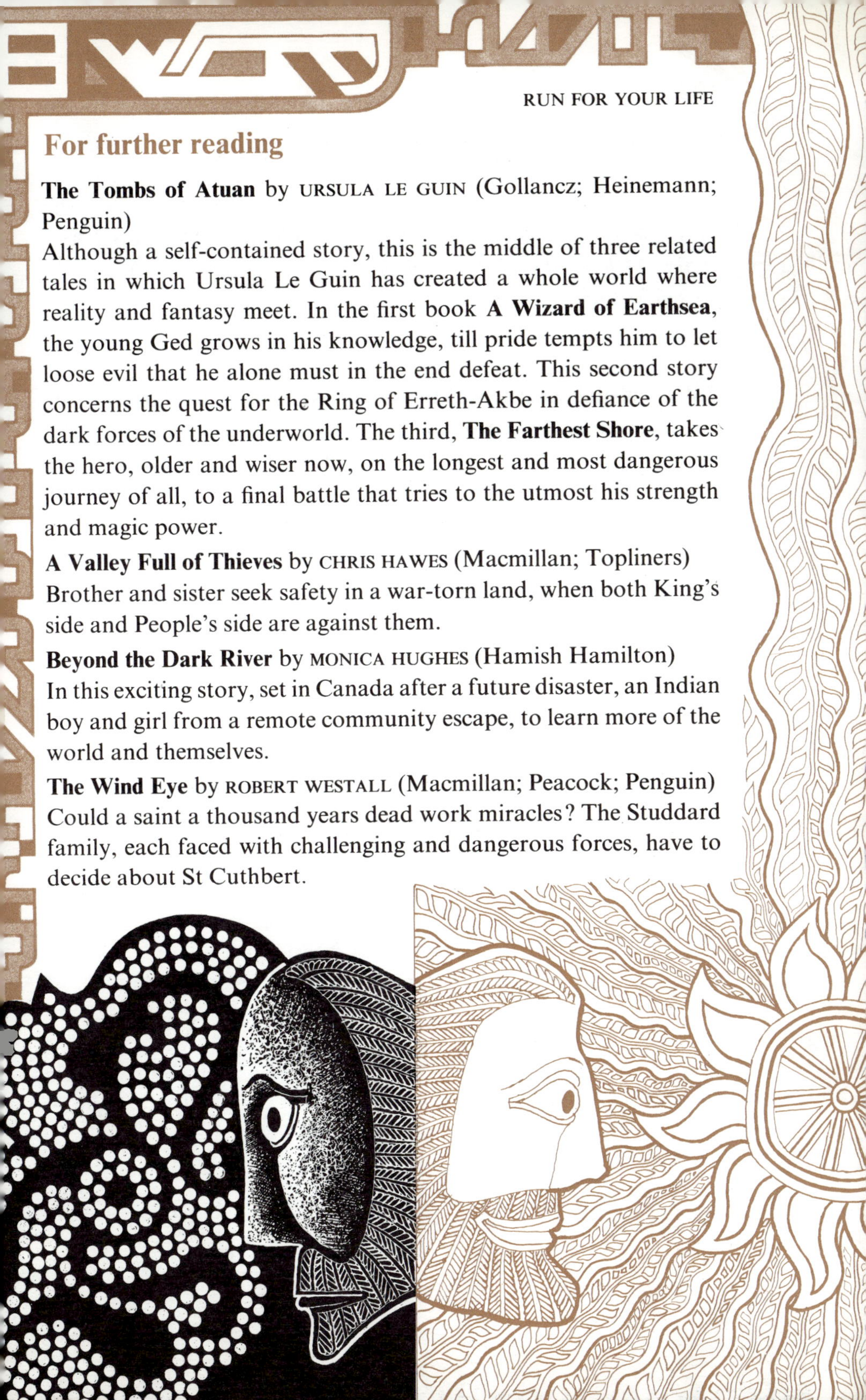

18 Sharpening Your Senses

This story is set in rural Scotland in the 1930s. Jinty and her older sisters, Meg and Linda, have taken to going for walks past the cottage where the blind boy, Toby, lives . . .

Toby was nine, and he was the son of Mr Gillan, the Earl's factor. He hadn't always been blind. That was due to an illness he'd had when he was a baby – before his mother died, they said. Now it was Mrs Tait, a sort of nurse-housekeeper, who looked after him; but Toby had very little company apart from her, because his father worked long hours on the business of the estate. The house that went with Mr Gillan's job, also, lay a good half-mile deep in the

woods, which meant that hardly anyone used the path leading past the foot of its garden. And Toby was desperate for company. They found that out the very first time they saw him in the garden playing about with a big coloured ball, kicking it into the air and then listening for the sound of it falling so that he could run and get it again.

He could do this quite easily, they noticed. There were no flowers in the garden, no bushes, nothing that could trip him up. The grass was cut very short, too, so that he could always run straight and quite fast, to the ball. He left the ball where it lay, however, that first day he heard their voices, and came running straight to the fence instead, crying out as he ran, "Speak to me! Speak to me, please!"

His hands came stretching through the fence, touching their clothes, feeling the baskets they were carrying for the bramble-picking. They were small hands, white and clean. Toby's skin was all white and clean – not like any other boy they knew. It was delicate, almost transparent, like flower-petals. His eyes were grey, and big. There was a fixed stare to them; and sometimes when he was listening, he flapped his hand in front of them in a sort of

fanning movement, as if this could somehow flap their blindness away.

"Who are you? What're your names? How old are you? Where are you going? What will you do with those baskets? May I touch your faces?"

Toby was full of questions. They told him about themselves, and gave him some of the brambles they had picked on the way to his house. They were big berries, black and ripe, with just the right touch of frost on them to make them sweet. Toby crammed them into his mouth, and the purple juice ran all over, staining his fingers and lips and white face till he looked like a little clown.

"Mrs Tait'll be cross with you," Meg said, and tried to scrub the stains away with her hankie.

"I don't mind. She's always cross," Toby said, and went on asking questions.

Every time they met him he had questions, and it wasn't long before he knew even more about them than they said, because Mrs Tait talked to everybody in the village and knew all the gossip ...

But Toby had other questions that he did persistently ask – all sorts of odd questions they had never expected to hear.

"What colour is the wind?" That was one of the things he wanted to know, and he wouldn't believe it when Meg and Linda said it was no colour at all.

"It is a colour. It is," he insisted. "*You* say which one, Jinty."

"It's the colour of the way it makes you feel," she told him. "A warm wind is gold, and a cold one is grey."

"Don't be daft!" Linda exclaimed. "What's the use of saying things like that when he doesn't even know what colour *is*?"

"I do, I do now," Toby contradicted. "Gold is warm, and grey is cold. How high is the sky, Jinty?"

"It's almost near enough to touch, in winter," she told him. "But in summer, the sky is forever."

Linda laughed at this, but Toby fanned his hand across his eyes and said eagerly, "I can see that! I can see how far away the sky is now."

266

Meg didn't say a thing about Linda laughing that day – not until they had gone on beyond Toby's garden and there was no danger of his hearing her. Then she really did speak her mind about it.

"There's a lot Toby hears that doesn't make sense to him," she said. "You can't expect it to do that – not with him being a blind boy that's never known anything in his life but being shut up in a bare garden. But if Jinty can help him to make his own kind of sense out of it, then you've no right to laugh at either of them. And you'd better not do it again." . . .

"Bring me flowers, Jinty," he begged her. "Please, will you? I want to see what flowers look like, and there's none in my garden."

Linda's mouth silently formed the word "See!", but the look in Meg's eyes stopped the sound of it.

"It's a bit late in the year for flowers, Toby." Cautiously, because she didn't want him to expect too much, she explained. But there were still Michaelmas daisies and dahlias and chrysanthemums to bring in single blooms so that she could let his fingers feel the shape while she tried to describe the colours in ways he could understand.

"Jaggedy-hot" for "red". That was easy. "A sunny day that's still cold." That was easy too, for "yellow". But what could she say for "purple"?

"It's like a taste," she decided eventually. "You think it's going to be jaggedy-hot, like red; but when you do taste it, it slides away into something smoother, and really cold."

Toby laughed at this, and fanned his hand across his eyes as if to make himself see purple, and stuck out his tongue as if he were tasting it. But once the frost had killed all the flowers in her own garden, and in the hedgerows as well, there was nothing she could do except to say she would bring more flowers in spring.

"Snowdrops," she promised. "They're the first through the ground; small flowers, like little white bells dancing around."

"Do they ring like bells?" Toby asked; and she told him, "Of course not, silly. Flowers don't make a noise. You'll have to make the ringing sound yourself if you want to hear bells."

"You really do understand that kid, don't you?" Meg asked, and she felt the sort of embarrassed pleasure she always got from Meg's approval. But Linda immediately said, "They're both crazy, that's why."

(from The Third Eye by MOLLIE HUNTER)

For discussion

1 What is a "factor"? Can you deduce from the extract what kind of job Mr Gillan did?

2 In what ways do (a) Toby's hands and (b) Toby's eyes seem to you appropriate for a blind person?

3 What is another word for "bramble-picking"? What were the girls doing on the day they first met Toby?

4 In what ways was it sensible and in what ways restricting to "shut" Toby "up in a bare garden"?

5 Why didn't Meg criticise Linda for laughing or sneering at Toby, out loud and in front of Toby? What would you have done in those circumstances?

6 In what tone was Linda about to say the word "See!", and why did Meg silently forbid her to say it? What do you think Linda's reaction had been when Meg "spoke her mind"?

7 To whom do you think Jinty "explained" her caution about bringing Toby flowers?

8 Can you describe in words the differences in shape between Michaelmas daisies, dahlias and chrysanthemums?

9 What *different* sensations of touch and taste does Jinty use to help describe various sights to Toby? Can you think of other, similar ideas for describing sights? Try sound and movement as well as touch and taste.

10 Do you think that Linda really does not understand what Jinty is doing, or is there some other reason why she condemns her (and Toby) as "crazy"?

11 How should blind, deaf, physically disabled or mentally handicapped children be treated? Should they be isolated, or kept in ordinary surroundings? Should they (or some of them) go to

special, secluded homes, schools, training centres or hospitals, or should they live as normal a life as possible, mixing all the time with the rest of the community? How do you think they wish to be treated? What do you think their parents want for them? Do you think we spend enough time and money helping handicapped people in this country today?

For written answers

1 What combination of circumstances made Toby "desperate for company"?
2 How did Toby manage to play ball, although he was blind?
3 Why do you think the girls noticed Toby's hands so much?
4 What impression does this extract give you of Mrs Tait?
5 Write a short character sketch of each of the three sisters, as you imagine them after reading this extract, and bringing out the contrasts between them. You should write at least three or four sentences on each one.

SMELLS

Why is it that the poets tell
So little of the sense of smell?
These are the odours I love well:

The smell of coffee freshly ground;
Or rich plum pudding, holly crowned;
Or onions fried and deeply browned;

The fragrance of a fumy pipe;
The smell of apples newly ripe;
And printers' ink on leaden type.

Woods by moonlight in September
Breathe most sweet; and I remember
Many a smoky camp-fire ember.

Camphor, turpentine, and tea,
The balsam of a Christmas tree,
These are whiffs of gramarye . . .
A ship smells best of all to me!

CHRISTOPHER MORLEY

Discussing the poem

1 Is it true that there are few poems about (or mentioning) smells? Can you think of any at all?

2 Do you agree with Christopher Morley's choice of well-loved smells? What would you add or take away?

3 What does "whiffs of gramarye" mean? Why do you think the last line is in italics? Is there any other difference between the last verse and the other four?

270

For learning about language

Exercise 1(a) Find out what the following adjectives mean; then rearrange them in eight groups of three, so that in each group there are three *synonyms* to describe **tastes** or **smells**.

acid	fragrant	piquant	salt	sweet
aromatic	hot	putrid	sharp	tart
balmy	insipid	rancid	sour	tasteless
briny	mordant	rank	spicy	vapid
candied	peppery	saline	sugary	

(b) Try to describe the following **colours** – perhaps in terms of a mixture of other colours.

For example:
Peacock blue is a strong greenish blue, as found in a peacock's tail feathers.

red ochre	olive green	yellow ochre	scarlet	buff
charcoal grey	cobalt	tangerine	crimson	purple
indigo	turquoise	cream	pink	mauve

(c) Discuss (or write down) the meanings of all the following thirty words describing **sounds**; they are in alphabetical order.

blaring	faint	hollow	rasping	shrill
clamorous	grating	hushed	raucous	sibilant
clanging	gruff	mellifluous	repetitive	soft
deafening	guttural	melodious	resounding	squeaky
distinct	harsh	piercing	reverberating	tuneful
echoing	high-pitched	piping	rhythmical	vibrating

It is possible to group these words in six groups of five words that have some qualities in common. For instance: echoing, hollow, reverberating, resounding and vibrating all have an element of repeated, gradually dying sound about them. Regroup the other words in five groups of five adjectives, and discuss what the words in each group have in common.

Exercise 2 As we saw in Book 1, tenses of verbs are often a source of confusion in standard written English. Rewrite the following sentences in the *past tense*, using a dictionary to check the correct form.

For example: The waves break relentlessly on the shore.

The waves broke relentlessly on the shore.

(a) She easily becomes jealous.
(b) The gale blows itself out.
(c) Their dog drinks water.
(d) The sun shines brightly on the water.
(e) I ring up my friend every Sunday.
(f) They run a club for spastic children.
(g) The old blacksmith shoes horses for the nearby stables.
(h) She swims beautifully.
(i) In autumn, trees shed their leaves.
(j) This loom weaves cloth faster than the others.
(k) Slow and steady wins the race.
(l) He always throws a party at Christmas.
(m) My father winds up the kitchen clock every Saturday night.
(n) The tiger springs on its prey.
(o) Nettles sting him all over.

272

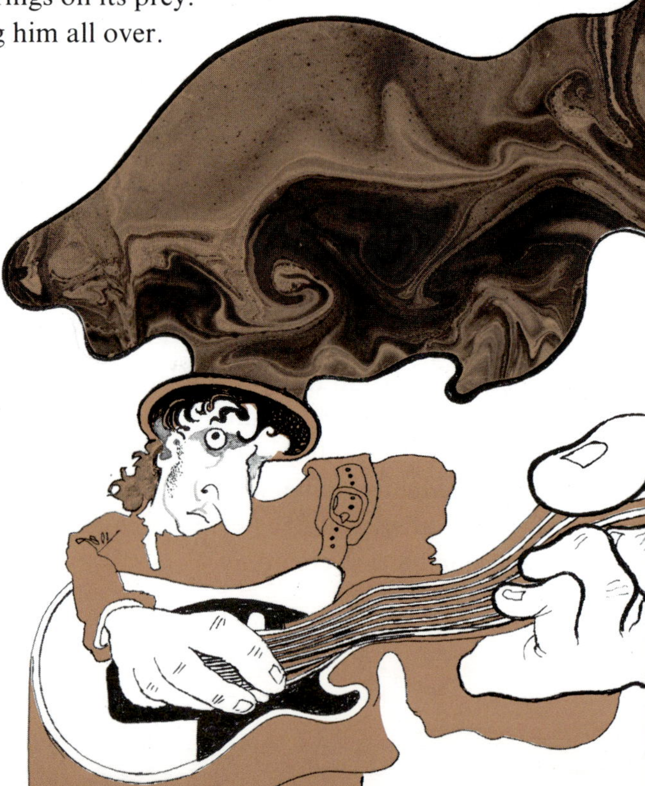

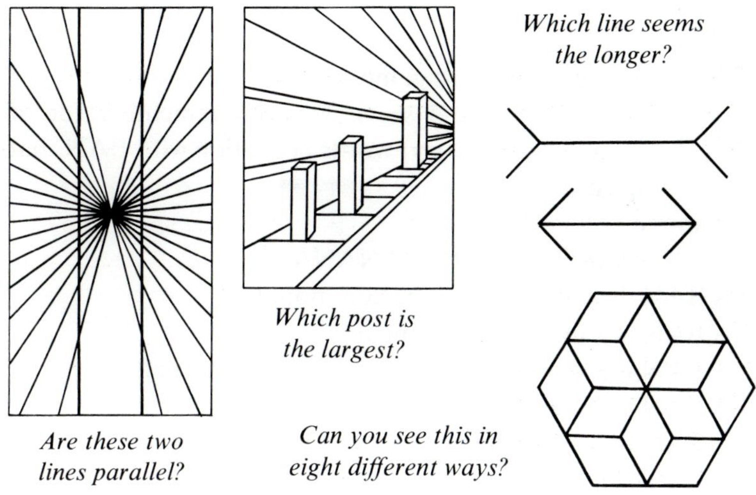

Exercise 3 Rewrite the following conversation about optical illusions, putting in all the punctuation necessary, including capital letters and apostrophes. The arrangement in paragraphs is already correct. Two of the paragraphs are comment, and are not spoken by John or his uncle.

ill believe it when i see it said john angrily

you think you can trust your own eyes then asked uncle bob

of course i can exclaimed john

uncle bob took a pencil and ruled two lines in the shape of an inverted T

which is longer he asked

john looked carefully the vertical one he said firmly

no replied his uncle taking the ruler and measuring them they are exactly the same length pass me that pair of compasses

he then drew two circles each 10 mm in diameter and began to draw a series of larger circles round one of them and a series of smaller circles round the other

you see he said triumphantly the 10 mm circles look different the way we see things is altered by their surroundings and we cannot always trust our own eyes

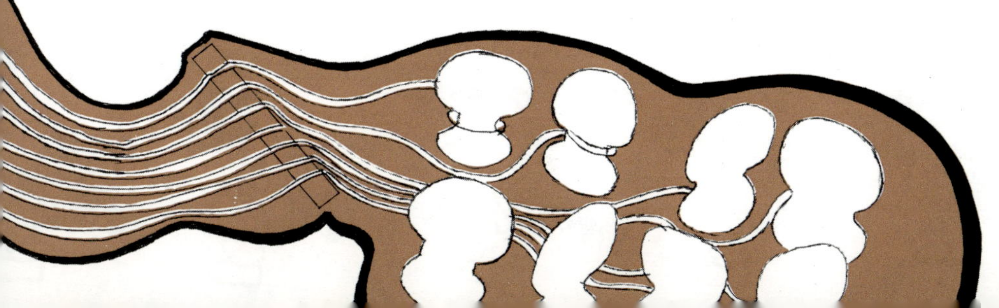

Exercise 4 Here are some word games.

(a) Take the letters BAN and see if you can remember (or, if necessary, look up in a dictionary) words beginning with BAN that fit the following clues.

For example:

This BAN is a tropical fruit – BANANA.

(1) This BAN describes something commonplace.

(2) This BAN is a musical instrument.

(3) This BAN is a richly coloured spotted handkerchief.

(4) This BAN is an outlaw.

(5) This BAN describes someone bow-legged.

(6) This BAN is a large destructive rat.

(7) This BAN is without money.

(8) This BAN is a Scottish loaf.

(9) This BAN is a female spirit of doom.

(10) This BAN is a small kind of hen.

Make up other lists of your own based on MAN, CAT, PAL or other groups of letters of your own choice. You will need a dictionary for finding words and making up suitable clues.

(b) See how many words you can make out of the letters in a given word. For instance, the letters in NAMELESS will make (at least):

name, less, seal, am, man, mane, mean, meal, lease, maneless, mess, measles, lame, lameness, same, seem, seam, seen, sane, male, mass, slam, lessen, lane, lass, lea, la, me, sale, see, sea, ass, alms, ale, an, a.

But "sameness" should *not* be in the list, because it would need *three s*'s.

See how many words (excluding proper names and abbreviations) you can make out of the letters in each of the following.

| homeward | passage | deliver |
| parole | testify | ourselves |

Similarly find other words that can be made into many more.

(c) Here is a **word chain** in which FOOL is changed into WISE in six moves, each move being the alteration of *one* letter only, to make another word that you would find in a dictionary.

F O O L

F O O D

F O N D

F I N D

F I N E

W I N E

W I S E

Change the following in the shortest possible number of moves:

BOAT to CASH   FALL to RISE

SHIP to ROCK   HEAD to TAIL

Make up others of your own.

(d) These are known as **word squares**:

I	N	T	O
N	E	E	D
T	E	N	D
O	D	D	S

S	T	R	A	P
T	R	A	S	H
R	A	D	I	O
A	S	I	A	N
P	H	O	N	E

E	L	S	E
L	E	E	R
S	E	A	R
E	R	R	S

Notice how the words are complete and make sense both across and down. How does this differ from the normal crossword? Try to make up a fourth word square from the following clues to the words that make it up.

1 Always replies when you call.
2 Underneath your mouth.
3 An indication or suggestion.
4 To a position on.

Now see if you can devise some word squares (with clues) of your own.

For your own writing

1 Jinty's attempt to describe colours to a blind child forces her to use language with precision and with feeling. The following exercises are intended to make you take a fresh look at things, and describe them as accurately and as fully as you can.

(a) Imagine that you are an ant, a butterfly, a fish, a skylark, or some tiny creature like the inhabitants of Lilliput in Swift's **Gulliver's Travels**. Describe what you would see and experience. The Lilliputians, who were only fifteen centimetres tall, made a list of the objects in Gulliver's pockets. What are they describing in this extract?

There were two pockets which we could not enter: these he called his fobs; they were two large slits cut into the top of his middle cover, but squeezed close by the pressure of his belly. Out of the right fob hung a great silver chain, with a wonderful kind of engine at the bottom. We directed him to draw out whatever was fastened to that chain; which appeared to be a globe, half silver, and half of some transparent metal; for on the transparent side we saw certain strange figures circularly drawn, and thought we could touch them, till we found our fingers stopped by that lucid substance. He put this engine to our ears, which made an incessant noise like that of a watermill: and we conjecture it is either some unknown animal, or the god that he worships; but we are more inclined to the latter opinion, because he assures us (if we understood him right, for he expressed himself very imperfectly) that he seldom did anything without consulting it: he called it his oracle, and said it pointed out the time for every action of his life. From the left fob he took out a net almost large enough for a fisherman, but contrived to open and shut like a purse, and served him for the same use: we found therein several massy pieces of yellow metal, which, if they be real gold, must be of immense value.

Your own description should also be full and accurate. Do not tell a complete story.

or: **(b)** Place a flower or small plant in front of you as you write, and attempt to describe it in detail without the aid of any illustration. Try to explain exactly what it looks like to someone who may never have seen one before, as Jinty did to Toby.

2(a) Write a short story or a full description in which you imagine what it is like to be blind, or deaf. Before you begin, study the following short passage from **Annerton Pit**, the story from which the extract in Chapter 4 (on pages 57–59) was taken. Jake, you will remember, was blind.

> Jake could have followed the man's footsteps without help, but he kept his fingers on Martin's wrist because he was aware of the tension building up in his brother, a mixture of panic and anger which might suddenly make him do or say something really stupid. They went down a long corridor but before they'd reached the end the man stopped, knocked at a door and opened it without waiting for an answer. Jake felt a pulse of surprise run through Martin's arm, followed by a sudden lessening of wariness.
>
> "Come in," said a woman's voice. "Sit down. It's a bit cramped for three, I'm afraid. You're Martin and Jake Bertold? I'm Sergeant Abraham."
>
> "Hello," said Jake, checking the position of the chair Martin had led him to.
>
> "Hello," she said. "Please sit down, Martin, I'm sorry to bring you along here like this."
>
> Jake began to build an idea of her in her tiny, office-smelling room. There were potted plants somewhere, recently watered. She wore quite strong-smelling scent and her voice was deep but not at all mannish. She knew she'd surprised Martin by not being a man and she thought that was funny. There was a vague suggestion of Mum about her, though she was shorter (or sitting on a very low chair) and a bit younger. She didn't have anything you could call an accent, but there was something a little careful about her vowels which suggested that she'd spoken differently when she'd been a kid and had taught herself to speak like this.

Notice all the non-visual details he uses to create his picture of their visit to a police station.

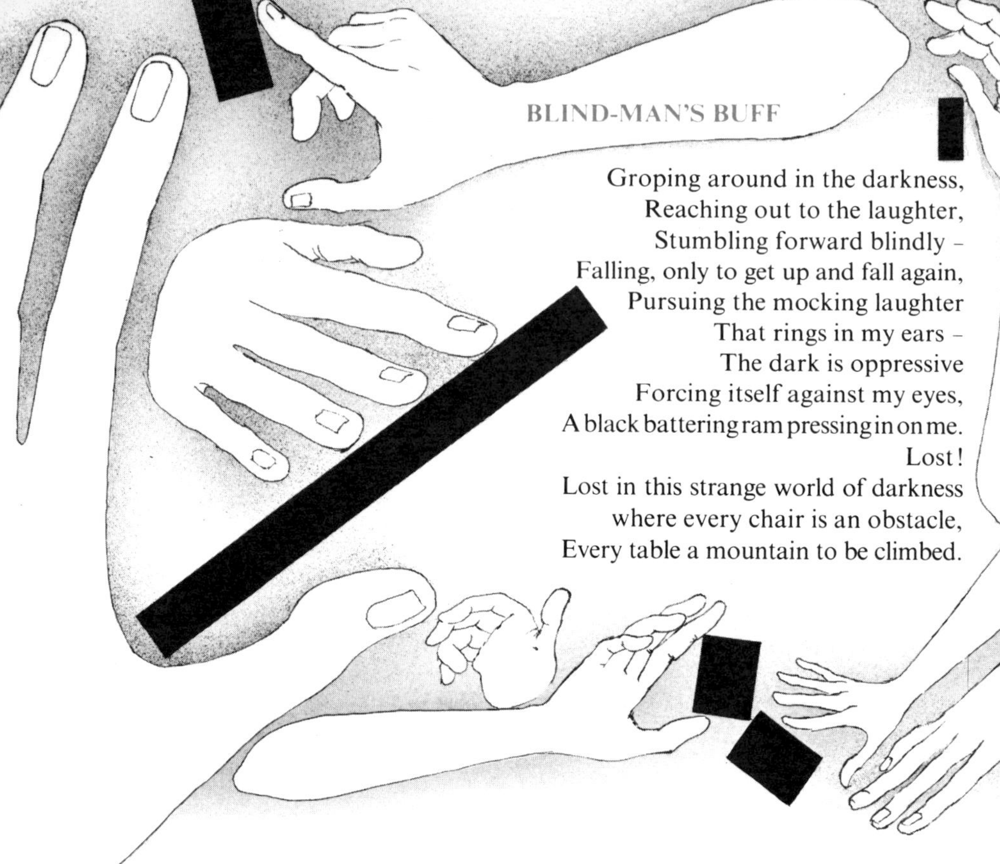

You may prefer to imagine deafness, rather than blindness. An advertisement by the Royal National Institute for the Deaf said: "Blindness cuts you off from things, but deafness cuts you off from people." Deafness from birth is usually associated with dumbness, and deaf people have great difficulty in learning to speak, which makes communication doubly difficult.

Concentrate on one particular scene –

in a restaurant   by a harbour   in a wood
in a street market or a covered market

and include the smells and the feel of the place, as well as the sights (if you are deaf) or sounds (if you are blind).

or: **(b)** Write a poem imagining what it is like to be disabled by blindness or deafness. Above is an example written by a pupil of 13.

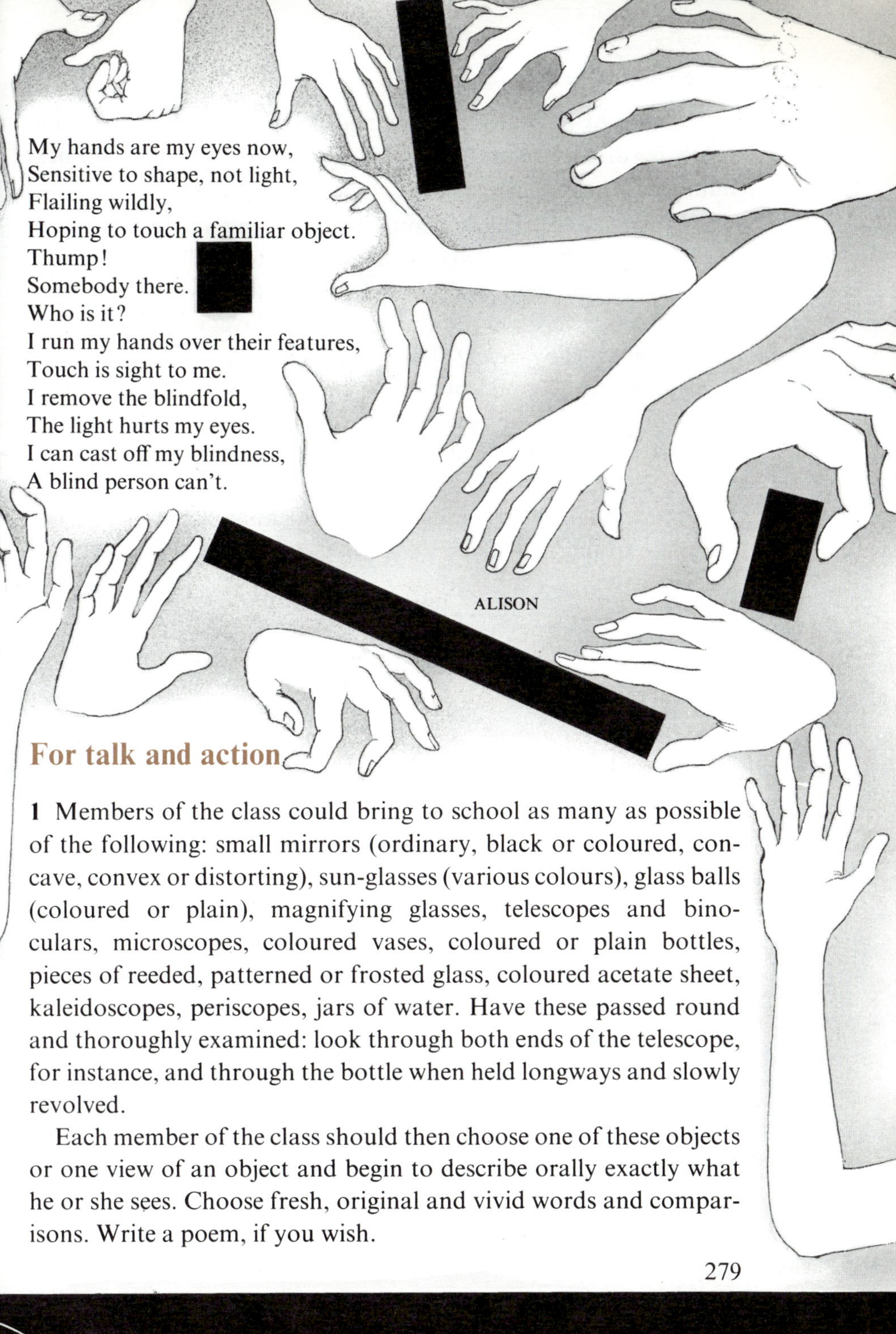

My hands are my eyes now,
Sensitive to shape, not light,
Flailing wildly,
Hoping to touch a familiar object.
Thump!
Somebody there.
Who is it?
I run my hands over their features,
Touch is sight to me.
I remove the blindfold,
The light hurts my eyes.
I can cast off my blindness,
A blind person can't.

For talk and action

1 Members of the class could bring to school as many as possible
of the following: small mirrors (ordinary, black or coloured, con-
cave, convex or distorting), sun-glasses (various colours), glass balls
(coloured or plain), magnifying glasses, telescopes and binoculars, microscopes, coloured vases, coloured or plain bottles,
pieces of reeded, patterned or frosted glass, coloured acetate sheet,
kaleidoscopes, periscopes, jars of water. Have these passed round
and thoroughly examined: look through both ends of the telescope,
for instance, and through the bottle when held longways and slowly
revolved.

Each member of the class should then choose one of these objects
or one view of an object and begin to describe orally exactly what
he or she sees. Choose fresh, original and vivid words and comparisons. Write a poem, if you wish.

The best of these descriptions and poems could be written out neatly for display on the board or in a folder; or included in the next number of the class magazine.

2 Small groups in the class could prepare some interesting games for the rest to play. One group should sew into small cloth bags dry samples of different well-known domestic substances: sugar, coffee-beans, rice, dried peas, peppercorns, cloves etc. The contents must be guessed by *feeling* alone.

Another group could put on to saucers samples of substances that can be *tasted* by someone when blindfolded: ginger, sugar, curry-powder, pepper, salt, celery salt, mustard powder, sherbet, flour etc. (Warn the victims not to take too much!)

A third group could arrange to make identifiable *noises* behind a curtain: striking a match, sharpening a knife, winding a clock, closing a book, tearing cloth etc.

For further reading

The Third Eye by MOLLIE HUNTER (Hamish Hamilton; Collins; Armada)
Jinty's intuition, sympathy and courage are put to a much more severe test before the end of this story. Behind local gossip about the Earl and his family lies a genuine fear of an ancient curse on the eldest son. Jinty's "third eye" finally helps break that spell.

In **A Sound of Chariots** (Collins; Hamish Hamilton) Mollie Hunter tells the moving story of Bridie McShane, growing up in Scotland in 1918, after her father's death, and gradually discovering her talent as a writer. Mollie Hunter sets **The Thirteenth Member** (Piccolo; Hamish Hamilton) further back in history. Adam is horrified to find that his friend Gilly is a reluctant member of a witches' coven (in an age when witches were burnt to death). Set in Scotland in 1590, this exciting story is also bound up with a plot against the King.

All in the Head by DAVID COHEN (Peacock)
David Cohen explains how the human senses work, describes various experiments that have been carried out on the senses, and suggests some tests that you can do for yourself.

The Phantom Tollbooth by NORTON JUSTER (Collins; Lions)
What sort of meal would you expect if you had to eat your own words? What happens when you eat subtraction stew? As Milo discovers when he visits Dictionopolis, where words are all-important, and Digitopolis, which is dominated by numbers, there is something to be said for the Wisdom of the Princesses Rhyme and Reason.

Marianne Dreams by CATHERINE STORR (Puffin)
Kept in bed by illness, Marianne finds a pencil with magic properties, and her drawings begin a dream-relationship and a weird adventure with Mark, who is also ill, until she learns to control the terror with her pencil.

Gulliver's Travels by JONATHAN SWIFT (Various publishers)
In these classic stories, Gulliver visits the lands of tiny people and of giants, and other countries strangely unlike our own; but the author makes merciless fun of the stupidity and narrow-mindedness of Europeans of his day.

Selected Short Stories by H. G. WELLS (Penguin)
In **The Country of the Blind** Nunez stumbles by chance into a completely secluded valley in the Andes where generations of inhabitants have all been born, lived and died totally blind. He remembers the old proverb: " In the country of the blind, the one-eyed man is king." But the story unfolds rather differently!

Supplementary Exercises

Revision Exercise 1

Revise the uses of commas discussed in Chapter 11. The following sentences contain examples of these, and the other uses of commas, as well as titles and special names that require inverted commas and some capital letters. In one case, there are *two* sentences in one question. Rewrite them all with the necessary punctuation.

(a) sea anemones called flower animals by the greeks are in fact animals

(b) many interesting creatures live along the sea-shore on the sands in the pools under the rocks and in caves

(c) along the edge of the sea by jill norman contains information about sea-nettles sponges shellfish of all kinds sand-borers crabs mussels shrimps worms and all kinds of sea-creatures

(d) jill norman who wrote the book did the illustrations of shells plants and sea-creatures herself

(e) the octopus with its large horny beak and eight arms feeds on crabs lobsters etc catching its prey by grasping it in its powerful arms

(f) octopuses shy but intelligent creatures will often make collections of crabs before eating them they will also stand guard over mussels or clams for hours knowing that eventually they must open their shells to feed when the octopus will quickly slip a stone in the opening so that his arms can easily extract the soft interior

Revision Exercise 2

(a) One way of representing contracted (or shortened) words is with an apostrophe to represent the omitted letter or letters. Write the contracted forms of the following:

(1) of the clock   (3) over   (5) he has   (7) shall not   (9) they will
(2) will not   (4) it would   (6) you are   (8) forecastle   (10) madam.

Write the full forms of the following contractions, which have apostrophes:

(11) 'em   (13) ain't   (15) we'll   (17) 'tis   (19) sou'wester
(12) they're   (14) it's   (16) we'd   (18) penn'orth   (20) e'er.

(b) Another kind of contraction is the abbreviation, using full stops and initial letters or some of the letters in the full word. Write the abbreviations for each of these:

(1) etcetera   (4) ante meridiem   (7) Bedfordshire   (10) Lieutenant-Colonel.
(2) nota bene   (5) assistant   (8) limited
(3) anno domini   (6) baronet   (9) for example

Write out the full forms (in English) of the following abbreviations:

(11) i.e.   (13) P.M.   (15) Oxon.   (17) q.v.   (19) kg
(12) p.m.   (14) recd.   (16) M.C.C.   (18) O.H.M.S.   (20) A.A.

Where the letters stand for Latin words, can you write these as well?

Revision Exercise 3

The other important use of the apostrophe is for the possessive – to show the owner of some thing or quality. Rewrite the following in a form using an apostrophe.

> For example: the death of Caesar – Caesar's death
> hats for ladies – ladies' hats

a vest for a boy	the duties of the teacher	a playground for boys
the snow of last year	the duties of the teachers	the favourite of the duke
lives of other men	progress during the term	pearls owned by a duchess
the tail of the ass	the square of St James	rainfall over three days.

Revision Exercise 4

(a) In each of the following you are given several *synonyms* and four or five sentences, each with a blank. Choose the synonyms that will best fit into these particular sentences; the first sentence has been completed for you. Rewrite the others.

(1) assigned, awarded, bestowed, conferred, gave, granted
      Example: They <u>assigned</u> me a place to park.
She . . . her friend a birthday present.
The Queen has . . . a title on the Prime Minister.
The magistrate . . . his petition.
They . . . the first prize to the new variety of rose.

(2) felt, fingered, groped, handled, touched
As soon as I . . . the hedgehog, it curled up.
I . . . the stove to see if it was still warm.
When you have . . . as many problem cases as she has, you will understand.
In the darkness we . . . for the door-handle.

(3) bid, offer, overture, proposition, tender
We put the . . . to him, that he could have all the goods at half-price, or not at all.
If it is auctioned, the necklace will go for the highest . . .
His firm put in a . . . for the contract, but their rivals were asking less.
We have made you a firm . . . for the property and you can take it or leave it.

(4) active, brisk, frisky, spry, vivacious
The committee has the matter under . . . consideration.
The . . . laughter rapidly dispelled the gloom.
The leader was . . . and energetic.
The lambs were . . .

(5) gradually, languidly, slackly, sluggishly, slothfully
He held the rope . . ., not expecting any strain on it.
In the dry season, the river flows . . . past the castle.
They were . . . reaching their goal.
She answered . . . and without interest.

(b) Try to compose sentences of your own to illustrate the subtle differences in meaning between these groups of synonyms:
(1) annex, earn, glean, procure, win (*verbs*).
(2) fodder, food, nourishment, provender, rations (*nouns*).

(c) Find one or more *antonyms* for each group of synonyms in **(a)**.

Revision Exercise 5

The following sentences use made-up words, in a similar way to those on page 35. Some of the verbs, nouns, pronouns, adjectives and adverbs are in italics. State first whether the word in italics is a verb, noun etc.; then, if it is a verb, say whether it is past, present or future tense; if it is a noun or pronoun, say whether it is subject or object; if it is an adjective or adverb, say what noun or verb it describes.
For example: *Will* some fids *be plinking wocks* here? (2)
               Will be plinking – verb, future tense
           wocks – noun (plural), object.

(a) All *fids* can plink.
(b) How bannily *it plinked*! (2)
(c) Most fids *plink bannily*. (2)
(d) They are then *banny* fids.
(e) Fids *are* always *plinking*.
(f) Little fids are called *fidlings*.
(g) Fids plink *wocks* and *swisps*. (2)
(h) This fidling *plinked* yesterday.
(i) Was its first *plink* a good one?
(j) *Has* this *fidling plinked* bannily? (2)
(k) A fid *was plinking* a wock bannily to show a little fid.

Revision Exercise 6

All the following words contain *silent letters*, that is, letters that are neither pronounced separately nor part of a combination of letters with a particular pronunciation (in -ch-, neither letter is regarded as silent). Rearrange them in seven groups of six words, so that each group is related by a particular silent letter.

For example, the following all have a silent -k-:

knapsack, knee, knell, knob, penknife, knuckle

pneumonia	knock	wren	gnat	build	knack	walk
pseudonym	psychic	talk	guilt	knit	guess	disguise
knowledge	ghost	wriggle	wreck	gnaw	aghast	guide
rheumatism	plague	wreath	knave	wrist	kneel	gnarled
rhododendron	wrinkle	psalter	stalk	gnash	gnu	psalm
psychology	folk	rhubarb	yolk	gnome	caulk	rhapsody

Revision Exercise 7

Rewrite the following short story in seven paragraphs (remembering that a new paragraph is required for each new speaker in a conversation), inserting all the necessary punctuation, including capital letters.

what did i hit then said mr reed to himself as he pulled up on a country lane one night i had better have a look he found that his car had run over a hare in the road another car drew up behind him and the driver got out whats the trouble asked the stranger i hit a hare and i think ive killed it replied mr reed the stranger looked at the motionless animal went back to his car and returned with a small bottle he poured some of the liquid over the hare which immediately jumped up and ran off my goodness what miracle-working liquid was that asked the astonished mr reed oh nothing special replied the stranger only hair-restorer

Revision Exercise 8

Rewrite the following description, inserting all the remaining punctuation and capital letters. It is all one paragraph.

there were ruddy brown-faced broad-girthed Spanish onions shining in the fatness of their growth like spanish friars; and winking from their shelves in wanton slyness at the girls as they went by and glanced demurely at the hung-up mistletoe there were pears and apples clustered high in blooming pyramids; there were bunches of grapes made in the shopkeepers benevolence to dangle from conspicuous hooks that peoples mouths might water gratis as they passed; there were piles of filberts mossy and brown recalling in their fragrance ancient walks among the woods and pleasant shufflings ankle deep through withered leaves; there were norfolk biffins squab and swarthy setting off the yellow of the oranges and lemons and in the great compactness of their juicy persons urgently entreating and beseeching to be carried home in paper bags and eaten after dinner the very gold and silver fish set forth among these choice fruits in a bowl though members of a dull and stagnant-blooded race appeared to know that there was something going on; and to a fish went gasping round and round their little world in slow and passionless excitement.

(from **A Christmas Carol** by CHARLES DICKENS)

Revision Exercise 9

(a) Write down the positive, comparative and superlative forms of each of these adjectives. For example: good – good/better/best.

In at least one case no comparative or superlative is possible – discuss why.

lovely	ugly	much	perfect	bad
hopeful	alone	many	poor	intolerable
sure	lively	feeble	comfortable	faithful

(b) Rearrange the following groups of words (now in alphabetical order) in order of "intensity"; thus "moon, planet, star, galaxy, universe" is a series that moves from smaller to larger.

284

(1) adequate, excellent, exceptional, fair, good.
(2) careful, frugal, grudging, mean, miserly.
(3) amble, race, run, streak, trot.
(4) dawdle, linger, plod, stroll, tarry.
(5) captain, corporal, lance-corporal, second lieutenant, sergeant-major.

Revision Exercise 10

Here are some common prefixes and suffixes.
  prefixes: dis-, im-, mis-, pre-, re-, un-
  suffixes: -able, -ation, -ful, -ible, -ion, -ly, -ment
By taking a simple short word and adding one or more of these additional syllables, see how many more words you can make. For example: present – presentable, unpresentable, presentably, represent, representation, misrepresent, misrepresentation etc.
  Using only suffixes and prefixes from the above list, make as many new words as possible from the following. You may drop a final -e or change -y to -i where necessary, but make sure that you spell words correctly and that you know what they mean:
  manage   charge   press   pronounce   organise   engage.

Revision Exercise 11

If you have studied Book 2 thoroughly, you should be able to rewrite the following statements inserting the correct word or words to complete each one. If you cannot do this, refer back to the appropriate chapter.
(a) Words of similar meaning are called ... and those of opposite meaning are called ...
(b) A direct comparison between two things in one or more particular respects is called a ...
(c) A *metaphor* is a ... comparison, in which one thing is treated as if ...
(d) A ... is a group of words (without a verb) which, as a group, does the work of an adverb, adjective or noun in a sentence.
(e) The verb "to be" and other "being" verbs often take ... instead of objects.
(f) When verbs have two distinct objects, the person or thing for whom or to whom the action happens is called the ... object.
(g) The repetition of similar consonant sounds is called ..., and ... is the use of words to suggest or represent actual sounds.
(h) The part or form of a verb ending in -ing is called a ... and this is frequently used as an adjective.
(i) Verbs that require objects to complete their sense are called ... verbs.

Books for Further Reading

Author	Title and Publisher
AIKEN, JOAN	**The Wolves of Willoughby Chase** Cape; Puffin
ALLEN, NEIL	**The Puffin Book of Athletics** Puffin
ANDREW, PRUDENCE	**Una and Grubstreet** Heinemann
ARLOTT, JOHN	**The Oxford Companion to Sports and Games** O.U.P.

Author	*Title and Publisher*
ASHLEY, BERNARD	**All My Men** Puffin
	Break in the Sun O.U.P.; Puffin
	Terry on the Fence Puffin
	Trouble with Donovan Croft Puffin
BARNE, KITTY	**She Shall Have Music** Dent
BECKWITH, LILLIAN	**The Spuddy** Hutchinson; Arrow
BERNA, PAUL	**The Mystery of the Cross-Eyed Man** Puffin
BLACKMORE, R. D.	**Lorna Doone** Various Publishers inc. Puffin
BONINGTON, CHRIS (ed.)	**Everest the Hard Way** Hodder & Stoughton; Arrow
BOSCO, HENRI	**The Boy and the River** O.U.P.
BROWN, PAMELA	**The Swish of the Curtain** Brockhampton
BURR, SYBIL	**Life with Lisa** Puffin
CAWLEY, WINIFRED	**Silver Everything** and **Many Mansions** O.U.P.
CHURCH, RICHARD	**The Cave** Heinemann; Pan
	Down River Heinemann
	Over the Bridge Heinemann
COHEN, DAVID	**All in the Head** Peacock
DAFTER, RAY	**Running out of Fuel – Solving the Energy Puzzle** Wayland
DAY LEWIS, C.	**The Otterbury Incident** Bodley Head; Heinemann; Puffin
DICKINSON, PETER	**Annerton Pit** Gollancz; Heinemann; Puffin
	The Blue Hawk Puffin
	The Dancing Bear Puffin
	The Devil's Children Puffin
	Heartsease Puffin
	The Weathermonger Puffin
DUNPHY, EAMON	**Only a Game? Diary of a Professional Footballer** Peacock; Penguin
ENRIGHT, ELIZABETH	**The Four-Storey Mistake** Heinemann
	The Saturdays Heinemann; Puffin
FISK, NICHOLAS	**A Rag, a Bone and a Hank of Hair** Kestrel
FOX, LILLA M.	**Instruments of Popular Music** Lutterworth
	Instruments of Processional Music Lutterworth
GALWAY, LANCE	**Forgers** Kestrel
GARFIELD, LEON	**Black Jack** Puffin
	Devil-in-the-Fog Longman; Kestrel; Puffin
	Jack Holborn Puffin
	Smith Puffin
	The Strange Affair of Adelaide Harris Puffin
GEORGE, JEAN	**Julie of the Wolves** Hamish Hamilton; Macmillan; Puffin
	My Side of the Mountain Bodley Head; Macmillan; Puffin
GRANT, MICHAEL	**The Olympic Games** Kestrel
GRENDER, IRIS	**An Old Fashioned Christmas** Hutchinson
HAMLEY, DENNIS	**Pageants of Despair** Deutsch; Puffin

<table>
<tr><td>Author</td><td>Title and Publisher</td></tr>
<tr><td>O'HARA, MARY</td><td>My Friend Flicka Methuen; Mayflower
The Green Grass of Wyoming Methuen; Mayflower
Thunderhead Methuen; Mayflower</td></tr>
<tr><td>OVERTON, JENNY</td><td>The Thirteen Days of Christmas Faber; Puffin</td></tr>
<tr><td>PATON WALSH, JILL</td><td>The Dolphin Crossing Macmillan; Penguin</td></tr>
<tr><td>PEARCE, A. PHILIPPA</td><td>Minnow on the Say O.U.P.; Puffin
Tom's Midnight Garden O.U.P.; Heinemann; Puffin</td></tr>
<tr><td>RANSOME, ARTHUR</td><td>Winter Holiday Cape; Puffin</td></tr>
<tr><td>RASKIN, ELLEN</td><td>The Tattooed Potato and Other Clues Macmillan; Peacock; Puffin</td></tr>
<tr><td>RUTGERS VAN DER LOEFF, ANNA</td><td>Avalanche Puffin</td></tr>
<tr><td>SADIE, STANLEY</td><td>The Great Composers series Faber
Beethoven and Handel</td></tr>
<tr><td>SCOTT, CAPT. R. F.</td><td>The Personal Journals of Capt. R. F. Scott Murray; Tandem</td></tr>
<tr><td>SERRAILLIER, IAN</td><td>The Gorgon's Head O.U.P.; Heinemann
The Ivory Horn O.U.P.; Heinemann
The Silver Sword Cape; Heinemann; Puffin
There's No Escape Cape; Heinemann; Puffin
The Way of Danger O.U.P.; Heinemann; Puffin</td></tr>
<tr><td>SOUTHALL, IVAN</td><td>The Fox Hole Methuen</td></tr>
<tr><td>STORR, CATHERINE</td><td>Marianne Dreams Puffin</td></tr>
<tr><td>STREATFEILD, NOEL</td><td>White Boots Collins; Puffin</td></tr>
<tr><td>SWIFT, JONATHAN</td><td>Gulliver's Travels Various Publishers</td></tr>
<tr><td>THEROUX, PAUL</td><td>London Snow Hamish Hamilton; Puffin</td></tr>
<tr><td>TREASE, GEOFFREY</td><td>Cue for Treason Puffin
The Maythorn Story Heinemann
The Seas of Morning Puffin</td></tr>
<tr><td>UTTLEY, ALISON</td><td>A Traveller in Time Faber; Puffin</td></tr>
<tr><td>VIPONT, ELFRIDA</td><td>The Lark in the Morn O.U.P.
The Lark on the Wing O.U.P.</td></tr>
<tr><td>WARNER, REX</td><td>Athens at War Heinemann; Bodley Head
Greeks and Trojans Heinemann
Men and Gods Heinemann
Stories of the Greeks MacGibbon & Kee
Vengeance of the Gods Heinemann</td></tr>
<tr><td>WELLS, H. G.</td><td>The Country of the Blind from Selected Short Stories of H. G. Wells Penguin</td></tr>
<tr><td>WESTALL, ROBERT</td><td>The Wind Eye Macmillan; Peacock; Penguin</td></tr>
<tr><td>WILLIAMS, JAY</td><td>The Time of the Kraken Gollancz; Macmillan; Topliner
Unearthly Beasts and Other Strange People Macmillan; Topliner</td></tr>
<tr><td>WOOLLEY, SIR LEONARD</td><td>Digging up the Past Greenwood</td></tr>
</table>